KIERKEGAARD AS PHENOMENOLOGIST

KIERKEGAARD AS PHENOMENOLOGIST

An Experiment

Edited by Jeffrey Hanson

Northwestern University Press
Evanston, Illinois

Northwestern University Press
www.nupress.northwestern.edu

Printed in the United States of America

10 9 8 7 6 5 4 3 2 1

Library of Congress Cataloging-in-Publication Data

Kierkegaard as phenomenologist : an experiment / edited by Jeffrey Hanson.
p. cm.
Includes bibliographical references.
ISBN 978-0-8101-2681-7 (pbk. : alk. paper)
1. Kierkegaard, Søren, 1813–1855. 2. Phenomenology. I. Hanson, Jeffrey.
B4378.P44K54 2010
198′.9—dc22
2010020992

∞ The paper used in this publication meets the minimum requirements of the American National Standard for Information Sciences—Permanence of Paper for Printed Library Materials, ANSI Z39.48–1992.

Contents

Abbreviations of Works by Kierkegaard

CA *The Concept of Anxiety: A Simple Psychologically Orienting Deliberation on the Dogmatic Issue of Hereditary Sin,* ed. and trans. Reidar Thomte, in collaboration with Albert B. Anderson (Princeton, N.J.: Princeton University Press, 1980).

CI *The Concept of Irony, with Continual Reference to Socrates: Together with Notes of Schelling's Berlin Lectures,* ed. and trans. Howard V. Hong and Edna H. Hong (Princeton, N.J.: Princeton University Press, 1989).

CUP *Concluding Unscientific Postscript to "Philosophical Fragments,"* ed. and trans. Howard V. Hong and Edna H. Hong, vol. 1 (Princeton, N.J.: Princeton University Press, 1992).

EO I *Either/Or Part I,* ed. and trans. Howard V. Hong and Edna H. Hong (Princeton, N.J.: Princeton University Press, 1987).

EO II *Either/Or Part II,* ed. and trans. Howard V. Hong and Edna H. Hong (Princeton, N.J.: Princeton University Press, 1987).

EUD *Eighteen Upbuilding Discourses,* ed. and trans. Howard V. Hong and Edna H. Hong (Princeton, N.J.: Princeton University Press, 1990).

FT *"Fear and Trembling" and "Repetition,"* ed. and trans. Howard V. Hong and Edna H. Hong (Princeton, N.J.: Princeton University Press, 1983).

JP *Søren Kierkegaard's Journals and Papers,* ed. and trans. Howard V. Hong and Edna H. Hong, 7 vols. (Bloomington: Indiana University Press, 1967–78).

MLW *"The Moment" and Late Writings,* ed. and trans. Howard V. Hong and Edna H. Hong (Princeton, N.J.: Princeton University Press, 1998).

Pap. *Søren Kierkegaards Papirer* (Copenhagen: Gyldendal, 1968–78).

PC *Practice in Christianity,* ed. and trans. Howard V. Hong and Edna H. Hong (Princeton, N.J.: Princeton University Press, 1991).

PF *"Philosophical Fragments" and "Johannes Climacus,"* ed. and trans. Howard V. Hong and Edna H. Hong (Princeton, N.J.: Princeton University Press, 1985).

SKS *Søren Kierkegaards Skrifter* (Copenhagen: Gad, 1997–2009).

SLW *Stages on Life's Way,* ed. and trans. Howard V. Hong and Edna H. Hong (Princeton, N.J.: Princeton University Press, 1988).

SUD *The Sickness unto Death: A Christian Psychological Exposition for Upbuilding and Awakening,* ed. and trans. Howard V. Hong and Edna H. Hong (Princeton, N.J.: Princeton University Press, 1980).

UDVS *Upbuilding Discourses in Various Spirits,* ed. and trans. Howard V. Hong and Edna H. Hong (Princeton, N.J.: Princeton University Press, 1993).

WL *Works of Love,* ed. and trans. Howard V. Hong and Edna H. Hong (Princeton, N.J.: Princeton University Press, 1995).

Introduction

Jeffrey Hanson

Kierkegaard and the History of Phenomenology

During April 1928, the Kiev-born philosopher Lev Shestov, then making his home in France and teaching at the Sorbonne, attended a conference in Amsterdam where he met Edmund Husserl, with whom he would maintain a cordial friendship for many years. He had already published on Husserl and indeed was instrumental in introducing Husserl to France, and Husserl, despite disagreements with him, had taken an interest in his intense polemical thought, which vigorously protested against the imperialism of reason and protected the unique privileges of religious faith. Husserl had assumed that Shestov was inspired by Kierkegaard, but Shestov confessed that he did not know the Dane's work. Shestov recalled that Husserl then practically forced him to read Kierkegaard; this was not a dispassionate suggestion, it was an insistence. Shestov would later argue that one cannot properly understand Husserl without coming to grips with his enthusiasm for Kierkegaard.[1] This incident, the source of some understandable surprise and speculation, is perhaps the first noteworthy one in a series of encounters between Kierkegaard and the founding figures of the phenomenological movement.

The second is doubtless Heidegger's extensive dependence upon Kierkegaard, remarked upon by Husserl to Shestov. Heidegger himself was less apt to acknowledge this debt, relegating Kierkegaard instead to the category of a psychologist or religious thinker, a dismissal that surely belies the depth of Heidegger's borrowings and betrays his discomfort with his underappreciated source.[2] The exact nature of Kierkegaard's influence is under ongoing discussion, but it is quite clear that Heidegger could not have thought through thrownness, anxiety, truth, or subjectivity in the way he did without the Dane. Emmanuel Levinas would later say that he felt Heidegger had imparted to Kierkegaard philosophical seriousness, especially with respect to the importance of feeling, a long-neglected topic in respectable philosophical circles.[3]

Yet Levinas's relationship with Kierkegaard is surely just as ambivalent as Heidegger's. Often Levinas was sharply critical, attacking what he perceived to be Kierkegaard's violence and immodesty and his attempts to transcend the ethical.[4] At the same time he repeatedly expressed appreciation for Kierkegaard's efforts at resisting totality and praised his novel understandings of belief and truth.[5] Even while accusing him of egotism, Levinas acknowledges that he had the most rigorous phenomenology of faith possible,[6] so recent scholarship on the ambivalent relation between these two thinkers is surely right to argue that Levinas cannot be read as having merely dismissed Kierkegaard without having also surreptitiously or not so surreptitiously borrowed from him as well.[7]

Derrida's retrieval of "a certain Abraham,"[8] which he reclaimed thanks to Kierkegaard and in opposition to Levinas as early as "Violence and Metaphysics" and again as recently as *The Gift of Death,* is another important milestone in this history.[9] As Mark Dooley points out in his contribution to this volume, Derrida was less abashed than some of his peers in his willingness to "stand up for" Kierkegaard, and he asserted that above Nietzsche, Rousseau, and Gide, "it is Kierkegaard to whom I have been most faithful and who interests me most."[10]

Less well known perhaps is the concluding meditation on *The Sickness unto Death* provided by Michel Henry at the end of his massive volume *The Essence of Manifestation.* It is no exaggeration to say that apart from an appendix on Hegel's concept of manifestation, Henry ends his magnum opus with a prolonged discussion of Kierkegaard's account of despair and the clues it provides to Henry's account of the fundamental affective tonalities that occupy a central place in his phenomenology.[11] At the end of his career in *Incarnation* Henry returned to Kierkegaard, this time with special emphasis on his account of innocence and anxiety.[12] It was Henry who precipitated the idea for this collection of essays on Kierkegaard as phenomenologist. It is he who in *The Essence of Manifestation* referred to Kierkegaard as a phenomenologist and interacted with him as if he were just another laborer in the field of phenomenological research.[13]

The precipitating insight for this collection is that while Kierkegaard has undoubtedly been an influence on phenomenological thinking, he has rarely if ever been read as a phenomenologist himself. This book is surely not the first such effort. Calvin Schrag for one has written on Kierkegaard as a kind of phenomenologist,[14] and Vincent McCarthy's book on Kierkegaard's phenomenology of moods is another early resource.[15]

But recent developments in phenomenology, many still in flux after the time of the predecessors immediately mentioned, have expanded our conception of what the discipline itself is and the varieties of experience it can address. Is it possible that Kierkegaard, a canonical figure by any measure, can be reappraised in light of these developments? Or more radically, is it possible that the frontiers of phenomenological investigation were already broached by Kierkegaard before phenomenology was even defined formally by Husserl?

The question that the collection hopes to answer is whether and how Kierkegaard can be interpreted as a phenomenologist. This work is an experiment inasmuch as the plausibility of the undertaking itself will only be proven by the outcome. Some of the contributors clearly regard it as possible to read Kierkegaard as a phenomenologist, though all concede that he is not in the classical, Husserlian sense. Others plainly do not and will contest the very hypothesis that forms the basis of this experiment.[16] Our shared hope is twofold: first, that Kierkegaard scholarship will be renewed, and second, that the meaning of phenomenology itself will be reconsidered.

With respect to Kierkegaard scholarship, it is worth remembering that Kierkegaard's first reception into the English-speaking world was mainly theological or devotional. At the same time, his influence on existential currents in Europe was remarked upon right away and is axiomatic in contemporary Kierkegaard scholarship. This collection does not explicitly address either Kierkegaard as religious thinker or existentialist but instead seeks to uncover the roots of his only recently acknowledged influence on phenomenological thought. As such we hope to provoke at least a small shift in the way Kierkegaard is viewed in the contemporary scholarship and to stimulate further research into Kierkegaard's thought, viewed through a new lens.

With respect to the meaning of phenomenology, the nature and limits of this path of thought have been in dispute from the very beginning. Particularly in the wake of the so-called theological turn, fundamental questions have arisen as to what sorts of phenomena are properly the objects of phenomenological inquiry and to what extent phenomenology can concern itself not only with what appears strictly speaking but with what may also be necessary to address as a condition of that appearance. Some scholars have argued that indeed such a "broadened" conception of phenomenology was implicit all along and only now is receiving the attention it deserves or that phenomenology was already theological and never needed to "turn" there in the first place. Kierkegaard's thought dances at the border of theology and philosophy and thus may be a fruitful source for examining contemporary debates within phenomenology that play out at this same border.

Kierkegaard the Phenomenologist: One Possibility

If we narrow the question to one specifically of method, which is a recurrent concern for phenomenology, we may find that Kierkegaard can supply underappreciated resources. In particular, the method that Kierkegaard called "psychology" represents a potential inspiration for phenomenological thinking, particularly for scholars interested in the relationship between phenomenology and theology. This method arose from Kierkegaard's earliest pseudonymous works and is directed at holding faith (whether understood in the eminent sense as specifically religious belief or in the ordinary sense [*PF*, 87–88]) and doubt together in tension. As such, it simultaneously navigates between theology and metaphysics and thus addresses itself neither to possible nor actual phenomena but to the "real possibility" of phenomena and speaks to experience that only the individual can undergo in the first-person perspective while unfolding from this experience implications of general human import.

Method was a preoccupation for Kierkegaard at least from the latter part of 1842 and early 1843. During this period Kierkegaard explicitly took up a variety of thematic issues characteristic of philosophizing in Greek and modern modes (*PF*, x). It was in this same period that Kierkegaard drafted a work that would never be finished, *Johannes Climacus or De Omnibus Dubitandum Est,* which can be read as a satirical but nevertheless clear repudiation of the method of thoroughgoing Cartesian doubt. In this unfinished text Kierkegaard imaginatively engages methodological doubt by dramatizing its effects upon the eponymous character who undertakes to live it out in all earnestness. To his chagrin, Johannes Climacus finds that if he begins philosophizing with doubt he fails to begin philosophizing at all, inasmuch as to doubt is precisely not to philosophize but only to doubt. Here the sensitive reader cannot help but draw a potential comparison with phenomenology's recurrence to beginnings, a trope inaugurated by Husserl himself and explored by Maurice Merleau-Ponty.[17] Both Kierkegaard and Husserl have been read as thinkers who were perpetually beginning anew.[18]

It is clear from *Johannes Climacus* that like Husserl, Kierkegaard did not regard the Cartesian insight as one that could be simply uncritically appropriated, though both acknowledge appreciation for the spirit of Descartes' effort.[19] It would be a caricature of Kierkegaard to paint him as then merely repudiating the need for philosophical skepticism in favor of uncritical faith. Though in his edifying writings Kierkegaard claimed that "wonder [is] the archenemy of doubt, with which it is never combined,"[20] in his pseudonymous corpus he developed a more subtle method of navigating between faith and doubt. *Fear and Trembling,* like *Johannes Climacus,* examines these issues by presenting dramatic or poetic[21] characters: Abraham, the Delphic bridegroom, Agnes and the merman, Tobias and Sarah, and Faust, among others. After his treatment of these characters and in preparation for the paragraphs on Abraham's paradoxical utterance to Isaac that God would provide the sacrifice, Kierkegaard wrote in a note to himself that was not included in the final text: "the believing *epoché*!" (*FT,* 255). While it would be too much to see in this aside a perfect coincidence of Kierkegaard's interests with Husserl's treatment of the *epoché,* both acknowledged a debt to Pyrrhonian skepticism.[22] What the reference to a "believing *epoché*" does indicate, however, is that Kierkegaard sought at least in some of his works a means of holding together faith or wonder and doubt. This tension is carried forward in Kierkegaard's texts that he designated "psychological," a moniker attached to the subtitles of *Repetition: A Venture in Experimental Psychology, The Concept of Anxiety: A Simple Psychologically Orienting Deliberation on the Dogmatic Issue of Hereditary Sin, The Sickness unto Death: A Christian Psychological Exposition for Upbuilding and Awakening,* and "'Guilty?'/'Not Guilty?': A Story of Suffering, An Imaginary Psychological Construction" from *Stages on Life's Way.*[23]

In the introduction to *The Concept of Anxiety* Haufniensis positions psychology as an intermediate discipline. It can draw upon dogmatic insights without itself being conflated either with dogmatic theology or metaphysical speculation. Haufniensis also distinguishes it from ethics and aesthetics (*CA,* 12, 14). As such, psychology is founded neither in revelation nor metaphysical constructs. It assumes no ethical theory and does not seek to satisfy any sentimental intuition. Instead, it calls for "altogether different categories" (*CA,* 17).

The need for different categories is imposed by the object of psychology, which is what Haufniensis calls "real possibility." The specific concern of the text is anxiety and by extension sin. Metaphysics treats only whatever "only *is,*" not what comes into being by transcendent leap, and thus can only be a disinterested speculation operative on the basis of logic and inappropriate to account for first-person experience (*CA,* 15). Sin therefore cannot be treated metaphysically inasmuch as sin is a free act brought into being uniquely by every individual. Dogmatics by contrast presupposes its object as a given of revelation and of actual fact. Sin is a possibility that is posited by theology and explained in terms that are only acceptable to a believer. Hence the need for psychology to account not for sin, since this is a dogmatic concept, but anxiety, which is "sin's real possibility" (*CA,* 21). This object is not a "what" but a "how," to paraphrase Heidegger and Henry.[24] "That which can be the concern of psychology and with which it can occupy itself is not that sin comes into existence, but how it can come into existence. Psychology can bring its concern to the point where it seems as if sin were there, but the next thing, that sin is there, is qualitatively different from the first . . . Psychology may abandon itself, so to speak, to the disappointment that sin is there as an actuality. But this last disappointment reveals the impotence of psychology and merely shows that its service has come to an end" (*CA*, 21–22). So psychology is sharply delimited in its scope. It cannot assume a dogmatic revelation as an actuality but traffics only in possibility. Haufniensis confirms this when he writes, "The actuality of sin as an object of thought is irrelevant to it . . . Only the possibility of sin still belongs to it" (*CA*, 22, 23).[25] By taking as its object anxiety as the real possibility of sin, psychology finds a way to talk about the dogmatic doctrine of sin *without presupposing it,* as dogmatics does, and *without taking into account any specific actual sin,* as ethics does.

How does psychology make sense of sin? First, while dogmatics presupposes that sin is, and ethics deals with its actual "manifestation," psychology makes sense of sin by explaining its "coming into existence" (*CA*, 21). It is therefore a science that mediates without mediation. Unlike speculative dogmatics, psychology explains movement by appealing to freedom and not the dialectical necessity engineered by what Haufniensis charmingly refers to as the "strange pixies and goblins who like busy clerks bring about movement in Hegelian logic" (*CA*, 12). Second, psychology explains sin in a manner that is of interest, and that word is chosen deliberately, to the individual. While dogmatics presupposes a concept that is of concern to the whole human race, and this is especially clear when it speaks of hereditary sin, and ethics copes with specific particular sins, psychology deals with the really possible sin of the single individual.

Darío González helpfully explains this point. "All through the book, the parallel treatment of both notions [anxiety and sin] will imply the encounter of two complementary perspectives: on the one hand, the description of a phenomenon (anxiety) that can only be observed in an individual life, but in such a way that this observation transcends the simple structure of self-reflection; on the other, the presupposition of a condition (sinfulness) that, according to the dogma, affects the human race taken as a whole, but in such a way that this presupposition becomes ethically relevant for each individual person."[26] It is hard to imagine a better description of the phenomenological project, even if in Kierkegaard's handling it takes on an ethically and religiously interested valence.

While much fine work has been done on this topic, much more

could be said about it, though this is not the place for a full exposition. But it should be clear that Kierkegaard's development of a method to address his peculiar concerns is sufficiently rigorous and promising for the questions that phenomenology pursues to merit more than a mere dismissal by the phenomenological tradition. Though he is doubtless an edifying writer who writes with the explicit aim of awakening possibilities in his reader, Kierkegaard nevertheless in his psychological works adopts an approach that relies not on dogmatic presumptions or metaphysical postulates but seeks to account for first-person experiences—sin, anxiety, despair, loss, heartbreak, disorientation—in a manner more rigorously defined than his critics have accredited.

The Contents of This Volume

While the phenomenological tradition is replete with inheritances from Kierkegaard with respect to these themes and more besides, this collection contains no papers on Kierkegaard's relationship to particular phenomenologists or their inheritance from him. While references to other phenomenologists are unavoidably present in these papers, inasmuch as the contributors bring their own understanding of what phenomenology is to their reading of Kierkegaard, the principal focus is on Kierkegaard himself and how his work contributes to phenomenology or expresses phenomenological insights previously unnoticed. The topics covered are familiar to students of Kierkegaard, but they never before have been systematically read as phenomenology.

The contributors represent many nations. Some come from theological backgrounds; most have philosophical training. Some are better known for Kierkegaard scholarship and others chiefly for phenomenological work. They represent a diversity of perspectives and approaches, and this variety of contributions comes together to create a genuinely multivalent experimental project.

The contributors to this volume address a variety of works from across the corpus and themes as wide ranging as intentionality, affectivity, angst, self-consciousness, the incognito, givenness, negativity, reduction, and temptation. These have been grouped into broader categories, beginning with, appropriately enough, the question of beginning and methodological concerns.

In the first essay, Kevin Hart surveys the history of phenomenology and catalogs a number of iterations upon the reduction found therein. His exploration reveals that the reduction was never received without alteration by Husserl's followers, such that one cannot easily speak of only one reduction, and in many cases the reduction was jettisoned by thinkers who nevertheless associate themselves with the phenomenological program. As a thinker who was just as much a writer, Kierkegaard like any poet would have to engage in some degree of phenomenological reduction, assuming an adequately broad notion thereof. More specifically, Hart goes on to show where in the Kierkegaardian corpus a more specific sort of reduction takes place. Often Kierkegaard pursues not a particular instantiation of an eidos but the eidos itself. Similarly, his pseudonymous works are not directed toward accounting for actualities but toward articulating possibilities. To fully account for the reduction in Kierkegaard's works, though, Hart argues we need to attend to the sort of phenomenality in which he is principally interested. Drawing on Jean-Yves Lacoste, Hart identifies in Kierkegaard a liturgical reduction that brackets both world and earth and dismantles the self-sufficient subject before the divine counterintentionality of desire and love.

Jeffrey Bloechl's paper takes its point of departure from Heidegger's rejection of Kierkegaard as a partner in the project of fundamental ontology and by implication, the project of phenomenology as well. Taking a tack from there at once more critical and sensitive, Bloechl indicates that the apparent problem posed to religious life and experience by phenomenological analysis committed to the thought of Being is also a promise. Such a promise is fulfilled by Kierkegaard in some of his upbuilding writings on love of God. If phenomenological analysis can attend to the religious way of being in the world, then it can in fact, Bloechl maintains, contribute in some way to an ontology and not merely an existentiell interpretation of religious life, and it is Kierkegaard, not Heidegger, who offers the more promising route to this possibility. Concentrating on "Purity of Heart Is to Will One Thing," Bloechl demonstrates that the text achieves its modest task of clarification without requiring the conversion or commitment of the reader. The discourse disrupts ordinary understanding from within by capitalizing on what understanding is already present, subverting it, and pointing the way to meaning in excess of traditional modes of understanding. Bloechl concludes by examining in turn the phenomena of paradox, enigma, and "the oblique" in Kierkegaard's communication.

The second section, on self-consciousness and self-givenness, features papers by Merold Westphal, Daniel Dahlstrom, and Arne Grøn. Westphal chooses to read Kierkegaard as substantively rather than historically phenomenological, and as such asks whether Kierkegaard is a thinker of the modes of givenness whereby "objects" are presented to consciousness, keeping in mind a wide range of possibilities for what counts as the given, inclusive of that which is given to the neglected capacity for faith. Turning to *Fear and Trembling,* Westphal reminds us that de Silentio's analysis of faith and the givenness of God to faith is hermeneutically phenomenological, inasmuch as philosophical speculation is for him anything but a pure unsituated intuition and that whatever understanding we have of such matters must detour through culture, language, interpretation, and narrative, holding to the story of the binding of Isaac not as theological ground but as cultural residue. This approach clears the way for philosophical meditation on the possibilities that theology affirms as fact. On Westphal's analysis God is given as personal speaker of commands and promises in the mode of inverted intentionality; God is given to faith, understood otherwise than as depleted knowing; and God is given as ultimate authority performing an *Aufhebung* on the morality of mores. Correlate to this theme is Kierkegaard's discussion of how the self is given, and to analyze this point Westphal turns to *The Sickness unto Death,* the notoriously difficult opening words of which he reads not metaphysically but phenomenologically. The self is given to itself, on Westphal's interpretation, as a dialectically incomplete relation. This relation is always a self-relation in turn, which encompasses an awareness of one's self as self-conscious, responsible, and free. The relation is at the same time one that also relates to another and is thus given to itself as task.

Daniel Dahlstrom's "Freedom Through Despair: Kierkegaard's Phenomenological Analysis" traverses similar territory textually but does so from the perspective of the question of freedom. Normally, Dahlstrom observes, debates on freedom have to do with the presence of alternative possibilities and whether these alternatives are compatible with wholly causal explanations for human decision making. Kierkegaard proceeds toward the issue of freedom instead by way of despair, which so often paralyzes freedom and inhibits awareness of our own power to choose. Kierkegaard shows how freedom can admit of degrees by way of its dialectical passage through the stages of despair. According to Dahlstrom, this process can be interpreted phenomenologically in conversation with Husserl's and Heidegger's analyses of the meaningful and essential characteristics of consciousness with some risk of anachronism but profitably nonetheless. Dahlstrom therefore reviews the formal account of freedom Kierkegaard proposes, interprets this account with a view to elucidating a Kierkegaardian critique of determinism and indeterminism, and catalogs the forms of freedom as they are concretized in the stages of despair. He reads Kierkegaard as eschewing metaphysical conceptions of the self and freedom in favor of a phenomenological analysis of the experience of the self's relating to itself in the ways in which that process can unfold either more or less successfully.

Arne Grøn's essay begins by reawakening the question of phenomenology itself, which on the one hand claims a return to the phenomena, but on the other must cope with the inherent dilemma of our very approach to those phenomena. Kierkegaard, like Heidegger, realizes that the most salient aspect of the phenomena in question is one that is precisely hidden and not immediately available to consciousness. As such, according to Grøn, he writes in such as way as to remind his reader of what she has overlooked, calling her back to her concern, both for herself and her world. Crucial to this linkage is the manner in which the dative of manifestation makes its appearance, the question of subjectivity, and Grøn averts to *The Concept of Anxiety* to articulate how the self is given to itself precisely as a self. This work provides a phenomenology of subjectivity, an analysis of how human subjectivity comes to itself as historical and situated. Anxiety shows how and that one is free or unfree in her relating to herself and to her world and others. These insights culminate in *The Sickness unto Death,* wherein is diagnosed a tension between self-givenness and self-understanding. While we are inevitably given to ourselves, our self-understanding is not simply given, and the relation between these problematics reopens the question of phenomenology itself.

The third section deals with aspects of experience that can be given to phenomenological discussion, including the question of God. Heiko Schulz provides a fresh approach to this contentious question in his piece, "A Phenomenological Proof? The Challenge of Arguing for God in Kierkegaard's Pseudonymous Authorship." Schulz furnishes a detailed exposition of the pseudonyms' objections against proofs for the existence of God, a point on which they all speak with one voice. Despite this unanimity, though, Schulz maintains that a phenomenological reading of *The Sickness unto Death* in particular opens up a proof for the existence of God that the author himself does not intend as conclusive but does have formal validity, leaving the question of its truth to be determined by the only one who can answer that question: each of Anti-Climacus's readers. Schulz demonstrates that there is a final incompatibility in Kierkegaard's thinking between the aim of proving God's existence and the goal of rendering a truthful account of Christian faith in its ideal structure. Schulz thereby renders a coherent and consistent account of Kierkegaard's theory of proofs for the existence of God and situates Anti-Climacus's formally valid phenomenological proof for God in this larger context.

Brian Gregor provides a thorough and systematic analysis of Kierkegaard's contribution to a phenomenology of temptation as it is articulated in a variety of works from the corpus. Gregor's treatment includes a careful distinction between temptation, anxiety, and the all-important category of spiritual trial. Turning to *Practice in Christianity* and the true heart of Kierkegaard's teaching on temptation, Gregor argues for the crucial role of the imagination in soliciting the self into temptation. It is imagination that gives possibilities to the self and allows it to "be drawn" into both temptation and, more positively, the imitation of Christ. Gregor fully limns Kierkegaard's typically keen psychological insights, describing the danger of lingering with temptation and imagining ourselves strong enough to defeat it on our own power. Temptation solicits us in weakness, befalling suddenly and announcing the prospect of a sin that is not yet either fully present or fully absent. And it at once allures the self with a new and dangerous possibility but one that at the same time appeals to something in the self already. Gregor concludes by arguing for the necessity of a hermeneutics of suspicion to complement the theory of temptation and gestures toward the possibility of a renewal of phenomenological analysis on the grounds of an acceptance of revelation as the precondition for discussion of new forms of phenomenality. Such a project would take the shape of a "second phenomenology," which would in turn be both hermeneutical and interested. Capitalizing on this option, Gregor finally turns to forgetting and remembering in relation to temptation as these themes are developed in the edifying writings.

The final piece in this section, Darío González's treatment of negative phenomena in Kierkegaard, places the issue of negative phenomena like the demonic in *The Concept of Anxiety* in relation to the questions of truth and freedom. González demonstrates that for Kierkegaard truth can only be produced by the individual in the consciousness of her untruth and thus in action, though this action can only be determined as the possibility of unfreedom. This paradoxical double formulation is in turn necessitated by the structure of human existence as spirit, the synthesis of the finite and infinite. The advantage of awareness of the negative then is to militate against the self-assured nature of the positive, which seeks security in speculation and sensate or historical certainty. Kierkegaard thus on González's reading ends up pursuing a deeper form of negativity peculiar to Christian consciousness than that of the Socratic or the merely ironic. This point of view requires a conception of time wherein the self experiences the future as primary, the temporal dimension that is the medium for the eternal. While irony preserves the past and the possibility of its recollection, sin forecloses the possibility of recollection and infinitizes inwardness. This form of negativity can only be described phenomenologically by the subject that itself exists negatively as anxiety, which reveals untruth and unfreedom as more than mere negations of their presumptive antonyms. The negativity of the self that has nothing for the object of its anxiety and the negativity of the unfreedom by which freedom reveals itself to itself as freedom form the two bookends of Haufniensis's exposition of anxiety as a whole: innocence and the demonic. González ties these analyses into a final discourse on the resistance of temporality to the syntheses that posit the self and the emergence of spirit in the "moment."

The final section includes perspectives from Mark Dooley and George Pattison, both of whom express some reservation about the association of Kierkegaard's work with the phenomenological tradition. Mark Dooley remarks on the clear differences between Kierkegaard's project and that of the phenomenologists and on the surprising fact that Husserl's most important disciples all acknowledge Kierkegaard's influence on their own thinking. The best way to read this affinity according to Dooley is to understand Kierkegaard as a thinker preeminently interested in reenchanting the lifeworld. In that sense he is akin to the late Husserl, who also sought to free thinking from the dominance of the natural sciences and like Kierkegaard, responded to a modern crisis in European society by attempting to revitalize the world of the characteristically human. For Dooley, then, Kierkegaard makes use of a mode of understanding that does not penetrate to the "really real" (or even aspire to do so) or do its work through causal explanation but seeks instead to be at home in a world of meaning. This sort of understanding takes the form of subjectivity, the values that allow for the personalization of ourselves and others. With the loss of these values the world becomes a leveled terrain wherein egocentrism, boredom, and suspicion reign, where the awkwardness and trials of the face-to-face encounter are supplanted by the purposeless and anonymous pseudointeraction characteristic of "chatter." If Kierkegaard is a phenomenologist, then, he is a phenomenologist of love. His work exists to move his readers from the isolation and self-obsession of the aesthetic into mature, responsible selfhood. Human beings are fundamentally characterized by their capacity for love, which must be expressed in concrete, rooted terms, not in a fantastical spectral "nowhere." The loss of faith is something that can be experienced phenomenologically, inasmuch as it plunges us into a loveless existence, for faith directs the self not just to God but to others too. Faith's task can only be realized by an education designed to sensitize the pupil to the sacredness of her own life and the lives of those around her.

George Pattison advances a reading of Kierkegaard as a fundamentally religious writer whose interests and aims are not easily assimilated to those of phenomenology. Following Heidegger's understanding of phenomenology as providing a methodological basis for all science in general, Pattison notes the particular problems this approach poses to religious thinking. The problems become even thornier when examined through the lens of Kierkegaard's notoriously difficult project. Nevertheless, given Kierkegaard's pivotal position between Hegel and Heidegger, Pattison contends he is of importance to the history of phenomenology, such that any self-accounting performed by phenomenology would have to include his work. That project according to Pattison must be subjected to sharp limits, but within those limits he examines the clear phenomenological tendencies discernible in Kierkegaard's works. These tendencies are clearly exhibited (as are their limits) in the structure of *The Sickness unto Death,* the first part of which is a formal existential phenomenology of despair clearly designed to be applicable to all humanity, while the second part consists of a hypothetical exploration of how the account of the first part would be radically revised on the basis of a theological supposition. Nothing in the first part or the strategy it adopts, Pattison argues, will motivate or much less compel belief in the substance of the second part. Insofar as Kierkegaard is desirous of inspiring belief, then he reaches the limits of phenomenological analysis (a limit reached not by abutting the transcendence of God but the complexities of human existence) and presents himself to his reader as neither phenomenologist nor dogmatist but Christian moralist.

Once again, all the essays included here are submitted in the spirit of furthering conversation and are intended both to provoke and edify.

Notes

1. Lev Shestov, "In Memory of a Great Philosopher: Edmund Husserl," *Philosophy and Phenomenological Research* 22, no. 4 (June 1962). See also Bernard Martin's introduction to *Athens and Jerusalem,* trans. Bernard Martin (Athens: Ohio University Press, 1966). An effort in the direction of explaining the parallels between Kierkegaard and Husserl is made by Michael Paradiso-Michau in his "Suspensions in Kierkegaard and Husserl," *The Lev Shestov Journal* 6 (Autumn 2006): 11–24.

2. The question is addressed by Michael Wyschogrod in his *Kierkegaard and Heidegger: The Ontology of Existence* (New York: Humanities Press, 1954), in the chapter on Heidegger in Walter Kaufmann, *Nietzsche, Heidegger, and Buber* (New York: McGraw-Hill, 1980), and Hubert Dreyfus, *Being-in-the-World: A Commentary on Heidegger's "Being and Time," Division I* (Cambridge, Mass.: MIT Press, 1991). See especially the appendix on Kierkegaard and div. 2 of *Being and Time.*

3. See Levinas's remarks published in an appendix to Jean Wahl, *A Short History of Existentialism,* trans. Forrest Williams and Stanley Maron (New York: Philosophical Library, 1949), 48–49.

4. Emmanuel Levinas, "Kierkegaard: Existence and Ethics," in *Proper Names,* trans. Michael B. Smith (London: Athlone Press, 1996), 70–71.

5. Ibid., 78; Emmanuel Levinas, "Enigma and Phenomenon," in *Basic Philosophical Writings,* ed. Adriaan T. Peperzak, Simon Critchley, and Robert Bernasconi (Bloomington: Indiana University Press, 1996), 70.

6. Levinas, "Kierkegaard: Existence and Ethics," in Smith, *Proper Names,* 70.

7. The most complete historical account of Levinas's influence from Kierkegaard is provided by Samuel Moyn in his *Origins of the Other: Emmanuel Levinas Between Revelation and Ethics* (Ithaca, N.Y.: Cornell University Press, 2005). See especially chap. 5. The most important philosophical work on the issues that jointly concern Kierkegaard and Levinas and their respective understandings thereof is *Kierkegaard and Levinas: Ethics, Politics, and Religion,* ed. J. Aaron Simmons and David Wood (Bloomington: Indiana University Press, 2008). For an exhaustive, encyclopedic treatment of all of Levinas's references to Kierkegaard, see my "Emmanuel Levinas: An Ambivalent but Decisive Reception," in *Kierkegaard Research: Sources, Reception, and Resources,* ed. Jon Stewart, vol. 11: *Kierkegaard's Influence on Philosophy, Tome II: Francophone Philosophy* (Aldershot, Eng.: Ashgate, forthcoming).

8. Jacques Derrida, "Violence and Metaphysics," in *Writing and Difference,* trans. Alan Bass (Chicago: University of Chicago Press, 1978), 111.

9. Jacques Derrida, *The Gift of Death,* trans. David Wills (Chicago: University of Chicago Press, 1996). I have written on the triangulation formed between Derrida, Levinas, and Kierkegaard in "Returning (to) the Gift of Death: Violence and History in Derrida and Levinas," *International Journal for Philosophy of Religion* 67, no. 1 (February 2010): 1–15.

10. Jacques Derrida and Maurizio Ferraris, *A Taste for the Secret* (Cambridge: Polity Press, 2001), 40. For more from Mark Dooley on Kierkegaard and Derrida, see his *The Politics of Exodus: Søren Kierkegaard's Ethics of Responsibility* (New York: Fordham University Press, 2001).

11. For further discussion of Henry's relationship to Kierkegaard, see my "Michel Henry's Problematic Reading of *The Sickness unto Death,*" *Journal of the British Society for Phenomenology* 38, no. 3 (2007): 248–60; "Michel Henry and Søren Kierkegaard on Paradox and the Phenomenality of Christ," *International Journal of Philosophic Studies* 17, no. 3 (2009): 435–54; and "Michel Henry's Theory of Disclosive Moods," in *Words of Life: New Theological Turns in French Phenomenology* (New York: Fordham University Press, 2010). See also Nicole Hatem, "Michel Henry, lecteur du 'Concept d'angoisse' de Kierkegaard," *Revue Philosophique de la France et de l'Etranger* 191, no. 3 (2001): 339–57.

12. See *Incarnation: Une philosophie de la chair* (Paris: Seuil, 2000).

13. See the pages beginning with 676 in his *The Essence of Manifestation,* trans. Girard Etzkorn (The Hague: Martinus Nijhoff, 1973).

14. See especially part 3, chapter 4, "Phenomenology of Despair," in Calvin O. Schrag, *Existence and Freedom: Towards an Ontology of Human Finitude* (Evanston, Ill.: Northwestern University Press, 1961).

15. Vincent A. McCarthy, *The Phenomenology of Moods in Kierkegaard* (The Hague: Martinus Nijhoff, 1978). See also Louis Pojman, "Kierkegaard's Phenom-

enology of the Stages of Existence," in *Faith, Knowledge, and Action: Essays Presented to Niels Thulstrup on His Sixtieth Birthday*, ed. George L. Stengren (Copenhagen: Reitzels, 1984), 116–45.

16. The variety of perspectives represented herein should, I hope, indicate that neither I nor anyone contributing is seeking anything as straightforward as a "yes or no" answer to the question of Kierkegaard as phenomenologist. The proposal is meant to stimulate thought on a variety of fronts both among ourselves and in the minds of our readers, not to "settle" the matter one way or the other.

17. Merleau-Ponty refers to Husserl on this point in the preface to *Phenomenology of Perception*, trans. Colin Smith (London: Routledge and Kegan Paul, 1962), xiv: "The philosopher, as the unpublished works declare, is a perpetual beginner, which means that he takes for granted nothing that men, learned or otherwise, believe they know. It means also that philosophy itself must not take itself for granted, insofar as it may have managed to say something true."

18. Husserl's *Cartesian Meditations*, *Ideas* I, *Paris Lectures*, and *Crisis* all present themselves as introductions to phenomenology. Kierkegaard's works also often take the form of repeated beginnings, as in the many "preliminary" sections of *Fear and Trembling* and the repeated reinterpretations of the central problematic of *Philosophical Fragments*.

19. Through his pseudonym Johannes de Silentio, Kierkegaard notably offers a more charitable reading of Descartes in the preface to *Fear and Trembling*, wherein de Silentio suggests that Descartes himself has been misunderstood by his enthusiastic imitators. These imitators imagine that doubt can be easily dispensed with and forgo the difficult work of doubt themselves by simply paying lip service to Descartes and proceeding on the assumption that they have doubted as rigorously as he. In this respect de Silentio actually draws parallels between doubt and faith. Both, he implies, are projects of a lifetime, something that the ancient skeptics realized about doubt and that Abraham understood about faith (*FT*, 5–7). Husserl's engagement with Descartes is of course familiar to us from *Cartesian Meditations: An Introduction to Phenomenology*, trans. Dorion Cairns (The Hague: Martinus Nijhoff, 1977).

20. *Eighteen Upbuilding Discourses*, ed. and trans. Howard V. Hong and Edna H. Hong (Princeton, N.J.: Princeton University Press, 1990), 135.

21. It is arguable that de Silentio's use of "poetic" figures and approaches is not an approach with which he himself is content. In every major such character study from Problem III de Silentio goes out of his way to say that he is changing the story in such a way as to make it *less* poetic. In the case of the Delphic bridegroom de Silentio states openly that the story is not being told poetically or as a poet would. He introduces it by saying, "If a poet were to make use of it" (*FT*, 89), as if his own usage is not poetic, and then he declares openly that he is not a poet himself (*FT*, 90). Similar disavowals of the role of the poet accompany the story of Agnes and the merman, which de Silentio alters in order to distance his own retelling from a poetic one. He recites, "The merman is a seducer who rises up from his hidden chasm and in wild lust seizes and breaks the innocent flower standing on the seashore in all her loveliness and with her head thoughtfully inclined to the soughing of the sea. This has been the poets' interpretation

until now. Let us make a change" (*FT,* 94), and again once his version of the tale has been told, in which the merman's lecherous intent is thwarted by the perfect innocence of Agnes, de Silentio admits, "I have taken the liberty of changing the merman somewhat, and essentially I have also changed Agnes a little" (*FT,* 95). Likewise in the case of Tobias and Sarah de Silentio writes, "If a poet read this story and were to use it, I wager a hundred to one he would make everything center on the young Tobias . . . this heroic courage would be the subject. I venture to propose another" (*FT,* 103).

22. For an interesting perspective on Kierkegaard's use of skepticism, see José R. Maia Neto, *The Christianization of Pyrrhonism: Scepticism and Faith in Pascal, Kierkegaard, and Shestov* (Dordrecht: Kluwer, 1995). On Husserl's use of Pyrrhonism, see Dermot Moran, *Introduction to Phenomenology* (New York: Routledge, 2000), 148–50.

23. George Pattison addresses the nature of Kierkegaard's psychology and whether it can be considered proto-phenomenological in his *The Philosophy of Kierkegaard* (Montreal: McGill-Queen's University Press, 2005), 46–48. Pattison and this author do not necessarily agree in every respect on this issue, but our conversation is ongoing both within this volume and in personal exchanges.

24. Martin Heidegger, *Being and Time,* trans. John Macquarrie and Edward Robinson (New York: Harper and Row, 1962), 50; and Michel Henry, *The Essence of Manifestation,* 57.

25. Insofar as phenomenology concerns itself with possibility, Kierkegaard's psychology may in fact be read as at least proto-phenomenology. Interestingly Louis Mackey too reads Kierkegaard as primarily concerned with possibility, though he attributes this to Kierkegaard's conception of himself as a "poet." He could just as easily be read not as a poet but as a phenomenologist. Louis Mackey, *Kierkegaard: A Kind of Poet* (Philadelphia: University of Pennsylvania Press, 1971), 289–90, 292.

26. "The Triptych of Sciences in the Introduction to *The Concept of Anxiety,*" in *Kierkegaard Studies. Yearbook* 2001, ed. Niels Jørgen Cappelørn, Herman Deuser, Jon Stewart, and Christian Fink Tolstrup (Berlin: W. de Gruyter, 2001), 15.

KIERKEGAARD AS PHENOMENOLOGIST

Part 1

Beginnings and Method

The Elusive Reductions of Søren Kierkegaard

Kevin Hart

If the idea of Kierkegaard as a phenomenologist is to be considered at all rigorously, the question whether there is one reduction (or more) in his thought must be posed and answered. Perhaps the question does not need to be answered in the affirmative, however, for there are people who subscribe to a phenomenology without any reduction. Not all of Husserl's students made the move from the realism of the *Logical Investigations* to the transcendental viewpoint of *Ideas* I. Perhaps it suffices to bring Kierkegaard into the fold of phenomenology to say that he is a philosopher for whom proving is less important than showing, and that the pseudonymous writings in particular show what no argument or exposition could ever manage to establish.[1] And with the writings presented over his signature, perhaps it is enough to indicate that they are concerned with the intentional structure of love and, indeed, the counterintentional structure of divine love. Further, it might be said, not without reason, that Kierkegaard is a phenomenologist preoccupied above all with God, and God is the irreducible par excellence, from which it would follow that it would be wrongheaded to look for one or more reductions in his writings.

Support for this relaxed attitude to Kierkegaard as a phenomenologist can be gained simply by looking at the history of phenomenology with respect to reductions. I say "reductions" partly because there are different steps and directions of abstention and ascesis that are in "the phenomenological reduction" and partly because there are other reductions that are sometimes in play.[2] To name only a few: the eidetic reduction and the philosophical reduction, the phenomenological reduction, and the transcendental reduction. If Husserl started by thinking of *epoché* (bracketing) and reduction together, he ended by seeing the one as the condition for the other.[3] Yet it might be said that one mark of a major phenomenologist, whether before or after the discovery of the reduction, is his or her refusal of "the reduction" as Husserl came to determine it and refine it in the period running from *The Idea of Phenomenology* (1907) to the second volume of *Erste Philosophie* (1923) to *The Crisis of European Sciences and Transcendental Phenomenology* (1934–37). Those philosophers with phenomenological insight who preceded Husserl—Descartes, above all—disappointed him by not recognizing the importance of reduction when they came across it.[4] Husserl remained interested only in the first two of the *Meditations on First Philosophy,* for with the third Descartes moved away from the phenomenology that was to be. The *Logical Investigations* (1899–1901) was of course a breakthrough for Husserl, but after 1905, with what he then called the epistemological reduction firmly in place, it was deemed by him to be "not an end, but rather a beginning."[5] With the second edition of the *Logical Investigations,* published the same year as *Ideas* I (1913), Husserl introduced what he now called the phenomenological reduction, and subtly changed the fabric of the entire work.

More disturbing for Husserl, though, were those phenomenologists, including former students from Göttingen such as Roman Ingarden and Hedwig Conrad-Martius, who declined to adopt the reduction in order to remain realists, or who failed to perform it in the way or ways he deemed necessary. Chief among the latter is Heidegger, who told his students as early as the summer of 1927 that for him the reduction was not the passage from the natural attitude to transcendental consciousness but from beings to being, and that it was not central to phenomenology in any case.[6] Similar stories can be told of other phenomenologists, including some that Husserl would never know. Jean-Paul Sartre dropped reduction because it sought to lead him to transcendental consciousness whereas phenomenology is endangered, he thought, if it does not determine the "I" as a relative existent.[7] Discharging reduction is one marker, an important one, of his half turn from phenomenology to existentialism. For his part, Maurice Merleau-Ponty insisted that the phenomenological reduction is never completed, and that we are always forced to begin again when trying to adopt the phenomenological gaze.[8] (Husserl would have agreed with him.) Jan Patočka held that reduction fails because it illegitimately identifies immediate givenness and subjective immanence, but that it nonetheless allows us to understand human transcendence as the subject's self-opening to being.[9] Yet others have adopted and adapted reduction. Derrida at first enlarged it so that the being of transcendent entities is suspended instead of suppressed, and then maintained that, properly understood, reduction is pure thought as the delay incurred in any origin having to refer back to an earlier origin.[10] And, more recently, Marion has extended reduction in order to bring out its intrinsic connection with givenness and phenomenality.[11]

Yet other later phenomenologists have rejected reduction in no uncertain terms. Emmanuel Levinas, for one, dismisses it on the ground that it is rooted in a theoretical attitude to the world, an intellectualism that phenomenology of all philosophies should resist in the name of concreteness.[12] He remains committed to intentional analysis, which he takes to be the core of phenomenology. Michel Henry, for another, argues that the reduction leads one to an ecstatic phenomenology whereas the proper procedure would enable one to elaborate an enstatic phenomenology in which originary phenomenality is the ground and abyss on which the quest for phenomena is based.[13] Yet we need to ask exactly what these later thinkers are rejecting and why they are doing so, and if one can in fact do phenomenology of any sort without some form of reduction, if not the phenomenological or the transcendental reduction. Should it turn out that there is no reduction, in any recognizable sense, in Kierkegaard's thought, we must ask what makes some people think that his writings abide in the neighborhood of phenomenology. And of course if there is a reduction of some kind, we must ask what it is, what prompts it, and where it leads.

Many readers of Kierkegaard are happy to regard him as an existentialist, or as a forerunner of that movement, but not as a phenomenologist.[14] After all, the existentialists took the word "existence" from him (as he took it from Schelling), and with it a stress upon the singularity and absolute nature of the individual. One highly influential text in this regard is a note that Heidegger appended to the last paragraph of the introduction to division 2 of *Being and Time* (1927): "In the nineteenth century, Søren Kierkegaard explicitly seized upon the problem of existence as an existentiell problem, and thought it through in a penetrating fashion. But the existential problematic was so alien to him that, as regards his ontology, he remained completely dominated by Hegel and by ancient philosophy as Hegel saw it."[15] Heidegger finds himself preferring the edifying discourses to the pseudonymous works, except for *The Concept of Anxiety* (1844), to which he is indebted in his account of *Angst.* The Kierkegaard who comes into focus for Heidegger in his first major work is a thinker of existence, although one still dominated by Hegel's concept of being as "empty thinking."[16] No mention is made of Schelling, and one might object that, despite Kierkegaard's growing disappointment with the philosopher's Berlin lectures on his "positive philosophy" of 1841, he was a tonic influence on the young Danish writer. It was Schelling's emphasis upon actuality, as distinct from Hegel's dialectical idea of being, which excited Kierkegaard. In its search for the concrete, Kierkegaard's is always a positive philosophy, not a negative one, and the Hegel to whom he comes close now and then—as in the very movement of *The Sickness unto Death* (1849)—is the author of *The Phenomenology of Spirit* (1807).

Adorno will wisely prompt us not to take Heidegger at his word as a reader of Kierkegaard, telling us that "in *Being and Time* . . . Kierkegaard's concept of existence had undone the posture on the part of the 'observer' in which the phenomenologist felt himself vindicated."[17] And in the same spirit we may recall that Heidegger's note on Kierkegaard in *Being and Time* was not his first mention of him. In the summer semester of 1921, when lecturing on Augustine's *Confessions,* he quoted favorably from *The Sickness unto Death* and from *The Concept of Anxiety.*[18] To develop a phenomenological reading of Augustine, Heidegger had to go by way of Kierkegaard's reflections on guilt and sin. Are these reflections phenomenological? They are certainly descriptive. But do they change the "what" question to the "how" question in the manner of phenomenology? Heidegger certainly does that himself when reading Augustine: "'Life'—a How of having, and indeed an experiencing of *tentationes* . . . 'Life': a How of a being of a determinate structure and categorial expression," he writes in his notes.[19] It is the movement from "What?" to "How?" that marks phenomenology, at least for Husserl and Heidegger. Yet Heidegger's mention in the note of Hegel's great work of 1807 reminds us that "phenomenology" was not a word of Husserl's coinage. (It entered philosophy in Johann Heinrich Lambert's *Cosmological Letters on the Arrangement of the World-Edifice* [1761].) Merleau-Ponty tells us in the *Phenomenology of Perception* (1945), "*Phenomenology can be practiced and identified as a manner or style of thinking, that it existed as a movement before arriving at complete awareness of itself* as a philosophy" (viii; my emphasis). Indeed, he begins that invaluable book by asking, "What is phenomenology?" and remarking how strange it is that the question must be posed half a century after Husserl's first publications appeared. He goes on to say that followers of the movement have found it ex post facto "in every quarter, *certainly* in Hegel and Kierkegaard" (viii; my emphasis). It is not a matter of finding all in all, the future already in the past, since only one aspect of phenomenology is to be found in the nineteenth century.

Phenomenology speaks about itself in a doubled way, Merleau-Ponty says. On the one hand, it is a transcendental philosophy and a rigorous science, while on the other hand, it is concerned with the world and with lived experience. We cannot locate Kierkegaard in terms of transcendental philosophy or rigorous science, yet he is deeply concerned with being in the world and with the texture of lived experience. Not that one will find any of Husserl's technical vocabulary for clarifying experience in Kierkegaard, no more so than one will find it in Hegel's *Phenomenology of Spirit.* Even so, we can, Merleau-Ponty says, find Kierkegaard in phenomenology considered as a "movement" before it became a "doctrine," if we focus on his attentiveness and wonder, awareness and the "will to seize the meaning of the world" (xxi). To which we might add that if phenomenology can be found in both Hegel and Kierkegaard, two figures associated in the modern philosophical imagination mainly by the latter's sharp disagreements with the former, we must assume that the movement to which Merleau-Ponty refers is a very broad one indeed.

Merleau-Ponty cites Eugen Fink as saying that the reduction is wonder in the face of the world, though the German does not say that in so many words.[20] He observes, instead, that "the phenomenological onlooker . . . does not remain thematically focused upon the transcendental experience of the world . . . but *inquires back* from *experience* of the world to *constitution* of the world."[21] And he also evokes "the awful tremor everyone experiences who actually passes through the phenomenological reduction," a tremor caused by realizing that the world has been "de-absolutized" by the reduction (144), and that its meaning has been coconstituted by the transcendental ego. For Fink as for Husserl, phenomenology secures the world so that phenomena may disclose themselves. There is no attempt to ground the world in terms of a theory; rather, by way of an intellectual ascesis, one takes a step back to the very edge of the world and assumes the viewpoint of the transcendental ego. One becomes an onlooker who is not committed to any theses about the being of the word or its contents, as was the empirical, psychological "I" before the reduction took place. Authoritative as Fink's account of the reduction is, the French philosopher offers the more winning description of it. "Reflection does not withdraw from the world towards the unity of consciousness of the world's basis; it steps back to watch the forms of transcendence fly up like sparks from a fire; it slackens the intentional threads which attach us to the world and thus brings them to our notice; it alone is consciousness of the world because it reveals that world as strange and paradoxical" (xiii). As already mentioned, Merleau-Ponty qualifies his account of the reduction by saying that no reduction is ever complete: we cannot step back all at once, we cannot quite leave our empirical "I" behind, and we cannot bring the strangeness and paradoxical nature of our being in the world fully and clearly into view. One reduction implies another, and then another, and so on. The sheer multiplication of reductions by Husserl in his later work gives credence to Merleau-Ponty's account of the reduction as incomplete, though we may wonder if the Frenchman is right to contain phenomenology within philosophy as he does. Does it not apply to all thinking and all writing?

Kierkegaard is a rare philosopher, for he is as much a writer as a thinker. Perhaps only Plato stands as a comparison with him in this regard. "To be an author—well, yes, this appeals to me. If I am to be honest, I must indeed say that I have been in love with being productive," the Dane wrote toward the end of his life.[22] One of his most admiring modern readers, Louis Mackey, insists on taking Kierkegaard at his word and thinking of him first and foremost as "a kind of poet."[23] "There has hardly been a poet before me," Kierkegaard told his journal in 1849, "who has known about life and especially about religion as profoundly as I do."[24] The word "poet" reminds us that Kierkegaard could write lyrically; also, it captures the spirit of some of the pseudonymous writings; and, furthermore, it indicates the status of those writings: they are "without authority," since he does not write about ethics and religion with the backing of the church.[25] Mackey explicitly sets Kierkegaard's claim to be a poet against what he is pleased to call "the jejune solemnities of the *epoché*" (xii). Now in most of his works, at least up until *The Crisis,* Husserl reserves the word *epoché* for the phenomenological reduction, through which we are led back to the position of transcendental onlooker, and this is quite distinct from the eidetic reduction that is performed while still in the natural attitude in order to disclose the eidos or principle of something. Without the eidetic reduction we could not do mathematics, write poems, or even think straight. There is nothing jejune here.

And yet the *epoché* is jejune, Mackey says. What might give him pause, though, is a line from a letter that Husserl wrote to Hugo von Hofmannsthal in 1907, the very year he started to lecture on the reduction.[26] He says there to the poet and playwright, "The phenomenological gaze is therefore a close relation of the aesthetic gaze."[27] Note that Husserl is not saying that the aesthetic gaze is close to the eidetic reduction, although he could have said that as well. When we see Shakespeare's *Othello* acted memorably we discern the eidos of jealousy, and when we read Hopkins's "Hurrahing in Harvest" we grasp what it is to have religious joy. One cannot be a poet without performing the eidetic reduction. (One cannot be anything much.) Yet Husserl goes further and says that the aesthetic gaze is kin to the *phenomenological* gaze. The writing or reading of a poem, such as Hofmannsthal's "Vor Tag," edges us out of the natural attitude, allows us to stand at the very limit of the world and to contemplate our experiences without holding a thesis about them. What may appear to be judgments made by the poet are really no more than quasi-judgments.[28] The aesthetic gaze encourages reflection without holding a position or a thesis about being, although of course Husserl would want to add that the phenomenological gaze is more rigorous and more radical than the aesthetic gaze: it disconnects us more thoroughly from the world of fact, neutralizes it more surely, and enables us to reflect more deeply on our experiences. Images can only go so far, the philosopher thought.

Husserl's insight has been taken up by others, writers as well as philosophers. In *Le pas au-delà* (1973), Maurice Blanchot reflects in the third person on his early practice as a novelist in the 1930s, saying, "During the day there were the daytime acts, the day to day words, the day to day writing, affirmations, values, habits, nothing that counted and yet something that one had confusedly to call life. The certainty that in writing he was putting between parentheses precisely this certainty [*il mettait précisément entre parèntheses cette attitude*], including the certainty of himself as the subject of writing, led him slowly, though right away, into an empty space, whose void (the barred zero, heraldic) in no way prevented the turns and detours of a very long process."[29] The writing of *Thomas l'obscur* (1941), *Aminadab* (1942), and perhaps also the stories written alongside *Thomas* and now gathered in *Le ressassement eternal* (1951), involved a reduction that called the ground of subjectivity into question. Notice that for Blanchot the aesthetic gaze (an expression that would make him uncomfortable) has quietly become the phenomenological gaze.[30] We remember Blanchot's evocation of Husserl in *L'Entretien infini* (1969), when he tells us, in a more philosophic voice, that phenomenology contributed greatly to the project of dismantling "man" in the human sciences. In thinking of consciousness by way of intentionality Husserl "empties consciousness of consciousness, and makes of this emptiness a relation that is always distinct from and superior to the terms in relation."[31]

No one can be a poet, not even "a kind of poet," without some degree of phenomenological reduction, it would seem. Certainly that is Jacques Derrida's view. Let us overhear him elucidating it in an interview:

> Poetry and literature provide or facilitate "phenomenological" access to what makes of a thesis a *thesis as such*. Before having a philosophical content, before being or bearing such and such a "thesis," literary experience, writing or reading, is a "philosophical" experience which is neutralized or neutralizing insofar as it allows one to think the thesis; it is a nonthetic experience of the thesis, of belief, of position, of naivety, of what Husserl called the "natural attitude." The phenomenological conversion of the gaze, the "transcendental reduction" he recommended is perhaps the very condition (I do not say the natural condition) of literature.[32]

The scare quotes around the word "phenomenological" make us recall Merleau-Ponty's distinction between phenomenology as a doctrine and as a movement. Poetry and literature are held to participate in phenomenology as a movement that is more general than the one Merleau-Ponty imagined. It goes back to Homer and Lascaux. Writing, in Derrida's extended sense of the word, allows us to suspend the inevitable relation with transcendence, whether it is meaning or reference, and to savor the experience at hand. This literary functioning may take place, at least to some degree, in all speech and writing, Derrida argues, and thereby he extends Blanchot's point. All the more surely this literary functioning occurs sharply and variously in a writing such as Kierkegaard's, much of which is characterized by aphorisms and irony, parables and stories, humor and satire. On this understanding, a reduction has always and already taken place before any of the works, especially the pseudonymous writings, get under way. It is an elusive reduction, a condition for writing, and one that never appears as such. Perhaps everything that has ever been said about rhetoric and genre, prosody and form, has been indirectly a discourse on reduction.

There can be no question then of the reduction, any one of them, being an "esoteric experience" that one must have in order to do philosophy or write poetry or compose music or paint a landscape.[33] No special experience is required for Husserl to write, "Natural cognition begins with experience and remains *within* experience," or for Kafka to write, "It was late in the evening when K. arrived."[34] No philosophy, except perhaps for reductive naturalism, and certainly no literature, not even a gritty realist novel, can be written by men or women who remain entirely within the natural attitude. A change of seeing is required, not an esoteric experience. If this is true, then Levinas and Henry, along with everyone who has written that the reduction should be rejected because it is intellectualist or even idealist, have been implicitly performing a reduction in order to do so. They and others may object that this understanding of the reduction, coming from Blanchot and Derrida (with some support from Husserl), is so broad as to be without use in reading Kierkegaard or anyone. I am not so sure: the thought of a reduction involved in writing and reading has the great benefit of deflecting naïve approaches to both. That said, it would be one thing to agree with the objection to reduction as a condition of possibility for writing but quite another to be beaten back to accept the reduction as a single methodology, deeply embedded in epistemology, found only momentarily in Descartes and then gloriously expounded in Husserl.

In one of his late seminars at the Collège de France, Merleau-Ponty observed that over the period from preparing the *Cartesian Meditations* (1929) to drafting *The Crisis,* Husserl shifted in his understanding of the reduction. Properly grasped, it is "less of a method defined once and for all than the index of a multitude of problems"; it "no longer involves a return to ideal being, but brings us back to the spirit of Heraclitus, to an interweaving of horizon, to an open Being."[35] To be sure, Husserl stepped back from the overly Cartesian aspect of the reduction, pointing out in *The Crisis* that it has an ontological as well as epistemological function.[36] It is "the gate of entry" (257) through which one must pass to pure transcendental consciousness and the world as its noematic correlate. That subjectivity and that world are doubtless the site of many problems, some of which call for further reductions, but it is doubtful that the precisions of *The Crisis* will help us very much in reading Kierkegaard. If we are to find a reduction in his work it may not closely resemble anything we find in Husserl, except of course for the aesthetic gaze that leads us to experience things without holding an ontological thesis about them, and for the "irreducible openness" of the inside to the outside, that aspect of the reduction that Derrida calls "*a theatre stage.*"[37] It will be a reduction, but not the phenomenological or the transcendental reduction.

With that caveat in mind we can begin to pick out in a preliminary way some sites, by no means all of them, where a reduction has taken place in Kierkegaard's writings. To begin with, note the title of one of Kierkegaard's most often read works, "Diary of the Seducer" [*Forførerens Dagbog*] in *Either/Or* (1843). This is not a diary of *a* seducer, a Casanova or a Don Juan, but a diary of *the* seducer. By way of Johannes the Seducer, Kierkegaard has given us the eidos of being a seducer: not an abbreviation of the being of a seducer, its *Wesen,* or a series of accidents that could make up various stories of seduction, but the mental and affective structures of a mind that is intent on seducing women.[38] (Kierkegaard is less successful in presenting the essence of marriage in the pastoral of Judge Wilhelm and his wife.) In the same year, 1843, *Fear and Trembling* might be taken to offer a "phenomenology of the inapparent," as Heidegger called it.[39] It is precisely the nonappearing of faith as a phenomenon in the daily actions of the knight of faith that is presented to us at length and in detail. Pass from here to a much later piece, the papers by Inter and Inter that constitute *The Crisis and a Crisis in the Life of an Actress* (1848). Not only does Kierkegaard seek the eidos of the actress in and through Johanne Luise Heiberg and finds it not in "feminine youthfulness" but in "expressiveness of soul" but also, in her second attempt to play Juliet in *Romeo and Juliet* (once at age sixteen, now at age thirty-four), he discerns there, by means of her more highly developed skill, the essence of Juliet's passion.[40] Repetition and craft serve here as prompts to reduction: we can know what adolescent passion is, in all its immanence, by watching the actress play her at the mature age of thirty-four, not sixteen.

Note too that in the pseudonymous writings there are no objective results that are presented for our acceptance. Kierkegaard may have thought that the pseudonymous writings, along with the uplifting discourses, were alike the work of a poet and penitent. All the same, it is important to recognize that the pseudonymous writings are disengaged from philosophical *theses* about being human or being a Christian. These writings present the reader with possibilities, not with actualities; and in saying that plainly it is good to recall Husserl speaking of the world beyond reduction as "a *world of absolutely pure possibility*."[41] That grasped, one should then look at the *Concluding Unscientific Postscript* (1846), where it is argued by Johannes Climacus that the differences between one period of history and another must be bracketed when considering the question of religious belief. What we are confronted with is the eidos of faith as a leap, and the preparations for that leap. And finally consider Johannes de Silentio's *Fear and Trembling* (1843), which anticipates the sort of reduction we associate with Heidegger's talk of *Befindlichkeit* (attunement) and *Stimmung* (mood). It begins with a "Prelude" (*Stemning*) that establishes a mood and attunes us to the dominant concerns of what will follow. The prelude consists of imaginative variations on the relationship between Abraham and Isaac that have the effect of awakening us to the concrete drama of the biblical story about him.

The reduction in each case just mentioned is elusive; it never announces itself, and yet its effects can be noticed: there would be no "Søren Kierkegaard" without it. So we look to Husserl for clarification, and there we find that the reduction has two aspects: a negative one of suspension and a positive one of leading back, whether in the service of a structural or a genetic phenomenology.[42] So far we have mostly identified an eidetic reduction in Kierkegaard, and a negative moment of phenomenological suspension in order to engage in pure showing, and we could locate these things in any concrete thought, whether in philosophy or literature. Is this sufficient to make it worthwhile to call Kierkegaard a phenomenologist? It is doubtful; and before regarding Kierkegaard as someone devoted at best to intentional analysis *avant la lettre* we need to look more closely to see if there is some sort of phenomenological reduction or close kin to it in operation. Is there, though, a leading back in Kierkegaard, and if so to where are we led? Certainly there is no step back into the transcendental structure of subjectivity such as the one that Husserl invited us to make in the writings of his final maturity. We were to take that step, he argued, in order to absolve ourselves of all presuppositions, those theses about being that entangle us while thinking in the natural attitude. In the midst of suspending those theses, however, Husserl quietly imported a very important presupposition of his own: that phenomenality was to be set strictly at the level of the objectness of the object. Phenomenology would bracket the natural attitude in order to divest itself of the metaphysics of the positive sciences but only so that it could finally address itself to the question of their constitution. On realizing this, one may begin a critique of Husserl's account of the reduction in order to reformulate it (as Patočka does, for example) or seek other modes of reduction that accord with other understandings of phenomenality. We begin to understand Kierkegaard when we grasp the phenomenality that compels his attention. There is an instant in which eternity crosses time, he tells us on many occasions, and we are invited to leap from a known state to another that is entirely unknown. The phenomenality of that leap is worked out by way of anxiety and faith, inwardness and passion. To where does Kierkegaard lead us in order to be attuned to this instant?

Jean-Yves Lacoste can help us answer the question. In his *Experience and the Absolute* (1994) he proposes a liturgical reduction. By "liturgy" he means not a specific rite of worship such as the Mass but more generally "the logic that presides over the encounter between man and God writ large."[43] Having considered Heidegger's distinction between world and earth, Lacoste tells us that "liturgy appears as a certain bracketing of world and earth" (175). Fink told us long ago that the one who performs the reduction becomes "the player of the world [*Weltspieler*]" and hence "like the gods" in the sense that Heraclitus gives to the expression when saying of Zeus, "He plays with worlds."[44] Lacoste tropes this figure, having the one who prays withdraw to the very margin of world and earth, not becoming a god but remaining *coram Deo,* in the presence of God. The one who prays brackets both world and earth while denying neither. If the liturgical being encounters God it is not by way of the ground of the world, as Husserl thinks, or religious experience (*Erlebnis*) but in love of God and the poverty of nonexperience. Exposure to God removes the ego from the center of life, Lacoste maintains, and thereby dismantles the subjectivity of the subject. The liturgical being is Dasein, a structure of "being there," but when exposed to God in prayer the "there" no longer directly impinges on the one who prays.

On hearing of this exfoliation of the subject one may well think that Kierkegaard, the fierce defender of the individual subject against the relentless advances of the System, has been entirely left behind. Not so: the affirmation of subjective truth turns not on approving one species of truth over another (which would commit him to "double truth") or floating an entirely new theory of truth as subjectivity (which would be unable to make sense of the veracity of mathematics and science), but on a subject's personal appropriation of truth so that it is lived in wakefulness, not tacitly confirmed in the half sleep of social convention. It is not the appearance of affirming the truth that matters, Kierkegaard repeatedly tells us, but the reality of having seized the truth for oneself without assurances given in advance. Needless to say, this impatience with appearance is one with Kierkegaard's criticism of state clergy and their tacit followers. The more apparent the clergy in a country, the more that God withdraws, for, as Kierkegaard wryly notes, in ecclesial matters "God relates inversely to phenomenon [*sic*]."[45] That there is a change in subjectivity when existing *coram Deo* is something Kierkegaard says in several voices. In the *Concluding Unscientific Postscript* Johannes Climacus says "to be known *in time by God* makes life enormously strenuous."[46] Anti-Climacus agrees, telling us that the self of the person who stands before God must change: "This self is no longer the merely human self but is what I, hoping not to be misinterpreted, would call the theological self, the self directly before God."[47] This transformation is no easy thing, for "man, as a particular individual, should have such a reality as is implied by existing directly in the sight of God" (214). And Kierkegaard, writing on his own account, agrees as well: "Having been looked at by God, I had to and have to look to God," he tells his journal in 1847.[48] The person in prayer is completely exposed to the counterintentionality of the divine gaze. Note, though, that Kierkegaard does not make the relation with God reciprocal and symmetrical. He does not look *at* God but *to* God. It is still an intentional relationship, but one marked by desire and love, which have become legible precisely because a reduction has taken place. This is of course everywhere apparent in Kierkegaard's prayers, and also in prayers that open his directly confessional works, such as the *Christian Discourses* (1848).

Perhaps then it is no great surprise that, after introducing the liturgical reduction, Lacoste turns to Kierkegaard. Liturgy is not an aspect of being in the world, and consequently we should not expect to find the person who is truly living *coram Deo* presenting himself or herself in worldly terms. Lacoste tells us, "the most profound break with the order of the world is not the privilege of whoever sets himself up most conspicuously against that order, but of whoever can do so in the strictest incognito, in the Kierkegaardian experience of the 'Knight of Faith'" (178). *Fear and Trembling*, as suggested earlier, gives us a phenomenology of faith by way of alerting us to the absence of faith as phenomenon. Consider the portrait of the knight of faith:

> He enjoys everything he sees, the swarms of people, the new omnibuses, the Sound. Encountering him on Strandveien, one would take him for

> a mercantile soul enjoying himself. He finds pleasure in this way, for he is not a poet, and I have tried in vain to lure the poetic incommensurability out of him. Toward evening, he goes home, and his gait is as steady as a postman's. On the way, he thinks that his wife surely will have a special hot meal for him when he comes home—for example, roast lamb's head with vegetables. If he meets a kindred soul, he would go on talking all the way to Østerport about this delicacy with a passion befitting a restaurant operator. It so happens that he does not have four shillings to his name, and yet he firmly believes that his wife has this delectable meal waiting for him.[49]

The portrait continues, each new detail rendering visible the invisibility of faith. A similar devotion to pure description occurs in the account of despair in *The Sickness unto Death* (1849). Here we see a dark side of living *coram Deo:*

> The God-relationship is an infinitizing, but in fantasy this infinitizing can so sweep a man off his feet that his state is simply an intoxication. To exist before God may seem unendurable to a man because he cannot come back to himself, become himself. Such a fantasized religious person would say (to characterize him by means of some lines): "That a sparrow can live is comprehensible; it does not know that it exists before God. But to know that one exists before God, and then not instantly go mad or sink into nothingness!"
>
> But to become fantastic in this way, and thus to be in despair, does not mean, although it usually becomes apparent, that a person cannot go on living fairly well, seem to be a man, be occupied with temporal matters, marry, have children, be honored and esteemed—and it may not be detected that in a deeper sense he lacks a self . . . The greatest hazard of all, losing the self, can occur very quietly in the world, as if it were nothing at all. No other loss can occur so quietly; any other loss—an arm, a leg, five dollars, a wife, etc.—is sure to be noticed.[50]

The eidos of despair is not always made manifest to us, yet only a phenomenologist would patiently describe its very invisibility, as Kierkegaard does here.

Heidegger reminds us that "it is precisely because phenomena are proximally or for the most part *not* given, that there is a need for phenomenology."[51] If, as he goes on to say, "Covered-up-ness is the counter concept to 'phenomenon'" (60), and if Kierkegaard reveals what hides itself, we may well wonder at his refusal to grant Kierkegaard the status of a phenomenologist. True, Kierkegaard is not an ontologist in Heidegger's sense of the word; his concern is to live *coram Deo* and not before being or before death, and we know that for Heidegger theology is an ontic, not an ontological, science.[52] Yet Heidegger oriented phenomenology to being, in his sense of the word, in *Being and Time*. If we demur over this restriction and retain from his analysis the idea that phenomenology is the gentle art of nudging phenomena so that they manifest themselves, Kierkegaard appears as a practitioner at a high level, for he allows us to see faith and despair even when they remain embedded in obscurity. The liturgical or theological reduction, as he practices it, calls into question the "I" that stands before God and the horizons that the "I" projects, for to be exposed to God is to live with those horizons perpetually breached, to be awakened both in one's study and in one's seat at church.

Yet does Kierkegaard pass from the "what" question to the "how" question? Let us listen to him writing in his journal about the author of the *Philosophical Fragments* and the *Concluding Unscientific Postscript:*

> In all the usual talk that Johannes Climacus is mere subjectivity etc., it has been completely overlooked that . . . he points out in one of the last sections that the remarkable thing is that there is a How with the characteristic that when the How is scrupulously rendered the What is also given, that this is the How of "faith."[53]

He is alluding to the following passage in the *Concluding Unscientific Postscript:*

> The decision rests in the subject; the appropriation is the paradoxical inwardness that is specifically different from all other inwardness. Being a Christian is defined not by the "what" of Christianity but by the "how" of the Christian. This "how" can fit only one thing, the absolute paradox. Therefore there is no vague talk that being a Christian means to accept and accept, and accept altogether differently, to appropriate, to have faith, to appropriate in faith altogether differently (nothing but rhetorical and sham definitions); but *to have faith* is specifically qualified differently from all other appropriation and inwardness.[54]

What is essential for Kierkegaard is how a Christian comports himself or herself with respect to God, and that "how" is given not in reason, which for Kierkegaard is socially received good sense (what Husserl calls the natural attitude), but in radical faith that cuts against "good sense."

Radical faith: this is not the belief that is suspended when performing the reduction, belief in the sense of holding a position or asserting a thesis about something. Belief in positions is put aside in the phenomenological reduction, and one may have nonthetic experience of it, which is precisely what Kierkegaard does in the pseudonymous writings. But radical faith is something different. It is faith born out of the absolute paradox.

Whether one is a Christian, for Kierkegaard, turns on how one lives, whether one merely follows an inherited social paradigm ("Christendom") or whether one has actually turned to believe in the God who is paradoxically eternal and in history ("Christianity"). The most important reduction for Kierkegaard is from Christendom to Christianity; it is prompted by the absolute paradox, thinking that which exceeds thought, namely the incarnate God. This reduction leads us back not to the past in which Jesus lived, a past about which we can never be entirely sure, or to a transcendental dimension of consciousness, but to God himself, indeed to God as Creator and Savior. Kierkegaard never forgot existence, the actuality of things, and the *reductio* he practiced always led back to the sheer fact that we exist and that we need to be saved. I say *reductio,* not reduction, partly to distinguish Kierkegaard from Husserl and partly to glimpse Saint Bonaventure in the distant background.[55] Not that Kierkegaard thinks that we are led back to theological distinctions; we are led back rather to a radical faith, not a way of viewing the world as mapped by Saint Augustine. Kierkegaard was not drawn to do theology better than others, not even the Danish Hegelians, but to a leap of trust in God no matter what. He was not drawn, like Husserl, to absolute presuppositionlessness, for he was all too aware that in life we need an absolute presupposition: not the Absolute of Hegel or Schelling but the God of Jesus, and Jesus as God, who is unconditioned and whose revelation one finds in Scripture. It is the paradox of Christ who prompts the *reductio* for Kierkegaard, and Christ who, by way of paradox, calls us to make an "inner transformation of the whole mind" and to be a "contemporary without, however, being contemporary," and who jolts us and makes us no longer at home in the world.[56]

Notes

I wish to thank Claude Romano for his comments on an earlier draft of this essay.

1. See, for example, George Pattison's comments on Kierkegaard as phenomenologist in his *The Philosophy of Kierkegaard* (Montreal: McGill-Queen's University Press, 2005), 82–89.

2. See Edmund Husserl, *Ideas Pertaining to a Pure Phenomenology and to a Phenomenological Philosophy,* first book, *General Introduction to a Pure Phenomenology,* trans. F. Kersten (Boston: Kluwer Academic, 1983), §33.

3. See Husserl, *The Crisis of European Sciences and Transcendental Phenomenology: An Introduction to Phenomenological Philosophy,* trans. David Carr (Evanston, Ill.: Northwestern University Press, 1970), §41.

4. See Husserl, *The Basic Problems of Phenomenology: From the Lectures, Winter Semester, 1910–1911,* trans. Ingo Farin and James G. Hart (Dordrecht: Springer, 2006), 41.

5. Husserl, *Logical Investigations,* trans. J. N. Findlay, 2 vols. (London: Routledge and Kegan Paul, 1970), 1:43. Husserl lectures on the reduction in *The Idea of Phenomenology,* trans. William P. Alston and George Nakhnikian (The Hague: Martinus Nijhoff, 1973), 4.

6. Martin Heidegger, *The Basic Problems of Phenomenology,* trans. Albert Hofstadter (Bloomington: Indiana University Press, 1988), 21.

7. See Jean-Paul Sartre, *The Transcendence of the Ego: An Existentialist Theory of Consciousness,* trans. Forrest Williams and Robert Kirkpatrick (New York: Hill and Wang, 1957), 42.

8. See Maurice Merleau-Ponty, *Phenomenology of Perception,* trans. Colin Smith (London: Routledge and Kegan Paul, 1962), xiv.

9. Jan Patočka, *An Introduction to Husserl's Phenomenology,* trans. Erazim Kohák, ed. James Dodd (Chicago: Open Court, 1996), 103–6.

10. See Jacques Derrida, *The Problem of Genesis in Husserl's Philosophy,* trans. Marian Hobson (Chicago: University of Chicago Press, 2003), 69, and *Edmund Husserl's "Origin of Geometry": An Introduction,* trans. John P. Leavey, ed. David B. Allison (Stony Brook, N.Y.: Nicolas Hays, 1978), 153.

11. See Jean-Luc Marion, *Reduction and Givenness: Investigations of Husserl, Heidegger, and Phenomenology,* trans. Thomas A. Carlson (Evanston, Ill.: Northwestern University Press, 1998).

12. Emmanuel Levinas, *The Theory of Intuition in Husserl's Phenomenology,* trans. André Orianne (Evanston, Ill.: Northwestern University Press, 1973), 150.

13. Michel Henry, *Incarnation: Une philosophie de la chair* (Paris: Seuil, 2000), §3.

14. See, for example, C. Stephen Evans, "Reductionism as Absentmindedness: Existentialism and Phenomenology as Strategies for Defending Personhood," *Man and World* 14 (1981): 181.

15. Heidegger, *Being and Time,* trans. John Macquarrie and Edward Robinson (Oxford: Blackwell, 1973), 494, note vi, div. 2, sec. 45.

16. G. W. F. Hegel, *Hegel's Science of Logic,* trans. A. V. Miller (London: George Allen and Unwin, 1969), 82.

17. Theodor W. Adorno, *Against Epistemology: A Metacritique,* trans. Willis Domingo (Oxford: Blackwell, 1982), 187.

18. Heidegger, *The Phenomenology of Religious Life,* trans. Matthias Fritsch and Jennifer Anna Gosetti-Ferencei (Bloomington: Indiana University Press, 2004), 186, 192, 199, 202.

19. Ibid., 184.

20. See Merleau-Ponty, *Phenomenology of Perception,* xiii. We are directed to Fink's essay "Die phänomenologische Philosophie Edmund Husserls in der gegenwärtigen Kritik," *Kant-Studien* 38, nos. 3–4 (1933), 331 and following. I am unable to find a passage there that resembles Merleau-Ponty's citation.

21. Eugen Fink, *Sixth Cartesian Meditation: The Idea of a Transcendental Theory of Method,* with textual notations by Edmund Husserl, trans. Ronald Bruzina (Bloomington: Indiana University Press, 1995), 21.

22. *MLW,* 91.

23. Louis Mackey, *Kierkegaard: A Kind of Poet* (Philadelphia: University of Pennsylvania Press, 1971), ix.

24. *JP* 6300. See also *MLW,* 36 and 129, but also Kierkegaard's comments on the danger of the poet, 225.

25. Kierkegaard, "The Whole in One Word," in *The Point of View,* ed. and trans. Howard V. Hong and Edna H. Hong (Princeton, N.J.: Princeton University Press, 1998), 235.

26. See Husserl, *Idea of Phenomenology,* 4.

27. See Husserl, "Husserl an von Hofmannsthal (12. 1. 1907)," in *Briefwechsel,* vol. 7, *Wissenschaftlerkorrespondenz,* ed. Elisabeth Schuhmann and Karl Schuhmann (Boston: Kluwer Academic, 1994), 135.

28. See Roman Ingarden, *The Literary Work of Art: An Investigation on the Borderlines of Ontology, Logic, and Theory of Literature,* trans. George G. Grabowicz (Evanston, Ill.: Northwestern University Press, 1973), §25.

29. Maurice Blanchot, *The Step Not Beyond,* trans. Lycette Nelson (Albany: State University of New York Press, 1992), 2. For Blanchot's views on Kierkegaard, see his "Kierkegaard's Journals," in *Faux Pas,* trans. Charlotte Mandell (Stanford: Stanford University Press, 2001), 17–22.

30. See Blanchot, *The Infinite Conversation,* trans. Susan Hanson (Minneapolis: University of Minnesota Press, 1993), xi.

31. Ibid., 250. Blanchot's remarks resonate with Fink's when he tells us that the person who has performed the reduction "inquires back before the 'world-character' of world-believing life, behind humanness, and thereupon to reduce that life to the transcendental constituting experience of the world that was concealed by the apperception of the human" (Fink, *Sixth Cartesian Meditation,* 10).

32. Derrida, "'This Strange Institution Called Literature': An Interview with Jacques Derrida," in *Acts of Literature,* ed. Derek Attridge (New York: Routledge, 1992), 46.

33. See David Bell, *Husserl* (London: Routledge, 1991), 162.

34. Husserl, *Ideas,* bk. 1, 5; Franz Kafka, *The Castle,* trans. Willa Muir and Edwin Muir (New York: Schocken Books, 1988), 3.

35. Merleau-Ponty, *In Praise of Philosophy and Other Essays,* trans. John Wild, James Edie, and John O'Neill (Evanston, Ill.: Northwestern University Press, 1970), 174, 176. See, for example, Husserl, *Crisis,* §§39–44.

36. Husserl, *Crisis,* §43.

37. Derrida, *Speech and Phenomena: And Other Essays on Husserl's Theory of Signs,* trans. David B. Allison (Evanston, Ill.: Northwestern University Press, 1973), 86.

38. Also see in this regard the speech of Johannes the Seducer, *SLW,* 71–80.

39. Heidegger, *Four Seminars,* trans. Andrew Mitchell and François Raffoul (Bloomington: Indiana University Press, 2003), 80.

40. Kierkegaard, "The Crisis and a Crisis in the Life of an Actress," in *"Christian Discourses" and "The Crisis and a Crisis in the Life of an Actress,"* ed. and trans. Howard V. Hong and Edna H. Hong (Princeton, N.J.: Princeton University Press, 1997), 311.

41. Husserl, *Experience and Judgment: Investigations in a Genealogy of Logic,* rev. and ed. Ludwig Landgrebe, trans. James S. Churchill and Karl Ameriks (Evanston, Ill.: Northwestern University Press, 1973), 351.

42. See Jacques Taminiaux, *The Metamorphoses of Phenomenological Reduction* (Milwaukee: Marquette University Press, 2004), 9.

43. Jean-Yves Lacoste, *Experience and the Absolute: Disputed Questions on the Humanity of Man,* trans. Mark Raftery-Skehan (New York: Fordham University Press, 2004), 2. In his *La phénoménalité de Dieu: Neuf études,* Lacoste writes of a "theological reduction" in connection with Kierkegaard. See *La phénoménalité de Dieu* (Paris: Cerf, 2008), 29.

44. Quoted by Ronald Bruzina in his *Edmund Husserl and Eugen Fink: Beginnings and Ends in Phenomenology, 1928–1938* (New Haven, Conn.: Yale University Press, 2004), 354.

45. *JP* 3099.

46. *CUP,* 449–50.

47. *SUD,* 79.

48. *JP* 6012.

49. *FT,* 39–40.

50. *SUD,* 32–33

51. Heidegger, *Being and Time,* 60.

52. See Heidegger, "Phenomenology and Theology," in *Pathmarks,* ed. William McNeill (Cambridge: Cambridge University Press, 1998), 41.

53. *JP* 4550.

54. *CUP,* 610–11.

55. See Bonaventure, *On the Reduction of the Arts to Theology,* trans. Zachary Hayes, Works of Saint Bonaventure, vol. 1 (St. Bonaventure: Franciscan Institute, 1996).

56. Kierkegaard, "He Was Believed in the World," in Hong and Hong, *Christian Discourses,* 246; and *PF,* 67.

Kierkegaard Between Fundamental Ontology and Theology: Phenomenological Approaches to Love of God

Jeffrey Bloechl

Heidegger sets the tone for a consideration of Kierkegaard's work as phenomenological when, on each of three occasions in *Being and Time,* he recognizes in some of the latter an extraordinarily penetrating grasp of our condition, but suggests that his insights are nonetheless without support by an adequate ontology.[1] Kierkegaard, we are told, has been a good "psychologist" with unsurpassed sensitivity to the existentiell dimension of the question of our existence: *existentiell* and not *existential,* which is to say posed strictly in terms of the relation to our own existence rather than in terms of our more primordial relation to Being. The implication of this claim is at least threefold: (1) to begin with, Kierkegaard will have only incompletely developed the phenomena in question—angst, being-in-the-world, and the "moment of vision" in which crystallizes authentic temporality—despite having "gone the farthest" until now; (2) the fuller interpretation will necessarily carry us beyond the theology and the psychology in which Kierkegaard's analyses are thought to be framed, and into the fundamental ontology that alone truly grasps their preconditions; and (3) this means that the theological and psychological interpretations cannot claim the support of fundamental ontology, which in Heidegger's severe estimation means that they cannot truly claim to *think.* This last point, of course, has been stated already in §10 of Heidegger's great book, where it is anticipated that the subsequent passages commonly called the "Existential Analytic" will at last, in the course of interpreting Dasein in its relation with Being, go beyond the essential limits of every other form of reflection on our existence (even if this has not in fact been Heidegger's guiding concern). So if Kierkegaard stops short of fundamental ontology, then in Heidegger's estimation to that degree he does not think—and, more seriously, the things of faith that concern him would appear to be, on Heidegger's terms, unthinkable.

Needless to say, this is not a claim that should go unchecked. At the simplest point of application, there is ample evidence against the notion that a theologian or psychologist must necessarily be unreflective even within the practice of her own work. Perhaps one might say of the reflective theologian that an ontological sensibility provides constant critical awareness of the limits of each proposition. Or of the thoughtful psychologist that it demands—as Gabriel Marcel once envisioned for good science—"a humility that belongs to the realm of true wisdom."[2] But these observations only confirm Heidegger's own claim for a distinct and deeper-reaching form of thinking that corrects and improves all other forms. But they also bring fully into view the special challenge that Heidegger presents to any thought of the absolute God. Can the thinking committed to such a God accept correction or improvement from a thinking that would arrive as if from outside? Is it possible to defend the view that our primary relation is with God, and yet also welcome the proposals of a thinking that instead takes the view that that relation is with Being? We are used to these questions. Do we yet agree on how to reply? An entire school of thought wishes to challenge Heidegger's claim, itself thoroughly consistent with the definition of fundamental ontology, that everything that is must appear within the horizon of our relation with Being. This leads inevitably to an insistence that some things can appear to us without entering that horizon, and thus without affirming the primacy of our relation with Being. Perhaps phenomenology can accommodate this thought. After all, already in Husserl there is an appreciation of dimensions not yet concentrated into meaning. Religious thinkers may be more hesitant. Would this not enforce an overt distinction, even an opposition, between the properly religious approach that touches us without ever coming to light (without ever entering a horizon), and everything belonging to the decline that begins the moment we embody or enact our inspiration? It is difficult to rule out such a conception of what amounts to being in the world toward God, yet one also cannot escape the impression of a certain impoverishment. After all, one would like to think that being toward God includes distinctive attitudes, comportments, and perhaps even gestures—none of which diminish the relation that defines them.

With this in mind, one might rather seek a more positive relation with the form of thinking that has proven so adept at interpreting the manifold dimensions of our being, even if one well knows that this has been undertaken without a positive commitment to the absolute God. Might the thinking that at least holds open the possibility of faith take up the phenomenological rigor of fundamental ontology without pretending to bring it into a religious orientation—without shifting it from its own orientation to the meaning of Being—as a means to get at what distinguishes a properly religious way of being in the world? In that case, the defining movement of phenomenology, its step back from the things themselves in order to contemplate their essences, becomes not only problematic for religious thought but now also promising. Upon stepping back from the attitude, actions, and things of religious life, phenomenology becomes capable of setting it off against what it is not, and in turn highlighting its defining features. Of course, this is a matter only of disclosure, and not of the rationality that may be embedded there. The disclosure of differences between ways of being in the world preserves the separate integrity of each. In itself, it is at best a soft apology for religion, one that upholds its distinct integrity by bringing into view elements that render it irreducible to anything else. At the same time, insofar as it does so from a perspective not already defined by an anterior religious commitment, it may also render those elements and thus that unique way of being in the world in terms that are broadly intelligible to those of us who do not share in them. At times, this procedure and these results are to be found in Kierkegaard's reflections on love of God.

All of this would mean supposing that Kierkegaard helps us with two pressing difficulties. On the one hand is the classical problem of providing a positive account of the relation with a God who every believer knows transcends complete understanding. If we address Kierkegaard as phenomenologist we propose to understand him as far as possible without ulterior appeal to any metaphysics. If there is a comprehensive account of faith in his works—and this is extremely doubtful, not least because he has something approaching antipathy to the very idea—it would have to be decidedly post-Scholastic. We may expect to find this expressed in a point of departure not in God divine as mysterious plenitude but instead in human being as wondrous movement toward that plenitude. On the other hand is the possibility that Kierkegaard's account of that movement may prove intelligible only to those who already read with the eyes of faith. And this, again, would return us to Heidegger's characterization of Kierkegaard in *Being and Time:* an author who thinks already in a religious context, or better, according to a religious determination, and moreover who writes for those who already recognize that context and share that determination, can only be a "psychologist" who elucidates a certain condition and a "theologian" who attends to its grounding principles.

Resources for eluding this reductive interpretation of Kierkegaard are present in Heidegger's own text. It was Heidegger, after all, who turned phenomenology away from a focus on act and evidence toward one on mood (*Stimmung*) and on the heart of moodedness in attunement (*Befindlichkeit*). The central claim is well known: anterior to my engagement with this world and everything in it, they are already manifest according to a basic disposition that I may find in myself—or first, find myself already in—and that hermeneutical phenomenology grasps as the root of a general orientation. It is far from certain that phenomenology itself has appreciated the full implication of this proposal in which thinking would recognize its own source and origin. To be sure, Heidegger himself returns to it often enough during the course of his long itinerary: true thinking originates in wonder or arises in anxiety but in any case abides in serenity, each of which is at this point said to return us to the Greeks and at that point interpreted differently. But in any case, all that stands between interpreting this appeal to attunement in thinking as the emancipation of its specifically religious form is an insistence on the preeminence of the one form that Heidegger finds in himself. And one is inclined to think that that insistence begs the question, What is fundamental ontology but the self-interpretation of Dasein, defined in advance by Heidegger as thrownness into the world? Yet if we wish to take the view that there is a distinctly religious attunement, or indeed many of them, this does not change the decidedly nonreligious attunement of phenomenology (i.e., to Being, as signaled in anxiety or serenity). When phenomenology takes up the work of interpreting a religious way of being in the world it must do so, according to Heidegger, in the context of its own orientation to the question of the meaning of Being. To come then to the essential point, whereas nothing prevents phenomenology from recognizing and interpreting the fundamental attunement proper to the way of being that is rooted in faith, its own interest will always be specifically in the being of the religious, which is to say as a specific disclosure of Being. Whatever phenomenology, as the hermeneutical expression of fundamental ontology, truly has to offer our understanding of religion must surely lie precisely here. And it is not insignificant. If without violating its essential principles, phenomenology can attend to the posture, the tonality, and, to repeat, the movement proper to a distinctive way of being in the world, then it may at least contribute to an ontology—and not merely a psychology—of religious life. How far could this ontology go toward admitting within its analyses a positive account of the transcendent orientation of the human religious being? Under what conditions?

This inquiry is best pursued in the works of Kierkegaard and not of Heidegger, and for reasons that are not only methodological. Heidegger, we may note, does not always seem to understand religion especially well. In some of his texts faith is said to be content with itself, as if it were a form of denial or lassitude. Faith stops short of living in the real "Why?" of our existence, or if it seems to participate in that questioning it proves to do so only in the limited form of acting "as if."[3] It hardly needs to be said that such a claim is perfectly consistent with the deeper and better-known claims in Heidegger's philosophy. And yet it so poorly matches the fervor and restlessness often available to even the simplest observer of religious life that one hesitates to take it seriously. This supports the view that for all of the importance just attributed to Heidegger's turn to a hermeneutics of attunement, one need not and no doubt should not concede everything to the fundamental ontology to which it belongs. Enough has already been said for this to be quite obvious: if there is anything distinctive about religious life as a form of being in the world, it must be found—must let itself be seen—in elements, events, or dimensions that resist definition within the horizon of a relation with Being. And this calls for particular attention to phenomena that are at once intelligible in the world and yet signal somewhat more than their intelligibility. Having come to this point, the phenomenologist can take great interest in Kierkegaard's facility with paradox, enigma, and what I will call "the oblique."

These many features are in evidence in, of all possible texts, the upbuilding discourse titled "Purity of Heart Is to Will One Thing."[4] I propose to comment on it here, with one eye constantly on the claims of the phenomenologist.

Kierkegaard's discourse is concentrated on the trajectory of a desire by which one approaches standstill before the God who transcends understanding. The topic is undoubtedly religious, and indeed any number of principles and practices that he takes up are unmistakably Christian, but this is not to say that the discourse as a whole is directed solely to those who already believe, and still less that only a believer could understand it. To the contrary, there is virtually nothing in the discourse, including both its terminology and its reasoning, that is unlikely to be grasped by the most uninitiated reader. Thus while the style of the text is plainly hortatory, it seems that its primary aim is not conversion but, more modestly, an improved understanding of the various themes brought forth. If the text "works," it does so without requiring those in whom it works to first accept either Christian dogma or the ecclesial authority thought to stand behind it. No special competence is needed for one to understand, for example, that repentance "is indeed the relation between a past and someone who is living in the present time" (*UDVS,* 11), or that the shame one feels when one is alone expresses a somewhat different vector of responsibility than does the shame one feels only in the company of others (*UDVS,* 51–52), or again that "immediate feeling selfishly understands everything in relation to itself" (*UDVS,* 71). Nor can any of us have any particular difficulty grasping Kierkegaard's guiding proposal that under ordinary conditions our state of mind is such that we are never given over to any single aim even if we do sometimes detect within ourselves a desire to achieve that condition. We are, he says, citing James 4:8, "double-minded," and that double-mindedness is sometimes haunted by a frustrated desire to truly settle on one thing.

The "one thing" in question is of course God, considered as the desirable par excellence. It is a subtle feature of the text to develop what we might be inclined to call "desire" into what eventually proves to deserve the loftier name "love," even while also making it clear that God is indeed uniquely desirable, which is to say lovable according to the most elevated sense of love. The definitions, in short, are not imposed on the reader—not stated up front, and then affirmed from all sides—so much as they are approached, as possibilities, by way of examples that make clear what they cannot mean. Some of his procedure therefore deserves to be called, in a limited sense only, dialectical: early in the text, it is demonstrated first that willing one thing can admit of no variety, since this would imply the contradiction that holds that any number of things are equally deserving of unqualified willing, and from this we are plainly to learn that willing one thing necessarily involves willing something that has absolute unity. But lest there be any doubt about the specific nature of this unity, Kierkegaard quickly adds that it cannot be won by worldly achievement, as seems to be the premise in those who seek above all else the singular esteem of their colleagues or friends. True unity would be unmixed with anything knowable in conformity with one who knows it and wills it, since the latter would be defined by the limitations and the distinctions that belong essentially to our finite human condition (*UDVS,* 34–35).

This can remind us of a question taken up by Thomas Aquinas in one of the initial movements of his *Summa Theologica:* how are we, as complex, related to our first and final aim, as simplex (Aquinas's God, it will be recalled, is characterized by perfect simpleness)?[5] I have already drawn attention to Kierkegaard's post-Scholastic perspective. On this point, we may recognize it in an interesting divergence from Aquinas. In the upbuilding discourses our relation, as homo complex to the Deus simplex, is never presented as a question for metaphysical theology in which, with all due regard for the subtleties of the doctrine of analogy, the idea of the revealing and creating God tends to define the idea of God's creature. And yet this does not lead Kierkegaard immediately into Christian psychology, in which a characterization of the experiences and constitution of the creature, as subject, sets the conditions for reflection on the meaning of God. Kierkegaard wants specifically to define the willing that would embody the very possibility of relating oneself to God. And so we are told, in a brilliant exercise of Kierkegaard's famous "maieutic carefulness," that if there is purity of heart, if someone truly wills one thing and one thing only, then this will entail having made oneself "simple" beyond any of the divisions or qualifications by which we know human willing and human knowing generally to function. But we are also told that if there is some one thing with simple unity, then it is the proper aim of a willing that cannot be the ordinary willing of double-mindedness, in which division and qualification necessarily rule. Again, as far as it goes, this dialectical procedure, no less than the examples it takes up, is readily understood by any careful reader. Its immediate effect is to settle the phenomenality of what is plainly an elevated form of love into a context of understanding that necessarily exceeds the one occupied exclusively by believers. In other words, to the degree that what is invoked in the *Discourses* is generally recognizable—whether or not this happens to be a matter of finding it already in oneself—Christian religious life may be considered continuous with human experience and understanding as such, which is to say beyond any proposed limitation to specifically religious experience and understanding.[6]

This then is how the *Discourses* edify: not by homiletic appeal to Christian piety or the lack thereof, but by an inner disruption of ordinary understanding, an untimely shattering of premises that come in the form of exhortations that, like Kierkegaard himself, run strongly against the grain of so-called common sense and received opinion. Perhaps there is support for this notion even in Kierkegaard's title: as it happens, there is nothing remarkable about his word for "upbuilding": *opbyggelig*, which one finds in almost any context where Anglophones might use the word "positive"—thus well beyond the contexts limited to moral or religious meaning. "Upbuilding" does not withdraw or depart from the conditions that might appear closed or at least indifferent to the religious, but intervenes in order to augment the thinking found there, enhancing it with a new range of possibilities. "Upbuilding" works with what is already present and already under way, not apart from it or against it. It is the opposite of breaking down (*nedbrydende*) and yet intent on breaking open. In Kierkegaard's text, to upbuild is to provoke a forward-looking gaze, toward a possibility that dawns in the realization that perhaps some phenomena are not to be explained solely in terms of ordinary understanding . . . and yet by all appearances are quite meaningful.[7]

A better case for this is made in a procedure that somewhat resembles what Husserl calls "eidetic reduction" and "imaginative variation." Upon registering a particular experience, we may wish to clarify its true meaning, whereupon we must attempt to distinguish what belongs to it essentially from what does not. This sort of reduction to the essential frequently calls for some experimental or hypothetical modification—that is, dropping this feature or altering that one, until it becomes clear precisely which features, and in what form, cannot be withdrawn from the experience in question without changing its proper nature. One thinks, perhaps inevitably, of Descartes' account of perceiving the same piece of wax even while it changes both in shape and consistency. However, whereas Descartes, who is concerned above all with grounding perception in an indubitable rationality, rules out any positive role for the clouded proposals of imagination, Husserl recognizes that without a capacity to imagine different versions or instances of what we have experienced there is no way for us to recognize the single one of them that includes everything essential and nothing accidental. After all, if one does not achieve immediate and apodictic knowledge of a thing, then one has no recourse but to approach it by way of comparison and contrast with (images of) other things. Interestingly, this signifies an important role for negativity: imaginative variation leads us toward a grasp of the essential by way of contrast with what it is not, until we arrive at the realization that it is impossible to imagine the thing without certain features we may take to be essential.[8]

This plainly invites us to ask whether it is Kierkegaard's intention that his reader undertake something close to eidetic reduction and imaginative variation when coming to terms with the purity of heart that wills one thing, but we should not forget that his interest is nonetheless with an entire way of life that professes an attunement extending to the absolute God who is by definition beyond the range of any possible intuition: this means that when applied to any encounter with religious life, and specifically to love of God, the "negative necessity" of eidetic reduction cannot rebound into the positivity of secure knowledge. But even if this procedure is therefore necessarily incomplete, it still can deepen the reader's understanding of religious love by showing how other, ostensibly plausible conceptions in fact fall short of the thing itself. Thus, when, for example, Kierkegaard takes up the impatience of those who cannot find their way to God soon enough, careful scrutiny uncovers there, buried in an attitude we may have been inclined to understand as genuine religious zeal, the subtle egocentrism of those who assure themselves, as it were in advance, that God is not present at all times and in all things (*UDVS,* 61–62). And to take this attitude—to hurry toward a God who one believes is not here but over there, not now but in the future—is to continue to function by the distinctions and oppositions that define double-mindedness. Such a person wills God, but also wills himself as source of criteria by which to measure or chart God's presence. Similarly, when at first Kierkegaard has us consider those who recognize that the world does not open itself easily to faith and who therefore reserve some of their time and energy for preserving that faith within themselves, it is only to then show us that this attitude betrays a willingness to compromise as much as it does a commitment to remain steadfast (*UDVS,* 74–75). To achieve purity of heart, it seems, we would have to break down the distinction between time and energy reserved for dealing with this world and its demands, and time and energy committed to love of God.

But Kierkegaard's phenomenology is not limited to an interpretation of the existential *paradox* by which human beings who are fundamentally double-minded sometimes also tend toward, or at least feel called toward, single-mindedness.[9] We are also presented with the *enigma* of those who do seem truly to embody the definition of religious life suggested by a degree of imaginative variation. How is it that some among us are capable of dedicating what certainly appears to be their full attention and efforts to a singular perseverance? By what thinking and on what extraordinary basis would all of a person's energy go into vigilance against any "evasion" of the straight path to purity of heart (*UDVS,* 93–99)? It is likely that we entertain some suspicion about the motives that drive a believer to seek the complete solitude and intense hardship entailed in true single-mindedness, but this is not enough for us to suppose that we actually see covert relief or unrecognized pleasure when none is evident, and indeed Kierkegaard would be the first to disallow such cases as single-minded. In any case, he is on solid footing here, since there certainly are asceticisms that do not merely forbid the pleasures of the world but also enjoin watchfulness against enjoying the deprivation itself. To this we may add, though Kierkegaard himself does not, that it belongs properly to psychology to assign hidden motives, ulterior causes, and a meaning that the subject herself may or may not recognize. And psychological explanation, even when it becomes quite complex, always traces phenomena to relations between separate and irreducible elements. For Kierkegaard's purposes, it is not merely enough, but in fact essential to let the thing appear in all its proper difficulty: by all appearances, there is a love that cannot be reduced to a dynamic that is solely internal.

This suggestion is reinforced at some length in Kierkegaard's treatment, late in the discourse, of those who are willing to suffer all for a Good that transcends the well-defined, lesser goods available in the world. Here it is a matter specifically of willing the suffering itself and not any pleasure that some may expect to gain from it. Kierkegaard does not use the word "kenotic," but of course this is what is meant when he does say that he has in mind a suffering that does not only forgo any comfort or cure but even turns resolutely against them. By what strange "wish," he asks, would it become necessary, even desirable, to surrender and do without everything else, which is to say everything that is knowable and perhaps obtainable starting from one's own capacities? Carried through to the end, such a wish—the one wish unlike all other wishes, and that destroys all other wishes—extinguishes every worldly hope, and in that sense weans a person from the temporal order. This is why it entails suffering, for living in the wish requires one to embrace the pain of relinquishing everything that might otherwise put one at ease. Living in "the wish," we might say, comes down to suffering one's individuality, without qualification or condition. In its extreme form it is the apotheosis of what Simone Weil calls the affliction of waiting for God. For only God, or what Kierkegaard certainly invites us to call the Good, could heal this pain—and only according to an approach that would have to come from beyond the range of everything that falls under our own power. Those who suffer everything for God commit themselves to waiting for a balm that only *may* eventually come.

A good phenomenologist will at this point object that this healing that can come only from God and that would thus involve an experience of God lies beyond the range of what can effectively be handled by either transcendental description or the hermeneutics of facticity. But this does not prevent us from recognizing something distinctive about the life in which these phenomena may be detected. The suffering of the one who wills one thing is a suffering that is irreducible to the suffering of those who are busy with many things. And this, according to Kierkegaard, testifies *obliquely* to what it is that such a person wills. "*And yet by observing such people* [sufferers], *one profoundly learns what the highest is*" (*UDVS*, 108; italics in the original). Now one can know what a thing is without necessarily believing in it, if "believing in" means committing one's full self to its presence. We can recognize a properly religious way of life, understand the one thing that it wills, and even admit that this is irreducible to anything else—and still do so without necessarily giving ourselves up to the fundamental commitment that defines the life in question. Perhaps this tells us how phenomenology might view the religious question in our own time: the virtue of faith is visible in its embodiment and its bearing, even if the commitment that secures it is rooted before and outside light.

After distinguishing between dialectical and phenomenological strands in "Purity of Heart Is to Will One Thing," I have touched on three sorts of phenomena by which his work attempts to render the religious intelligible without, however, thereby pretending to render it fully present and knowable: the paradoxical, the enigmatic, and the oblique. Their important differences notwithstanding, they have in common a phenomenality that refuses the standard conditions of phenomenality but without becoming either meaningless or obscure. What is striking about Kierkegaard's manner of attending to them is the movement of a thinking that manages to elicit meaning from examples without attempting to contain them entirely within concepts. A complex and important discussion with classical phenomenology could be centered on this very point. But if one follows Kierkegaard's procedure only slightly further, along the guiding thread of a desire that simplifies itself, until willing one thing reveals itself to be love of God, there might also be something to say to theology. We have just seen that in this discourse Kierkegaard proposes something like a phenomenology of the religious way of being in the world, and that in the end it proposes that its defining commitment of that way remains necessarily anterior to its visible forms. Faith in the absolute God is expressed in attunement and indeed in an attitude and a dynamism that show up *in* the world without belonging entirely *to* the world. This is also substantially the position of his *Works of Love,* which explores a life that is hidden yet recognizable by its fruit (this being the title of the first reflection). But the *Works* also says explicitly what is only implicit in the *Discourses:* as a work of transformation, purification, and vigilance, love gives expression to an awakening.[10] It is of little consequence whether this signals a possibility that is present in all but slumbering in most or else produced in only some of us. In either case, the "work" is provoked, or if one prefers, called. Kierkegaard's reasoning is not unexpected: what could call forth love if not love itself, since anything else—anything less—would instead call forth need or hunger or, perhaps closest to love, pity? And it stands to reason, then, the most elevated love, constituted in willing one thing, would thus have to respond to the perfect love that is, Kierkegaard reminds us, what Christians call "God."[11]

Yet this need not be taken as recourse to theology—need not signify a proposition about the (revealed) nature of God. Should we not rather say, certainly if we read the *Works* in light of the *Discourses,*[12] that the notion that God is love imposes itself in the course of describing and interpreting the remarkable love that wills only one thing? This would mean that love, at least in this one form, is in the final analysis irreducibly theocentric. It would also give new support to the idea that God is not only absolute but also somehow *personal.* The God who is love—the love whose call alone explains the love of those who truly will one thing—is thus a God who in some meaningful sense acts. Of course, this still cannot mean that phenomenology has somehow proven that such a God truly exists. But perhaps it can come to the aid of those who endeavor simply to acquire an adequate account of what it means to live as if that is so. And it leaves us with the final thought that such an account will come eventually, and indeed urgently to the very element—divine personhood—that our modern mind-set has been most eager to avoid.

Notes

Parts of this essay have appeared previously in Jeffrey Bloechl, "Kierkegaard and the Phenomenality of Desire," *Revista Portuguesa de Filosofia* 64, nos. 2–4 (2008): 909–20.

1. Martin Heidegger, *Being and Time,* trans. John Macquarrie and Edward Robinson (New York: Harper and Row, 1962), 492, note iv; 494, div. 2, sec. 45, note vi; 497, note iii.

2. Gabriel Marcel, "Science and Wisdom," in *Searchings* (New York: Newman Press, 1967), 34.

3. Martin Heidegger, *Introduction to Metaphysics,* trans. Gregory Fried and Richard Polt (New Haven, Conn.: Yale University Press, 2000), 6–8.

4. Perhaps this is the moment to recall that Heidegger considers the "edifying" writings more philosophically rewarding than his theoretical works. See Heidegger, *Being and Time,* 278, note vi (found on p. 494).

5. See Aquinas, *Summa Theologica* I–I 3, especially art. 7.

6. For this way of reading the upbuilding discourses I am indebted to George Pattison, *Kierkegaard's Upbuilding Discourses: Philosophy, Theology, Literature* (London: Routledge, 2002), 204–15.

7. In a few pages of his *Works of Love,* Kierkegaard expounds on the word "upbuilding" along lines similar to these. I have learned from my colleague Vanessa Rumble that much of the sense proposed there remains alive in contemporary Danish. See *WL,* 200–202.

8. Robert Sokolowski thus refers to the "negative necessity" by which we achieve eidetic intuition. See his *Introduction to Phenomenology* (Cambridge: Cambridge University Press, 2000), 184.

9. This approaches the definition of "paradox" given in *PF,* 37.

10. Kierkegaard describes love in these terms in the first reflection of the second part of the *Works,* titled "Love Builds Up."

11. *WL,* 205: "God, He who himself is love . . ."

12. It is not within my competence to insist on this way of relating the two

genres—the *Discourses* seeming to exhort with universally intelligible claims and categories, and the *Works* provoking or perhaps sharpening an understanding that is already Christian. That said, it is my view that the latter do not qualify or suspend the conditions of the former, but complete and fulfill the same line of reflection. For more on the relation between these texts, see M. Jamie Ferreira, "'The Next Thing': On the Maieutic Relations Between the *Upbuilding Discourses in Various Spirits* and *Works of Love*," in *International Kierkegaard Commentary* 15: *"Upbuilding Discourses in Various Spirits,"* ed. Robert L. Perkins (Macon, Ga.: Mercer University Press, 2005), 371–96.

Part 2

Self-Consciousness and Self-Givenness

Divine Givenness and Self-Givenness in Kierkegaard

Merold Westphal

There is an obvious sense in which Kierkegaard is not a phenomenologist, whether in his own name or through his pseudonyms. He is not inspired by or working in the tradition of Husserl, or Heidegger, or Scheler, or Merleau-Ponty, or even Levinas, who insists that he is a phenomenologist[1] even though he seeks to develop "an intentionality of a wholly different type" and holds that "not every transcendent intention has the noesis-noema structure."[2]

But we can ask of Kierkegaard's various writings whether they can be fruitfully read as phenomenological in a substantive rather than a historical sense.[3] In particular, we can ask whether they provide us with analysis of the ways in which various "objects" of consciousness are given to us, both in terms of how they appear to us (noemata) and of the intentional acts by virtue of which they appear (noeses). Of the wide range of the latter it is useful to recall the Cartesian listing. A thing that thinks is a thing "that doubts, understands, affirms, denies, wills, refuses, and which also imagines and senses."[4] In the immediately following paragraph Descartes adds desire to the list and later will add memory. Conspicuously missing from the list, for present purposes at least, is faith in Kierkegaard's Lutheran sense; for while it necessarily involves elements of both understanding and affirmation, it is reducible to neither, nor to the two together.

Let us begin with *Fear and Trembling* and ask the questions, How is God given to human experience according to this text?[5] What mode of intentionality is involved, and what sort of intentional object?[6]

The pseudonym Silentio is, we might say, a hermeneutical phenomenologist, for (1) he not only recognizes that philosophical reflection is a matter of interpretation and not the pure intuition of some unsituated, unconditioned, presuppositionless "view from nowhere;"[7] but (2) he also allows his interpretation to appear as the interpretation of a prior interpretation, in this case the biblical story of Abraham and the *Akedah,* the binding of Isaac (Gen. 22 and Heb. 11). Thus he follows Ricoeur in making "the detour through the contingency of cultures, though an incurably equivocal language, and through the conflict of interpretations."[8]

Note well: The phenomenologist's appeal to this story is not to the Bible as Scripture but as a cultural residue. That is the difference between the theologian and the phenomenologist, and it is why the phenomenologist who pays attention to religious texts and religious phenomena has not betrayed the phenomenological project, as charged by Dominique Janicaud. What the phenomenologist describes as a possible experience, the theologian affirms as actual fact.[9]

The God in question is, of course, the biblical God, and we are within a horizon where other gods are considered idols, including not only the gods of pagan polytheism but also the gods of modernity's pure reason and onto-theology, philosophical "counterfeits," in William Desmond's helpful term.[10] This God is at once Jewish and Christian, for the basic story is found in the Hebrew Bible, while Abraham is the father of the faithful in Romans, Galatians, and Hebrews. Moreover, Mary in her *Magnificat* and Zechariah in his *Benedictus* interpret the events celebrated at Christmas as the fulfillment of the promises to Abraham (Luke 1:46–79).

Fear and Trembling suggests at least three distinctive features of the way this God is given in human experience. First, God is given as personal. The decisive indication of this is that God speaks. In good Lutheran fashion, according to which revelation comes in the modes of Law and Gospel, the God of Abraham performs two different kinds of speech act: command and promise.[11] Silentio's focus is obviously on a very particular command, but he calls our attention to the fact that the command is tightly linked to promises. "By faith Abraham emigrated from the land of his fathers and became an alien in the promised land . . . By faith Abraham received the promise that in his seed all the generations of the earth would be blessed."[12]

Already this means that the intentionality of this phenomenology will be an inverted intentionality.[13] God is not given as the noematic content or theme constituted by an act of *Sinngebung* (meaning-bestowal) on my part. God is given as a subject by whom I am addressed; nor am I an object but rather a decentered subject. In inverted intentionality we have a subject-subject relation, not a subject-object relation.[14] The inversion leaves me as subject, but a radically changed one by virtue of having been given this "object," the God who speaks. The intentional arrows emanate not from me but toward me from an Other; the *Sinn* (meaning) in which God is given to Abraham and that defines Abraham and his situation is *gegeben* (given) by God and not by Abraham. He has been decentered by a voice not his own, at once a voice of promise and command. So far from being an origin that gives birth to himself and his world,[15] he is born as a responsible and graced self by the creative word of God.

There is an important element of passivity here, especially over and against theories that make the self an origin or foundation of itself, its "objects" and its world; so we can say that the decentered self is the "object" of the vision and voice of God. But Abraham has not been reduced as an object in the sense of a thing, whether present at hand or ready to hand. What has been given to him by a creative power not his own is a new subjectivity, one responsible for his response to the commands and promises of God. He is still an agent; but just as in his biological facticity he is not The Agent, so here in his moral and spiritual identity he is not The Agent, The Origin, The Foundation, but one given the freedom to respond to the First Speaker. The inverted intentionality in which God is given to Abraham as a personal performer of speech acts simultaneously gives Abraham to himself in a new way. It is altogether fitting that his name will eventually have to be changed (Gen. 17:5).

Second, in *Fear and Trembling* the God who promises and commands is given to faith and not to reason. We might speak here of a shift from the noematic to the noetic perspective, but we must be careful not to forget that this "noesis" is not a founding, grounding, *sinngebende* (meaning-bestowing) act of constitution but the free response of the founded, constituted, decentered self to the *Sinn,* promise and command, *gegeben* by God.

Silentio proposes a multifaceted *Wesensschau* (intuition of essence) of faith.

Unlike the *pistis* on the lower half of Plato's divided line, faith is not the failed attempt to achieve knowledge that therefore deserves to be called mere belief or opinion, *doxa,* lacking both the certainty and the clarity of genuine noesis, episteme, or even dianoia. It is not a lower species of the genus with which philosophy has become infatuated.

Since God is personal, faith cannot be a merely cognitive relation to some physical, psychological, or metaphysical facts. It is a relation of person to person, of I to Thou. In particular, it is trust in God's promises and obedience to God's command. While trust and obedience presuppose beliefs, neither is reducible to its doxastic dimensions. Nor can the promises and commands be derived from a "pure" reason, a power present in all humans at all times and places.

Faith seems to be a kind of virtue (as it was earlier in the Thomist tradition), and not just an intellectual virtue. For it is inextricably linked both to courage and to humility (*FT,* 33–34, 48–49, 73).[16] It is not too hard to see how being willing to be decentered while remaining responsible could require this kind of character. Silentio keeps telling us that he does not have Abraham's faith precisely because he lacks these virtues. There is an incipient unity-of-the-virtues thesis here as a phenomenological datum.

Like Sartre, Levinas, and Derrida after him,[17] Silentio is fully aware of the trauma involved in the encounter with a dramatically decentering Other, and like Rudolf Otto, he knows that the Holy is the *mysterium tremendum.* He speaks of the "shudder" and the "*horror religiosus*" evoked in Abraham and in us by the Abraham story (*FT,* 9, 61), and speaks of being terrified, shattered, repelled, even paralyzed in the encounter with this God (*FT,* 23, 33). He seems to say, If it isn't scary, it isn't God.[18]

Not surprisingly Silentio does not find faith to be an easy achievement. It isn't even an achievement. In addition to repeatedly confessing that he does not have it, implicitly asking whether anyone in Christendom can confidently say, I have the faith of Abraham, he tells us two things about faith's difficulty. First, he sandwiches his entire essay between two reminders that faith is the task of a lifetime (*FT,* 5–7, 121–23),[19] satirizing in the process the Hegelian claim to have gone beyond faith to something better, the System. Second, he affirms that faith is a marvel, "over and beyond human powers," and thus a miracle (*FT,* 48, 37). It seems Silentio is a good Thomist, for whom faith is an infused virtue. When he reads the apostle telling us, "For by grace you have been saved through faith, and this is not your own doing; it is the gift of God" (Eph. 2:8), he understands not only the grace and the salvation but also the faith by which they are received to be a gift of God.

And we haven't even talked about the traumatic tension between faith and reason.

Silentio has much to say about this tension, and he is not subtle or rhetorically reticent about it. He uses the language of paradox, absurdity, and madness to describe faith's relation to reason.[20] It cannot be stressed too much that these are relational rather than intrinsic characteristics of faith. They describe how faith looks *from the standpoint of reason.* And what might reason be?

When Abraham left for the promised land he left his "worldly understanding behind" for from its perspective what he was doing was "unreasonable." Similarly, and from the same perspective, the longer he waited in hope (another virtue closely linked to faith), the more his hopeful faith became unreasonable (*FT,* 17). What is this "worldly understanding" that congratulates itself with being the voice of reason? It is "human calculation," which is the "stockbroker" of the finite and finds everything else absurd (*FT,* 35–36).

For reason as understood here, God is not an independent variable in the situation, no more an agent than a speaker. Faith thinks that "for God all things are possible," so the knight of faith believes that even if he does have to go through with the sacrifice, he will get Isaac back *in this life* (for Isaac is an essential part of the promise in which he trusts). But for the understanding, "humanly speaking" that is, this is impossible and the faith that doesn't recognize this is absurd (*FT,* 46–47). The "worldly understanding" that finds faith to be unreasonable is a *human understanding* in relation to a *finite world* from which *God* has been excluded. Of course, faith, which trusts God's promises and obeys God's commands, will be paradoxical, absurd, sheer madness within that horizon.

But what about the "heaven-sent madness" that is superior to every "man-made sanity"?[21] Silentio reminds his readers that the pagans admired this "divine madness" (*FT,* 23) and recognized that their Logos was not the lord of all truth. He reminds his fellow phenomenologists that they cannot be engaging in presuppositionless, rigorous science if the God for whom all things are possible is excluded a priori. For phenomenology "it is forbidden to forbid."[22]

It would seem that Silentio is setting up Johannes Climacus, a subsequent pseudonym. He develops a thought experiment in which he contrasts what turns out to be the biblical concept of revelation with the Platonic (Socratic) notion of knowledge as recollection. Reason finds itself offended at the suggestion that important, even crucial knowledge about matters divine exceeds its own power to discover, even to recognize when staring it in the face. Revelation, as distinct from recollection, means not only that a Teacher is necessary to give to the learner the truth, but that the very condition for recognizing it as the truth must also be given. Climacus is not surprised at this offense and suggests that since the offended ones have wrapped themselves in the flag of Reason, the viewpoint at which they take offense might call itself the Paradox. Then he accuses the former of an acoustic illusion for thinking they are the ones who have discovered and announced the tension between faith in divine revelation from a God who speaks and autonomous, self-sufficient human reason that thinks it can get along without God, thank you. On the contrary, "The discovery, if it may be put this way, does not belong to the understanding but to the paradox, for . . . [the] offense does not understand itself but is understood by the paradox." That there is an opposition cannot be doubted. "It is just as you say, and the amazing thing is that you think that it is an objection."[23]

There is more to be said about the conflict between faith and reason, but it comes as part of the third dimension of Climacus's analysis. Firstly, God is given as personal. Secondly, God is given to faith and not to reason. Now, thirdly, God is given as an absolute norm for human life in relation to which all merely human norms are only relatively authoritative. The issue here, of course, is the (in)famous teleological suspension of the ethical, or, as I like to put it, the *Aufhebung* of the morality of mores in the commandments of God. A teleological suspension or an *Aufhebung* is a relativizing of something that might otherwise be taken (or might take itself) to be absolute and self-sufficient. It is now seen as part of a larger whole of which it is not the essential, organizing principle. It has been relativized.

The question is whether the (near) sacrifice of Isaac is to be considered, from the ethical standpoint, murder, or from the religious standpoint, sacrifice. The same dilemma is posed at the beginning of each of the three Problems that make up most of Silentio's text: if the ethical as the universal is the highest, Hegel is right, but Abraham is lost, merely a murderer rather than the father of the faithful, for he clearly intended to kill Isaac.

We must not think that the ethical as the universal is some form in a Platonic heaven or a principle of pure practical reason in a Kantian heaven. The reference to Hegel makes that clear, for Hegel thinks that there is no such ahistorical purity to be found by means of philosophical reflection. "Whatever happens, every individual is a child of his time; so philosophy too is its own time apprehended in thoughts. It is just as absurd to fancy that a philosophy can transcend its contemporary world as it is to fancy that an individual can overleap his own age, jump over Rhodes."[24]

So what gets teleologically suspended or relativized here is not eternal truth apprehended by an unsituated reason but the laws and customs of a particular people. Hegel's name for it is *Sittlichkeit,* usually translated as "ethical life," but meaning precisely the laws and customs of a people, the rules of the language game that is their form of life.[25] That this, not some Platonic or Kantian timeless truth, is what Silentio has in mind is clear not only from the explicit references to Hegel but also from the fact that he uses the Danish equivalent of *Sittlichkeit* (*det sædelige* or *Sædelighed*) for the ethical as the universal (*FT,* 55n7). He makes it, if anything, even clearer when he identifies the ethical universal as the nation, the state, society, even the church or the sect (*FT,* 57–59, 62, 74, 79). For Silentio each of these communities, concrete universals as wholes whose parts are individuals, has legitimate authority over the individuals who are their members, but from the standpoint of faith, only relative authority. Within the horizon of Abrahamic faith, only God is absolute.

Silentio argues that unless there is this difference between the absolute authority of God's commands and the relative authority of the laws and customs of one's people, "then the ethical is of the same nature as a person's eternal salvation" (*FT,* 55). That may be fine for paganism, for which "the ethical is the divine" (*FT,* 60), but when Christendom treats socialization into any human community, be it state, society, or even church, as salvation, it lapses into paganism and abandons biblical faith. As a phenomenologist, Silentio is not trying to validate biblical faith in relation to its rivals but to describe it so carefully that the two will not be confused, that a counterfeit will not get passed off as the real thing. Silentio would appreciate Johannes Climacus's epigraph for *Philosophical Fragments:* "Better well hanged than ill wed."

Throughout this discussion Silentio continues to use the language of paradox and the absurd with reference to faith. In the normative realm biblical faith is paradoxical and absurd because it is unwilling to grant absolute authority to the human communities in which it lives, although it grants them relative authority (*FT,* 70). Is there a connection here with the earlier conflict between faith and reason in the theoretical domain, as might be suggested by the continued use of the language of paradox and absurdity? Perhaps. Perhaps what counts as Reason in the theoretical domain is as tied to and reflective of a historically contingent and particular community as the ethical life (*Sittlichkeit*) of a people. Theoretical and practical Reason would be two sides of the same coin; and from the standpoint of biblical faith, the intentionality of Reason would be the intentionality of idolatry in which human, all-too-human communities absolutize themselves. "Reason" turns out to be ideology in the Marxian sense and thus idolatry in the biblical sense, the self-congratulatory, self-legitimization of the language game that goes by this honorific title.[26]

In the Kierkegaardian corpus we find not only phenomenological accounts of how the biblical God is given in human experience,[27] but also phenomenologies of how the self is given to itself, the self who just might be the decentered subject of faith. We have seen the two as two sides of the same coin in *Fear and Trembling.* The way that God is given to Abraham is simultaneously the way he is given to himself as decentered or relative both individually and socially. The same can be said of *The Sickness unto Death.* Since we are dealing with a different pseudonym, Anti-

Climacus, we should not assume a perfect match with the account of *Fear and Trembling*. For one thing, the movement is in the opposite direction, from the self's givenness to itself to the mode of God's givenness to that self. But since *Sickness* is also an account of faith, as the overcoming of despair, we can expect some significant overlap.

Our point of departure can be that dense definition of the self to be found at the outset. The self is "a relation that relates itself to itself and in relating itself to itself relates itself to another."[28] This could be read as a metaphysical claim, but let us try to read it phenomenologically.

Firstly, the self is given to itself as a relation or, to be more specific, as a dialectical incompleteness. It is dialectical in the sense of being a series of polar oppositions in tension with each other. These include infinite/finite, temporal/eternal, freedom/necessity, and psychical/physical (*SUD*, 13). Anti-Climacus speaks of the self as a synthesis of these in each case, but this language is misleading if it is taken to suggest that the antitheses rest in peaceful harmony. His own account shows them to be in unresolved tension with each other. The notion of an unresolved chord is an appropriate metaphor; Wagner's *Tristan and Isolde* comes to mind, where dissonance is disseminated indefinitely. In Hegelian language we are at the dialectical stage of thought in which oppositions arise that are internal to each other so that each side "passes over" into the other in perpetual movement. It is only in the speculative stage of thought that their unity is grasped and the tension between them resolved.[29] But neither Kierkegaard nor Anti-Climacus is a friend of Hegelian speculation, and their self is an ongoing dialectical tension.

Ongoing or, in other words, incomplete. The Cartesian/Sartrean desire is to become a whole by becoming the foundation of oneself, only to be reminded by Sartre that the for-itself is always dialectically intertwined with both its own in-itself (facticity) and its for-another. It never has the simple self-identity of the in-itself.[30] The Heideggerian self seeks to become a whole by outstripping its temporality, only to be shown by Heidegger that the completion of its journey is only possible by ceasing to be itself. The only "whole" that Dasein can be is being-*toward*-death; it is "wholly" incomplete, always *unterwegs*. Similarly, by virtue of its dialectical structure the Kierkegaardian self is always *in medias res*, an unfinished story not yet at its denouement. Existence itself, and not just faith as a mode of existence, is the task of a lifetime.

Secondly, the self is given to itself as self-relating, as a relation that relates itself to itself. One dimension of this self-relation is self-consciousness, which comes in varying degrees and various modes (*SUD*, 42–74). At one level the self is not aware of having a self and, a fortiori, an eternal self. But this is not the total absence of self-awareness; it is only the all-too-real possibility of being self-conscious only in "sensate" categories rather than those of spirit (*SUD,* 42–43). I am hungry. I am horny. There is, of course, an irony in a self's being aware of itself only as something less than a self. But that is the case in the aesthetic stage as presented in *Either/Or.* Far from lacking self-awareness, the aesthete is highly reflective.[31] Anti-Climacus does not explicitly distinguish between prereflective and reflective self-consciousness, but he might well be read as describing prereflective modes of self-awareness in order to bring them to reflective understanding and thereby, since his theme is sickness, to therapy.

The other dimension of the self's relation to itself is freedom. The self "relates itself to itself, which is freedom. The self is freedom. But freedom is the dialectical aspect of the categories of possibility and necessity" (*SUD,* 29). In other words, this freedom is not absolute. But necessity is not the only constraint on it; there are also normative constraints. As we shall see, the self is given to itself as a task and eventually as a "prodigious responsibility" (*SUD,* 5). In sum, the self is given to itself as self-conscious, responsible freedom.[32]

Thirdly, the self is given to itself as other-relating, but not as if its self-relating and its other-relating were two atomic realities externally juxtaposed. They are rather like the hydrogen and the oxygen that dissolve into each other to form water as H_2O. For the text reads that the self "*in relating itself to itself* relates itself to another" (*SUD,* 13–14; my emphasis). The latter is integral to the former; the other is the middle term between the self and itself. It is never *merely* present to itself, just as, in its incompleteness, it is never *wholly* present to itself. Here is a double phenomenological challenge to the metaphysics of presence.

It would be a mistake, however, to take this threefold account of the way in which the self is given to itself as culminating simply in the claim that subjectivity is always intersubjectivity. To understand why we must turn to a point noted above.

So, fourthly, the self is given to itself as a task. That task is to become itself (*SUD,* 29, 35, 68). Here Anti-Climacus begins to cash in the earlier analysis of the self as essentially incomplete, as *immer unterwegs.* Whither? To itself. At least that is the task. As Judge William puts it in *Either/Or,* the self's task is to choose itself, which means to receive oneself and thereby to become oneself.[33] Formally the task is to become a self; materially it is to become oneself.

One might object: "If the phenomenologist is describing essential structures of the human individual, how could I fail to be a self, indeed to be myself? Or, if I take the dialectical, temporal incompleteness of the self seriously, how could I fail to be in process of becoming a self, indeed my very own self? I will confess here for the sake of argument what I usually try to hide or disguise, namely that I am very good at being very selfish."

Anti-Climacus's response is quite direct. Becoming a self, becoming oneself is a task precisely because it is not automatically and inevitably accomplished or even attempted. It is not, for example, my task to breathe. What is most natural, precisely for the selfish self, the *conatus essendi* of Spinoza and Levinas, is the desire to be rid of oneself. This is the default setting, and its name is despair.[34] "To despair over oneself, in despair to will to be rid of oneself—this is the formula for all despair" (*SUD,* 19–20). Anti-Climacus gives a rich and detailed description of various modes of this despair, ways in which the self is given to itself as fleeing from itself. A detailed analysis of these descriptions might well reveal, in a manner Sartre would recognize, that what the self is fleeing is the alterity that is always already integral to itself, the alterity of both facticity and intersubjectivity. The self wants to be absolute and unconditioned. So let us direct our attention to the task of becoming oneself in terms of the other-relation that belongs essentially to every self-relation.

Anti-Climacus's first definition of this task is highly formal and abstract: "In relating itself to itself and in willing to be itself, the self rests transparently in the power that established it" (*SUD,* 14). We might even read this as follows: the task is to relate to oneself in such a way as to rest transparently in the power that established oneself and in this way to will to be oneself. The challenge is to accept the alterity that absolves the self from any absoluteness. The response can be resistance, resignation, or love. That Anti-Climacus will give the name of faith to this third option raises the question of the relation of faith to love.[35]

Anti-Climacus will soon enough identify the power that established the self as God (*SUD,* 30) and this willing and resting as faith (*SUD,* 49, 131), so that the full formula reads, "Faith is: that the self in being itself and in willing to be itself rests transparently in God" (*SUD,* 82).[36] But we need not be in a hurry to get there, for two reasons. First, in a gesture that is typical within the authorship, Anti-Climacus sometimes speaks quite specifically of God, meaning the biblical God, while at other times he speaks more abstractly of the self's Most Significant Other. In this case it is the eternal or eternity that is often presented as the alterity both within and beyond the self (*SUD,* 13, 17, 27–28, 42–44, 51, 64, 72, 123–24, 143, 155). This leaves it open to the reader to explore understandings of the eternal different from the biblical God.

Second, as if to encourage such reflection and in spite of his own passionate interest in the eternal precisely as the biblical God, Anti-

Climacus calls our attention to other candidates for the self's Most Significant Other. In doing so, and in harmony with his claim that other-relation is integral to self-relation, he suggests that the measure of the self's Most Significant Other is the measure of its selfhood. Thus he writes, satirically,

> A cattleman who (if this were possible) is a self directly before his cattle is a very low self, and, similarly, a master who is a self directly before his slaves is actually no self—for in both cases the criterion is lacking. The child who previously has had only his parents as a criterion becomes a self as an adult by getting the state as a criterion. (*SUD,* 79)[37]

So we can consider candidates other than God for the role of the power that has established the self. Two significant alternatives suggest themselves immediately: Nature and Society. It is not immediately clear what is meant by "resting transparently" in whatever power is understood to have given the self to itself. But the reference to transparency would seem to mean at least that the power in question is recognized as a power, or in this case, as *the* power that is not the self but gives the self to itself; and the reference to resting would seem to mean a certain acceptance or affirmation, the replacing of resentment with reconciliation.[38] The Sartrean war against any and all alterity is replaced by a genuine peace. By "genuine" here is meant more than peaceful coexistence, like North and South Korea separated by a demilitarized zone and without a peace treaty but not shooting and bombing each other, or like the United States and the Soviet Union during the cold war, kept at "peace" with each other by MAD, mutually assured destruction. A genuine peace is instead like that between Germany and the Allies after World War II, in which they are reconciled and become partners economically and in NATO.

To see Nature as the highest of the powers that have established the self is to think of fate or destiny. It is to enter the world of the Greek *Moirae* (Fates) and the Roman *Fortuna,* of Stoic resignation, and of Spinoza's neo-Stoic *Deus sive Natura.* It is worth recalling the contrast in *Fear and Trembling* between the knight of infinite resignation and the knight of faith. For *infinite* resignation, the power that has established the self is ultimate but impersonal. There is loss, but there is neither command nor promise.

It is also to enter the world of Heidegger's authentic being-toward-death in which one accepts one's thrownness and anticipates death without fleeing the anxiety this brings with it. Making peace with anxiety may not sound very restful, but Kierkegaard will not object. His faith is not without its own strenuousness. Resting transparently in the power that has established the self is not to be confused with the "wretched contentment" that defines Christendom.[39]

Some of Anti-Climacus's modes of despair can be read, at least in part, as having Nature as the power that has given the self to itself. These include the despair of finitude without infinity (*SUD,* 33–35), the despair of necessity without possibility (*SUD,* 37–42), and the despair "over the earthly or something earthly" (*SUD,* 50–60).

It can be argued that while Nature is clearly a power that has established the self, a source of its facticity, Society is a more ultimate source of the self, one in which the natural is subsumed (*aufgehoben,* teleologically suspended, relativized) under a supervening power.[40] On the basis of what I am by nature, for example, embodied, temporal, mortal, and so forth, I become more specifically myself as I assume social roles and am shaped by social norms that I internalize or resist. Thus I become, for example, a husband, a father, an academic, a driver, a sports fan, an opera buff, and so forth. Even my sexuality, it is widely argued, is not merely a matter of biological gender but also a matter of social formation.

So another candidate for the power that has established the self is Society. Anti-Climacus notices this possibility in the passage cited above where the master's criterion might be the slaves,[41] the child's criterion is the parents, and the adult's criterion is the state. Putting it this way reminds us that we have entered the world of Hegel's social philosophy, where the task of the self is to make peace with the social order, to find freedom in one's thoroughgoing integration into the rights and privileges of the social institutions of property, civil and criminal law, family, economic systems, and the state as a network of political structures.

Anti-Climacus is not terribly sanguine about this way of being a self. He speaks of those who abandon the task of becoming themselves "out of fear of men" and of the self that is

> tricked out of its self by "the others." Surrounded by hordes of men, absorbed in all sorts of secular matters, more and more shrewd about the ways of the world—such a person forgets himself . . . finds it too hazardous to be himself and far easier and safer to be like the others, to become a copy, a number, a mass man . . . Just by losing himself this way, such a man has gained an increasing capacity for going along superbly in business and social life, indeed, for making a great success in the world. (*SUD,* 33–34)[42]

In critiques such as this Kierkegaard has in mind not only Hegel's social philosophy, but Christendom as well, both of which have a veneer of religion that is superficial and self-deceived.[43]

To even the most casual reader it is obvious that Anti-Climacus wants to explore in detail neither of these possibilities but a third, namely that God is the power that gives the self to itself. "Before God" (*coram Deo*) is a constantly recurring motif (*SUD,* 5, 27, 35, 46, 77–79, 85). He identifies "Christian heroism" as the venture "wholly to become oneself, this specific individual human being, alone before God, alone in this prodigious strenuousness and this prodigious responsibility" (*SUD,* 5).[44] Here the task of becoming oneself reaches its greatest intensity, and here, as already indicated, faith as resting transparently in God as the power that has established the self is not a holiday from strenuousness and responsibility but making peace with them in their "prodigious" urgency.[45] Anti-Climacus sandwiches his comments on cattle, slaves, parents, and the state as Most Significant Others between a reference to the "*infinite* reality" gained by "the theological self, the self directly before God" and a reference to "what an *infinite* accent falls on the self by having God as the criterion" (*SUD,* 79; my emphasis).

Although Anti-Climacus speaks occasionally of God in part 1, titled "The Sickness unto Death Is Despair," the theological dimension is recessive, overtone rather than tone. It is in part 2, titled "Despair Is Sin," that "before God" is explicitly thematized. Thus the opening sentence reads: "Sin is: *before God, or with the conception of God, in despair not to will to be oneself, or in despair to will to be oneself.*[46] Thus sin is intensified weakness or intensified defiance: sin is the intensification of despair . . . what lawyers call 'aggravated' despair" (*SUD,* 77).

Before God the self is given to itself as sinner. The focus could have been on God as Creator and thus on the self as created with a further emphasis on (1) the finitude of the self as neither its own arche nor its own telos or (2) the *imago Dei* as a reflection of and participation in the divine glory. But as in the Pentateuch, where creation is prologue to covenant, and as in Luther, who thinks primarily in terms of Law and Gospel, and as in Silentio, who thinks of God not primarily as First Cause but as First Speaker, the one whose speech acts are command and promise, so Anti-Climacus sees the self, "Christianly understood" (*SUD,* 77, 5, 7–8, 17, 81, 96, 101), as the one who has been unfaithful to the covenant, who has broken the Law and not trusted in the Gospel, who has resisted the command and not rested in the promise. Sin is the misrelation of the I to its highest Thou.

For this reason the task of becoming a self, of willing to be oneself by resting in the power that has established the self, becomes very specific. "Thou shalt believe in the forgiveness of sins" (*SUD,* 115).[47] The Lutheran category Law and Gospel is especially visible here, for it is before the Law that the self is a sinner, and it is in the Gospel that forgiveness of sins is offered.

Here we find repeated two aspects of Kierkegaard as phenomenologist already noted. First, he is a hermeneutical phenomenologist who, instead of seeking to go directly "to the things themselves," turns rather to prior interpretations in terms of which to develop his own interpretations. In this case it is the biblical interpretation and especially the Lutheran interpretation of that interpretation of the human self as a sinner to whom forgiveness is offered. The task of becoming oneself is the task of acknowledging the former and accepting the latter. As in *Fear and Trembling,* this is called faith and is said to require both humility and courage. But then we shouldn't be too surprised, for behind the two pseudonyms stands one and the same Kierkegaard.

Second, we find a dialectical relation between the way in which God is given to the self and the way in which the self is given to itself. In Hegelian language, the two "pass over" into each other. At this point Kierkegaard is a good Calvinist. For it is Calvin who opens his *Institutes of the Christian Religion* as follows:

> I. *Without knowledge of self there is no knowledge of God*
> Nearly all the wisdom we possess, that is to say, true and sound wisdom, consists of two parts: the knowledge of God and of ourselves. But, while joined by many bonds, which one precedes and brings forth the other is not easy to discern . . . Yet, however the knowledge of God and of ourselves may be mutually connected, the order of right teaching requires that we discuss the former first, then proceed afterward to treat the latter.[48]

Kierkegaard seems in our two texts to be a more dialectical thinker, and while he distinguishes these two aspects of wisdom, biblically understood, he does not proceed in such a linear fashion. He enacts the interdependence of the two dimensions by never letting either gain apparent independence of the other. Whether this is because of his Lutheran heritage, his proximity to Hegel, or his fear of lapsing into either Feuerbachian anthropologism (theology is anthropology) or what Heidegger will call onto-theology—that would be a nice debate for a cold winter's evening.

Notes

1. "I think that, in spite of everything, what I do is phenomenology." Emmanuel Levinas, *Of God Who Comes to Mind,* trans. Bettina Bergo (Stanford: Stanford University Press, 1998), 87.

2. *Totality and Infinity,* trans. Alphonso Lingis (Pittsburgh: Duquesne Uni-

versity Press, 1969), 23, 29. On the convergences and divergences between Levinas and Kierkegaard, see my *Levinas and Kierkegaard in Dialogue* (Bloomington: Indiana University Press, 2008).

3. I call those writings Kierkegaard's that he gave to us to consider. I shall attribute particular pseudonymous writings to the appropriate pseudonym.

4. Meditation II, *Meditations on First Philosophy*, trans. Donald A. Cress (Indianapolis: Hackett, 1979), 19.

5. "Experience" here is meant to be as open and nontechnical a term as possible. Cartesian/Husserlian thought would speak of consciousness, but the term has been rendered problematic by post-Husserlian phenomenologists who would rather speak of being in the world, of concernful dealings, of comportment, of embodied awareness, and so forth. I use "experience" as Levinas does when he says that the transcendent, the "beyond" that indeed overflows being, objective experience, totality, thematization, and so forth, must necessarily show up in some way "*within* experience" (*Totality and Infinity*, 23). It must be given to me in such a way as to make a difference.

6. Here I follow Jean-Luc Marion who, on the basis of Husserl's *The Idea of Phenomenology* (1907), takes givenness to be even more basic to phenomenology than intentionality. See *Being Given: Toward a Phenomenology of Givenness*, trans. Jeffrey L. Kosky (Stanford: Stanford University Press, 2002).

7. For a phenomenology that is overtly not a transcendental phenomenology by virtue of its emphasis on the place or location of the self, see Jean-Yves Lacoste, *Experience and the Absolute: Disputed Questions on the Humanity of Man*, trans. Mark Raftery-Skehan (New York: Fordham University Press, 2004).

8. *Freud and Philosophy* (New Haven, Conn.: Yale University Press, 1970), 42. Ricoeur speaks of "the long detour of the signs of humanity deposited in cultural works" and of "the detour of understanding the cultural signs in which the self documents and forms itself . . . [so that] reflection is nothing without the mediation of signs and works." *Hermeneutics and the Human Sciences*, ed. and trans. John B. Thompson (New York: Cambridge University Press, 1981), 143, 158–59. In *Oneself as Another* (Chicago: University of Chicago Press, 1992) the detour is through the four "who" questions that structure the book. The self, so far from being the origin of meaning and the foundation of truth, is that which is sought in a reflection whose detours preclude total transparency. See pp. 16–19. For a related but different argument against the transparency of the self to itself, see Judith Butler, *Giving an Account of Oneself* (New York: Fordham University Press, 2005). With reference to the conflict of interpretations, I have a colleague in theology who gives an entire semester course on various interpretations of the *Akedah*.

9. In *The Theological Turn in French Phenomenology*, trans. Bernard G. Prusak, in Janicaud et al., *Phenomenology and the "Theological Turn": The French Debate* (New York: Fordham University Press, 2000). Jean-Luc Marion makes the point quite clearly. See *Being Given*, 4–5, 234–36, 242. To forbid phenomenology the right to do this is to lapse into dogmatic secularism. See "Metaphysics and Phenomenology: A Summary for Theologians," in *The Postmodern God: A Theological Reader*, ed. Graham Ward (Oxford: Blackwell, 1997), 289, where Marion says that for phenomenology, "It is forbidden to forbid."

10. See *Hegel's God: A Counterfeit Double?* (Aldershot, Eng.: Ashgate, 2003).

11. In *Divine Discourse: Philosophical Reflections on the Claim That God Speaks* (New York: Cambridge University Press, 1995), Nicholas Wolterstorff argues that "speaking is not revealing" (chap. 2), that is, does not consist exclusively or even primarily in making factual assertions or communicating information; then he calls attention to the centrality of promises and commands as distinctive speech acts of the biblical God.

12. *FT,* 17. The rhetoric here echoes Heb. 11:8–12, but the reference is to Gen. 12, where the Abraham story begins with the command to emigrate and the promise of a land and a blessing.

13. For the background of this notion in Sartre, Levinas, and Derrida, see my "Inverted Intentionality: On Being Seen and Being Addressed," *Faith and Philosophy* 26, no. 3 (2009): 233–52.

14. The objection that inverted intentionality simply reverses the subject-object relation simply misses the point.

15. Is Sartre's argument that existence precedes essence in "Existentialism Is a Humanism" the logical conclusion of Husserlian phenomenology? This essay is found by itself and in several anthologies, including *Basic Writings of Existentialism,* ed. Gordon Marino (New York: Modern Library, 2004).

16. *SUD,* 85.

17. See note 13 above.

18. In addition to Otto's *The Idea of the Holy,* see Jean-Luc Marion's account of the saturated phenomenon in "The Saturated Phenomenon," in *Phenomenology and the "Theological Turn"* and in *Being Given.*

19. Gilbert Ryle's distinction between task words and achievement words is helpful here. It is developed throughout *The Concept of Mind* (New York: Barnes and Noble, 1949).

20. For paradox, see *FT,* 33, 51–53, 55–56, 62–66, 85, 88. For the absurd, see *FT,* 34–37, 40, 46–51. For madness, see *FT,* 17, 23, 76–77.

21. Plato, *Phaedrus,* trans. R. Hackforth, in *The Collected Dialogues,* ed. Edith Hamilton and Huntington Cairns (Princeton, N.J.: Princeton University Press, 2005), 244d.

22. See note 9 above.

23. *PF,* 50, 52. Climacus may be thinking here of the Pauline contrast between the wisdom of the world and the wisdom of God in 1 Cor. 1–2. "For the message [*logos*] about the cross is foolishness to those who are perishing, but for us who are being saved it is the power of God" (1:18). See the sermon Kierkegaard preached in February 1844, just a few months before the publication of *Philosophical Fragments,* on 1 Cor. 2:6–9, which contrasts "the wisdom of the world" with "the mysterious Wisdom of God" (*"Johannes Climacus or, De Omnibus Dubitandum Est" and "A Sermon,"* trans. T. H. Croxall [Stanford: Stanford University Press, 1958], 159–73).

24. *Philosophy of Right,* trans. T. M. Knox (Oxford: Clarendon Press, 1945), 11.

25. It is what Nietzsche so often refers to as the morality of mores (*die Sittlichkeit der Sitten*).

26. In this frame of mind, Kierkegaard would find it dangerous to speak of

desecrating the flag, as if either the flag or the republic for which it stands were something sacred rather than, for better and for worse, something human, all too human. Whereas Sartre, in the Cartesian tradition, thinks it is as individuals that we are the desire to be God, Kierkegaard, closer to Hegel, thinks this possible mode of being given to ourselves in social rather than individual terms. His (in)famous individualism is best read as a form of ideology critique.

27. *Fear and Trembling* is by no means the only such account. While it is merely monotheistic, other accounts, including but not limited to the writings of Johannes Climacus, are explicitly Christian (that is, Trinitarian) by reflecting on how God incarnate is given.

28. See *SUD,* 13–14.

29. G. W. F. Hegel, *The Encyclopedia Logic,* trans. T. F. Geraets, W. A. Suchting, and H. S. Harris (Indianapolis: Hackett, 1991), §§79–82.

30. That Descartes acknowledges the creation by God that Sartre denies is perhaps little more than window dressing, whether sincere or merely tactical. The Cartesian self still thinks that through methodical doubt it can become the onto-theological god, the ground of itself and the measure of the world. See Jean-Luc Marion, "Descartes and Onto-theology," in *Post-Secular Philosophy: Between Philosophy and Theology,* ed. Phillip Blond (New York: Routledge, 1998), 67–106.

31. But nevertheless immediate in the sense of being unmediated by ethical or religious categories and norms. See my "Kierkegaard and the Role of Reflection in Second Immediacy," in *Immediacy and Reflection in Kierkegaard's Thought,* ed. P. Cruysberghs et al. (Leuven: Leuven University Press, 2003), 159–79.

32. The self who lives in "sensate" categories is "ignorant" of this, but this ignorance is best understood as the bad faith in which it manages not to notice what it nevertheless knows about itself. I believe Anti-Climacus would welcome this Sartrean gloss. See my "Kierkegaard's Psychology and Unconscious Despair," in *International Kierkegaard Commentary* 19: *"The Sickness unto Death,"* ed. Robert L. Perkins (Macon, Ga.: Mercer University Press, 1987), 39–66.

33. *EO II,* 177. See the illuminating commentary by Edward Mooney, "Kierkegaard on Self-Choice and Self-Reception: Judge William's Admonition," in *International Kierkegaard Commentary* 4: *"Either/Or, Part II,"* ed. Robert L. Perkins (Macon, Ga.: Mercer University Press, 1995), 5–31.

34. See *SUD,* 22–28, on the universality of this sickness.

35. In *Fear and Trembling* faith is related to the virtues of humility and courage. There are numerous passages in *SUD* that encourage us to think about the relation of faith to love and, perhaps, to read *SUD* in relation to *Works of Love.*

36. Anti-Climacus does not distinguish his role as phenomenologist from his role as theologian. But we can do so, if we wish to, and read him as asking the question, How is the self given to itself when it takes the power that established it to be God? This mode of experience is not inevitable, but it is possible and, so far as phenomenology can say, possibly veridical, that is, an experience in which we "let that which shows itself be seen from itself in the very way in which it shows itself from itself." This formula is Heidegger's definition of phenomenology. See *Being and Time,* trans. John Macquarrie and Edward Robinson (New York: Harper and Row, 1962), 58.

37. As a commentary on the first option here, I have a *Garfield* cartoon in which Jon says to Garfield, "I am not pathetic! Am I?"—to which Garfield's mental response is, "Jon, you're asking a cat's opinion." Had there been a next frame, it would have shown Garfield thinking, "I rest my case."

38. With regard to resting, Lacoste's account of relating to God as absolute is helpful here. "[T]he man who finds complete repose in God escapes the world's rule over him, and participates in God's lordly reign over the universe" (*Experience and the Absolute,* 26). Not incidentally, Lacoste describes the God who is absolute as someone . . . who promises . . . and over whom there is no supreme and impersonal authority" (21). If nature or society were to be taken as absolute as the self's ultimate place, it would involve a different escape and a different participation. Spinoza and Hegel come to mind, and it is important to note that insofar as this repose is an escaping and a participating it is not the passive inertness of the couch potato.

39. The phrase is from Nietzsche's *Thus Spoke Zarathustra,* though it nicely fits Kierkegaard's attack on Christendom. See especially sec. 3 of Zarathustra's Prologue.

40. See, for example, Peter L. Berger and Thomas Luckmann, *The Social Construction of Reality* (Garden City, N.Y.: Doubleday, 1966), especially pt. 3, "Society as Subjective Reality," with its analysis of internalization and identity.

41. Here, I suppose, the task of the self is to become a member of the ruling class and to exercise the rights and privileges thereof.

42. This comes in the analysis of the despair of finitude without infinity.

43. See my "Paganism in Christendom: On Kierkegaard's Critique of Religion," in *International Kierkegaard Commentary* 17: *"Christian Discourses" and "The Crisis and a Crisis in the Life of an Actress,"* ed. Robert L. Perkins (Macon, Ga.: Mercer University Press, 2007), 13–33. The focus is on *Christian Discourses,* but the critique of Christendom in earlier texts, including *SUD,* is sketched. See also the satirical "jury trial" to which Jesus is put in Christendom as described in "Kenosis and Offense: A Kierkegaardian Look at Divine Transcendence," in *International Kierkegaard Commentary* 20: *Practice in Christianity,* ed. Robert L. Perkins, (Macon, Ga.: Mercer University Press, 2004), 30–36.

44. This is a reminder that the loneliness of Abraham in *Fear and Trembling* is not the expression of an individualistic existentialism for the simple reason that Abraham is alone—before God. His being is an essentially relational being.

45. The strenuousness of faith is an important theme of Johannes Climacus in *Concluding Unscientific Postscript.*

46. These two modes of despair, without the focus on "before God," have been carefully analyzed at the end of pt. 1 (*SUD,* 47–74).

47. At this point, if not sooner, it becomes clear that "Christianly understood" signifies, in this text, a contrast with the universally human understanding, if there is such a thing, and with "paganism," but not with Judaism, for the forgiveness of sins is as central to biblical Jewish faith as to biblical Christian faith.

48. John Calvin, *Institutes of the Christian Religion,* trans. Ford Lewis Battles (Philadelphia: Westminster Press, 1960), bk. 1, chap. 1, sec. 1, 3.

Freedom Through Despair: Kierkegaard's Phenomenological Analysis

Daniel Dahlstrom

> And to me an even more horrible expression of this most terrible sickness and misery is that it is hidden—not only that the person suffering from it may wish to hide it and may succeed, not only that it can so live in a man that no one, no one detects it, no, but also that it can be so hidden in a man that he himself is not aware of it!
>
> —Kierkegaard, *The Sickness unto Death*

Despair is not a common theme in contemporary philosophical treatments of the issue of free will—the freedom, in some sense, to choose and make decisions. Dominating these treatments for the most part are two closely related questions, the question of the necessity of the presence or perception of alternative possibilities for this freedom and the question of its compatibility with a completely causal account of human behavior, with or without an indeterministic component. By contrast, Kierkegaard takes the question of despair—what it is, how it develops, and what forms it takes—to be central to the issue of human freedom, the free exercise of an ability to choose and make decisions for oneself. To be in despair is, among other things, to feel hopeless and paralyzed on some level; in despairing, we are unable to act in a way that frees us from that self-inflicted paralysis. Whether or not, following Kierkegaard, we also define it as something that we do to ourselves, despair is a constant threat to our existence, precisely insofar as we regard ourselves as freely self-developing, more or less. Kierkegaard accordingly portrays human freedom as an inherently personal and fragile, dynamic and unfinished reality, constitutive of existence, that is, constitutive of who we are, rising and falling as a function of our struggle with different possible forms of despair. The possibility of a certain stage of despair accompanies and challenges a corresponding breakthrough to a higher form of freedom, such that the highest form of freedom is, among a good many other things, a freedom from despair.

The following paper offers an interpretation of Kierkegaard's analysis of human freedom in the face of specific forms of human despair identified by him.[1] The main objective of the interpretation is to identify his conception of the nature of properly human freedom by elucidating precisely how, according to his analysis, it comes about only through despair and admits of degrees corresponding to different stages of despair. To the extent that this elucidation is successful, it demonstrates that the connection between freedom and despair is a dimension of human freedom that contemporary philosophers can ill afford to neglect. A secondary objective of the interpretation is, in keeping with the theme of the present volume, to highlight the phenomenological character of Kierkegaard's method of analysis.

In regard to the latter objective, certain qualifications are in order. The term "phenomenology" is often bandied about in contemporary philosophy as a label for something like the immediate contents of consciousness or the identification and examination of what is immediately given to the mind in human experience.[2] Although Kierkegaard carefully avoids the epistemological as well as ethical slipperiness of the notion of "immediacy," his analyses are phenomenological in a sense analogous to this contemporary usage, given their focus on the inwardness of consciousness and subjectivity. However, the term "phenomenology" also designates two philosophical methods, one introduced before, the other after Kierkegaard's life of writing. The former is the Hegelian variety of phenomenology, designed to investigate scientifically "the experience of consciousness," in all its basic forms as it allegedly unfolds—dialectically and purposefully—in history. There are, as several scholars have amply demonstrated unmistakably Hegelian dimensions to Kierkegaard's analysis, emphasizing dynamic relations among opposites at the heart of human consciousness.[3] But in the present paper I shall be calling more attention to phenomenological sensibilities that Kierkegaard shares with Husserl and the early Heidegger. For this tradition, "phenomenology" designates a particular sort of foundational analysis of the various forms of consciousness (Husserl) and/or self-disclosing existence (Heidegger), with a view to determining what is meaningful and essential about them.[4] Talk of Kierkegaard's phenomenology in connection with this tradition obviously incurs the risk of anachronism. However, the following considerations of Kierkegaard's analyses of freedom and despair in *The Sickness unto Death* (1849) hopefully demonstrate that these risks, while worrisome, are worth running.[5]

Kierkegaard's characterization of despair as a "sickness unto death" suggests the agony of someone in the throes of death. But the malady that Kierkegaard signals by this metaphor is an affliction from which even death itself provides no relief. At the same time, he regards the possibility of despair as a condition of human freedom. Indeed, freedom is inherently dialectical and that dialectical character is manifest in its intrinsic connection with despair. For, while we freely succumb to the stages of this beleaguered state, we also only experience freedom as the release from them in the course of exercising our freedom to transcend these stages. Herein lies perhaps the basic theme of Kierkegaard's remarks about freedom in *The Sickness unto Death:* despair is something that we do, the effects of which are painful, and yet at the same time the inevitable, necessary condition of the constant, more or less progressive task of human freedom (where positive and negative senses of "freedom" converge). On the one hand, every moment a person is in despair, she is bringing it upon herself and, indeed, as a constraint that she feels (*SUD,* 15–16/148–49). Despair is not simply an emotional state that we undergo but also, and more importantly, an activity for which we are responsible. As Kierkegaard puts it in his journals, "It is by virtue of freedom that a person despairs—of freedom"; in short, despair is "self-inflicted" (*Supplement* 145, 147). On the other hand, freedom develops as a capacity to choose, precisely to the extent that a person manages, more or less, to overcome despair. In short, while giving rise to despair, freedom also grows precisely in the process of transcending its proclivities to despair.

But the key words here are "develop" and "process" since freedom, like the existence constituted by it, is never static, never over and done with—something that can only be said of phenomena without mortal constraints (importantly unlike the phenomena on which later phenomenologists famously focus). The process, however, is punctuated by certain phases or stages of despair. Kierkegaard begins his analysis of the process with an abstract, formal account of this basic theme. The following reconstruction of his analysis begins with (1) a review of that initial account, aimed at unpacking its general significance. As a means of determining more precisely the senses of "freedom" at work in his account, I offer (2) an interpretation of these senses in the course of exposing what Kierkegaard takes to be the shortcomings of determinism and indeterminism. Finally, I sketch (3) an outline of the general forms of freedom before turning to (4) an elucidation of the concrete forms they take in passing through the stages of despair.

1. The Basic Theme: Freedom Through Despair

In the opening passages of *The Sickness unto Death,* after declaring a human being to be spirit and spirit to be the self, Kierkegaard characterizes the self in relational terms. But the self here, he advises, is to be understood not as a relation simply but as a relation "relating itself to itself in the relation." For all its abstruseness, this formulation suggests that the self is an unfinished, reflexive process. The observation that immediately follows in the text confirms as much: "A human being is a synthesis of the infinite and the finite, of the temporal and the eternal, of freedom and necessity, in short, a synthesis. A synthesis is a relation between two. Considered in this way, a human being is not yet a self" (*SUD,* 13/146). For our purposes, what is important in this observation is the direct inclusion of freedom in an unfinished, reflexive process of coming to selfhood and its dependence upon necessity or, better, upon its synthesis with necessity in that process. Soul and body can also be regarded as factors in this synthesis, but such that the soul is not identical to the self or the spiritual process through which the self emerges. In order for a self freely to come to be (itself an endless "task"), this reflexive process must relate freely to its freedom and the synthesis of its freedom with necessity. Thus, in an abstract, structural sense, the reflexivity involved in the (unfinished) emergence of human selfhood entails two levels of freedom at any moment in the process. We shall try to make this clearer and more concrete below (see section 3). But it is important to stress from the outset that coming to selfhood is not a matter of simply recognizing or being reflectively conscious of the (potential) synthesis but deliberately choosing and, to the extent possible, actively engaging in its emergence. Thus, reminiscent of Pindar, Kierkegaard contends: "The self is the conscious synthesis . . . whose task is to become itself."[6]

To be sure, if we approach this contention with certain suppositions, it appears contradictory or even senseless.[7] One might suppose, for example, that if something already exists, then it cannot become itself; if it becomes anything, then it can only become something else, something other than itself. Nor is it clear how someone can have a task to become herself, to come to be who she is. Normally when we speak of a person being assigned a concrete task to do one thing or another, it is in view of some future state or condition of that very person. So, for example, it might be someone's task to be diligent or work hard, to better herself in the interest of becoming a better employee, citizen, mother, human being, and so on. However, for these tasks to be meaningful at all, they can only be assigned to someone who already is.

While perhaps tendentious, these reservations with Kierkegaard's contention cast light on the specific phenomenon of freedom that forms the subject of his analysis. We experience freedom precisely because what we already are (and thus in a sense necessarily are) is undeveloped yet in our hands (at least in part) to develop and refine. This basic tension—the phenomenon of self-emergence as an unfinished necessity placed in the hands of the emerging self to shape—enables and characterizes the freedom that we experience as human beings. This phenomenon, moreover, is falsified if a conception of reality as something inherently already fully formed and developed is foisted upon it. Here, at the outset of his analysis, Kierkegaard already displays distinctively phenomenological sensibilities, not letting some metaphysical conception of things preempt him from heeding the phenomenon itself.

At the same time the self-relating process—the process of achieving a synthesis of body and soul, freedom and necessity, and so on as the constitutive condition for selfhood—can go well or badly. It goes well if that self-reflective process contributes to realizing the genuine potential of the synthesis. In the final analysis that means, among other things, acting in the recognition of its essential dependence or, to put it more paradoxically, the dependence of its freedom and necessity upon a power beyond it. The possibility of despair, like gravity for a leaper, is a condition for this liberating process; in this important sense, Kierkegaard observes, it is an "advantage," providing for "pretty nearly the best thing that can be said of a man."[8] The comparison with gravity ends there, however, since, as already noted, the actuality of despair, "a misrelation in the relation of a synthesis that relates to itself," is always the act and responsibility of the one who despairs; accordingly, despair amounts, as Kierkegaard puts it, not only to "the worst misfortune and misery," but even to "ruination" or "perdition" (*SUD,* 15/148).

Despair expresses itself in anguish and despondency but, given its structure and dynamic (as just described), to identify it with those emotional states without further ado is to misrepresent this phenomenon profoundly. Alert to this possibility, Kierkegaard advises that despair is not to be confused with "transitory states, such as dejection, inner conflict," with feelings of anxiousness or insecurity or, for that matter, the absence of any thought or feeling of being in despair (*SUD,* 23–26/156–59). Far from being a matter of any immediate disposition, despair is instead a sickness unto death, the sickening realization, not that death is the last thing, but that even death will not provide surcease or closure. "The hopelessness in this case is that even the last hope, death, is not available" (*SUD,* 18/151; Lowrie translation used). As Kierkegaard also puts it, despair is "veritably a self-consuming, but an impotent self-consuming that cannot do what it wants to do" (*SUD,* 18/151). This despair over oneself, this impotent will to be rid of oneself and, indeed, a self with an eternal vocation, is, Kierkegaard submits, "the formula for all despair" (*SUD,* 20/153, 60/194). Accordingly, the very attempt to rid oneself of despair on one's own terms and by one's own power is itself an expression of despair. In other words, while despair is something that we do in the course of carrying out the reflexive synthesis of body and soul, it is not something that we can undo by ourselves.

This fact along with the self-directedness of despair—the fact that one despairs, properly speaking, of oneself—has a direct bearing on Kierkegaard's conception of freedom since he understands the emerging self as precisely the synthesis of freedom and necessity (as noted above). As the disruption of the "synthesis *that relates to itself*" (more precisely, "the misrelation in the relation of a synthesis that relates itself to itself"[9]), despair is the condition for freedom much as fear is the condition for courage. Like fear, despair is something we feel, though, as noted above, the feeling, like many a fear, can be quite complex, pervasive, and enduring. Yet despair is not inherent in human nature in quite the way that fear is. Despair is far more the result of a way of relating to oneself and, indeed, oneself as the very relation of freedom and necessity (*SUD,* 16–17/150). As noted above, that means, among other things, that despair can take the form of the presumption that freeing oneself from despair is up to oneself alone. In this sense, despair is generally a misuse of freedom, a self-deceptive arrogation of power, indulging a pure figment of imagination, indicative of a failure in the reflexive synthesis of freedom and necessity. For a self who does not despair is precisely a self who "in relating itself to itself and in willing to be itself . . . rests transparently in the power that established it."[10] While despair is not eliminated by an exercise of human will alone, freedom from despair consists in willing to be oneself, to be who one is, where *who one is* is grounded "transparently" in the power that posited it. What the relationship is between this freedom from despair and the grounding power remains to be seen, but it seems prima facie that this power (in its relationship to the person free from despair) cannot be understood as a necessity determining it.[11]

2. Possibility, Necessity, and Prayer

In the opening passages of *The Sickness unto Death,* Kierkegaard initially construes freedom by locating it in relation to necessity where, as noted above, that relation is a condition of the reflexivity that plays a constitutive role in achieving and sustaining a self. A human being can be said to have a self to the extent that her individual synthesis of freedom and necessity is reflexive or, in other words, to the extent that she relates freely (thoughtfully, intentionally, and actively) to this very relation as her own. So whatever freedom is more specifically for Kierkegaard, human beings define themselves by synthesizing that freedom with necessity of some sort via a reflexive process that is also essential to human freedom. As noted above, this bare-bones analysis of the emergence of selfhood entails at least two sorts or levels of freedom.

Kierkegaard claims that the determinist or fatalist is in despair in a superficial way, having lost his self in a certain sense "because for him everything has become necessity" (*SUD,* 40/173). This claim underscores the fact that the self-establishing, reflexive synthesis involves a recognition of both freedom and necessity and, equally important, of their basic connection in our lives. In this context Kierkegaard also observes that "personhood is a synthesis of possibility and necessity" (*SUD,* 40/173). If we take this observation as indicating that "possibility" and "freedom" are at least metonyms, we gain a further insight into the sense of freedom, precisely in relation to necessity.[12] In other words, it is likely that, because freedom, while not identical to possibility, entails it in some relevant sense, Kierkegaard substitutes "possibility" for "freedom" in characterizing personality as a synthesis of possibility and necessity.

Kierkegaard provides some illumination about the sort of possibility and necessity he has in mind here when he adds that because the fatalist's god is necessity, the fatalist cannot pray. Prayer, at least in the form of supplication, supposes precisely that "for God all things are possible." But Kierkegaard is also quick to add that possibility and necessity are jointly conditions of prayer (*SUD,* 40/173). We pray because possibilities exist, but we pray, too, because we are subject to various necessities, ever-present necessities as well as those of the unchanging past that together determine the possibilities of the situation in which we pray. To put the point in another medium, the indeterminist no less than the determinist is caught up in a fantasy, a failure to appreciate what Kierkegaard calls "actuality": a "unity of possibility and necessity" (*SUD,* 36/169). From a phenomenological point of view, both the indeterminist and the determinist are blind to the phenomena in question, namely, their own existential reality. Moreover, this myopia is a function of not being able to disengage or bracket a theoretical conception of things or, equivalently, a function of not heeding the primacy of perception and its presentation of the things themselves over what we might merely picture or think things to be.[13] If a person can despair by imagining that everything is necessary and nothing possible for her, a person can equally despair from imagining that everything is possible for her and there is no necessity to which she has to submit. Pride, the deliberate failure to appreciate one's limits and thus to become aware of who one is, is a recipe for despair.

The appeal to prayer also makes it clear that the possibilities involved in freedom are not simply logical, physical, or surreal possibilities but existential possibilities, as a latter-day phenomenologist might put it. While existential possibilities may also conform to the law of noncontradiction and the statistical probabilities governing physical occurrences, this conformity is not what renders them possible in an existential sense. At the same time, while requiring imagination, the medium in which the self must reflect itself "in order to become itself" (*SUD,* 35/168), existential possibilities are not the possibilities imagined in some surreal world of fantasy.[14] Existential possibilities are the "serious" possibilities that pertain to "the reality of personal existence" (*SUD,* 5–6/142; Lowrie translation used). They are lived possibilities, not only in the sense that they are experienced as open to us within the realm of our capacities and responsibilities, but also in the sense that they are part of our lives, the history that we make of ourselves.

It is important to keep in mind that Kierkegaard is concerned not simply with the theory of determinism or indeterminism but with the phenomenon of living and practicing either one of two forms of despair: fatalism or autonomy. In practice, as noted, determinists and indeterminists alike fall prey to theoretical fantasies contrary to the phenomena, namely, the lived experience of the conditional freedom of personal existence.[15] So, too, the focus in so many contemporary debates between compatibilists and incompatibilists is typically juridical, directed at an individual action or an action within a particular scenario. The missing dimension in these discussions is precisely the agent's experience of existential possibilities as part of her life, concretely delimited possibilities of her history for which she nonetheless experiences herself as responsible. To his credit once again as a phenomenologist, Kierkegaard struggles to keep open this concrete dimension of the experience of freedom, defying metaphysical claims from determinists and indeterminists alike that contradict it.[16] Even the most elementary form of freedom for Kierkegaard is, as noted earlier, in the process of being synthesized with necessity, a synthesis that is a condition for every further form of freedom as well. The determinist denies that she is faced with existential possibilities, the indeterminist that she must submit to necessities of one sort or another and, indeed, not least the derivativeness of her body and soul as well as the synthesis of them that is the condition of her (emerging) selfhood. Human freedom is constituted by existential possibilities and what renders possibilities existential is, among other things, the fact that they are choices that an individual alone is forced to make, precisely at the threshold of necessities and constraints, including certain ideals or values, enveloping and pervading the concrete possibilities of the situation in which she finds herself.[17]

3. The Forms and Dialectical Formation of Freedom *in Abstracto*

Although Kierkegaard does not formally distinguish his uses of "freedom" in *The Sickness unto Death,* his opening remarks entail, as already noted, at least two different (albeit related) exercises and experiences of freedom. Given his taciturnity about these various senses of freedom, in the following I offer a speculative interpretation of what I take to be three strata of freedom entailed by his analysis of different stages of despair. Each of these forms of freedom is reflexive and thus represents a "dialectical" stage in the formation or, better, the maturation of freedom (always to be understood as its reflexive synthesis with necessity). By "dialectical" (a word Kierkegaard himself employs in this connection), I mean something reminiscent of Hegel's use of the term, namely, that a reflexivity (self-relatedness) issues in a subsequent level that includes (preserves yet reforms, in one sense lifts up or elevates, in another sense cancels: *aufhebt*) the freedom exercised initially.

The first and most elementary sense of "freedom" designates part of the synthesis, indeed, the self-relating part of the synthesis that is a condition of human selfhood (*SUD,* 29/162). Freedom of this first sort presumably corresponds to the experience of engaging one possibility or course of action rather than another in a situation that, while allowing for both possibilities, is already defined by necessities. Freedom of this sort can be as rudimentary as pivoting off my left leg rather than my right leg, indeed, consciously or not, prereflectively or reflectively. The freedom is self-relating, since I pivot with my body (that is to say I literally exert a force with one part of my body on another part). But at the same time this freedom is a relation to a necessity, for example, the requirements of and constraints on mobility (including those of a physical, electrical, and gravitational nature). Note that freedom in this elementary sense is not the exercise of a purely arbitrary will (*liberum arbitrium*), something repeatedly rejected by Kierkegaard.[18] Freedom in this elementary sense is both a real power of acting and moving, limited by its own capacities and its environment, and the experience of this power under constraints. This elementary freedom may be, as noted, prereflective or reflective. Given the contrast with the next form of freedom, however, I refer to this elementary sort of freedom as "reflective freedom," with the acknowledgment that it is rooted in and continuous with prereflective senses of freedom.[19]

The second sort of freedom is a manner of relating not directly to necessities alone (as in the first sense of freedom) but to the necessity of the relation of freedom and necessity. This second stage of freedom defines the self. More precisely, it is the manner of achieving a self as the reflexive relation or synthesis of freedom (in the first sense) and necessity. This reflexive relation takes the form of willing (choosing, deciding), involving the consciousness (reflection and/or imagination) of one's initial freedom and possibilities *as one's own*, relative to the necessities constraining them. Accordingly, I refer to this second sort of freedom as "self-reflective" or "autonomous" freedom. This second sort of freedom has remote kinships with Kant's sense of freedom as autonomy and with Harry Frankfurt's account of freedom of the will in terms of second- or higher-order volitions. Exercising and experiencing freedom in this second sense—reflexively relating to one's foregoing actions and willing or not one's ongoing actions as syntheses of capacities and constraints—is equivalent to coming to think and have a self. By "equivalence" here, I mean that, while not identical, this exercise of freedom and one's particular self-conception and degree of self-possession stand and fall together. That is also to say that, insofar as I think and have a self, it is not an option for me whether I exercise this self-reflective freedom or not. It is incumbent on me to do so or, as Kierkegaard pithily puts it, "The self is freedom" (*SUD*, 29/162).[20]

Herein lies ostensibly an important difference between the first two senses of freedom in Kierkegaard's account. Freedom in the second sense, in contrast to freedom in the first sense, is not a mere capacity to realize one possibility rather than another (in Frankfurt's jargon, to act on first-order desires that rule out others). Instead, this self-reflective freedom is the very actualization of itself as a capacity, since it is the reflection itself—and only the reflection—that necessarily presents the person reflecting with a choice of *her* alternatives, namely, to actualize or continue to actualize a capacity *of hers* or not (to indulge or not certain first-order desires). In becoming reflectively conscious of my capacities and imagining their possibilities, I necessarily present myself with alternatives and situations that call for decisions, but precisely as acts of will in which I come to define my self. Ignoring the situation and the alternatives as mine is a euphemism for choosing to ignore them and a recipe for despair (for despairing over oneself). Kierkegaard seems to be trying to capture this insight when he writes: "Generally speaking, consciousness, i.e., consciousness of self, is the decisive criterion of the self. The more consciousness, the more self; the more consciousness, the more will, and the more will the more self" (*SUD,* 29/162; Lowrie translation used). The hallmark of this second sort of freedom is personal choice, decisions through which, via a dialectical process, a person consciously makes herself, giving shape to her life. This second sort of freedom is, in more pedestrian terms, the sort of freedom enjoyed by someone who is reflectively conscious of her state and actions as her own, chooses them or not, and holds herself responsible for her choices.

Kierkegaard formally manages the difference between the first two stages of freedom by associating freedom in the first sense, the sense of reflexive relation to necessity, with the *soul* in relation to the body; and freedom in the second sense, the self-reflective relation to necessity (including the necessity of the first sense), with *spirit.* This duality captures once again, I submit, the concrete complexity of the way we experience freedom. That is to say, we experience freedom not as the capacity to choose in a vacuum among merely logical possibilities or possibilities in some imaginary scenarios but rather in the form of something that is both *accorded* us and *demanded* of us in the (spiritual) process of achieving selfhood (*SUD,* 21/154). What is accorded us is the capacity to choose and to choose among possibilities concretely given to us and/or created by us. What is demanded is that we choose those possibilities that make transparent our inherent dependency—though, as explained in the next paragraph, the transparency of this dependency is itself ultimately empowering. Moreover, this choice is a progressive one and the condition of this progression—again, somewhat like gravity for leaping and fear for courage—is despair (*SUD,* 27/160). For I can have the experience of myself for who I truly am, only by experiencing the temptation that despair represents. To paraphrase Augustine, temptation alone tells me what sort of person I am.[21]

Kierkegaard has least to say directly about the third form of freedom, the idea of the endgame, as it were, in a game without end. He merely refers to the rare person who "truly is devoid of despair" (translated by Lowrie as "truly free from despair") and to the self "willing to be itself" as a condition of despair's eradication.[22] This freedom from despair is presumably that ideal state of power and experience of power that coincides with the self's genuine emergence through willing, by the grace of God, its synthesis of freedom and necessity and willing it as a synthesis dependent upon God. Characteristic of this ideal state is the transparency that comes of freely being in "the power of the good," the divine freedom responsible for human freedom. "The true relation of freedom is this: freely to be completely in the power of the good, of freedom, or in the power of that in whose power one can be only by being free and through being in whose power one becomes free" (*Supplement* 147).

Given this emphasis on the goodness that envelops this third sense of freedom, we might characterize it as "benevolent freedom." By "benevolent freedom," I mean the freedom that embodies, realizes, and enacts a good will by acknowledging that this benevolence is the source of its power and goodness. The benevolence in question, moreover, is not only the benevolence of others or even divine benevolence but a shared benevolence, a benevolence that a person acting in good will receives and bestows. Just as self-reflective, autonomous freedom pivots off rudimentary (prereflective and reflective) forms of freedom, so this benevolent freedom supersedes that self-reflective freedom as a law unto itself.

The foregoing interpretation has been abstracted from Kierkegaard's remarks about freedom in the context of his study of despair. The phenomena of freedom present themselves, more concretely, in the context of the stages of despair. For human freedom is a process that concretely takes shape in the way we generate, battle, and forever attempt to elude forms of despair, since no human being on earth is ever completely free from despair of one sort or another.

4. Stages of Despair and Freedom *in Concreto*

Kierkegaard prefaces his account of the forms of despair with the observation that they are not always so neatly separated from one another in the continuum of real life (*SUD,* 42/175, 48/182). With this important caveat in mind, however, he distinguishes three progressively more intense gradations of despair, each entailing a respective degree of clarity about oneself and about the nature of despair. The first general form of despair is *unconscious despair.* "Unconscious despair" is, Kierkegaard acknowledges, something of an oxymoron and yet, precisely because it is in a certain sense unconscious and even innocent, it is also the most common and potentially the most dangerous form of despair. Unconscious despair may be also dubbed "spiritless despair" since it is an obliviousness to one's potential to be spirit, namely, the process of coming to be a self. This relatively lower and even *weak-kneed* opinion of oneself goes hand in hand typically (but not exclusively) with a failure to make the synthesis of soul and body properly reflexive, that is, self-reflective. This obliviousness to one's spiritual potential amounts, in this case, to a life immersed in aesthetic categories of what is agreeable and disagreeable, not subjecting oneself to categories of truth and, not least, the truth about one's derivative existence. But, more broadly, any form of human existence not conscious of itself as spirit, resting in God's hands, is in despair of this sort, including those syntheses of soul and body that merge with some abstract universality such as a nation or find satisfaction in exercising its powers while ignorant of their source.

That despair in such cases of spiritless existence is not fully unconscious is suggested by the resentment and irritation that the person despairing feels toward those who suggest that there might be something more to life, feelings that veil and thus betray an underlying despair. In any case, in this unconscious despair, one takes oneself (and herein lies an exercise of freedom) to be precisely not who one is. One thus falls into or, better, freely succumbs to despair over oneself and about one's eternal vocation, without knowing it, that is to say, without knowing that one is doing this to oneself (*SUD,* 42–47/175–79). For the most part, the soulful but not spirited freedom of this succumbing seems to be chiefly an exercise of prereflective or reflective freedom, falling short of the self-reflective freedom described above.

As with the stages of despair generally, so with conscious despair, there is a continuum of degrees of despair, even if we bracket, as Kierkegaard does, the question of whether being in despair is compatible with being fully cognizant of being in despair (*SUD,* 47–48/181). Our conscious lives are simply not of one cloth, and the degree of a person's consciousness of despair can shift dramatically with life's mottling of distractions and repressions, both serendipitous and protracted. But within this continuum, Kierkegaard distinguishes two general forms of *conscious despair,* (α) a weak and (β) a defiant form of despair: despairing by not willing to be oneself and by willing to be oneself (or, at least, what in bad faith one insists is all there is to oneself), respectively. Inasmuch as these forms of despair are ways of deliberately relating to oneself (willing or refusing to will to be oneself), each form as well as the development from one to the next is the work of a developing self-reflective freedom, as described above.

Within the category of weak conscious despair, there are further distinguishable stages and substages of despair. Despair over the earthly

(α1) and despair of the eternal (α2) are the two stages; despair over the earthly can take shape in a purely immediate existence (α1a) or an immediacy modified by a degree of quantitative reflection (α1b).[23] The former sort of despair (α1a) results from a person being immediately bound up (passively identifying) with something external to her, for example, something she craves or desires. When misfortune strikes, she despairs or, more precisely, she says that she "despairs," meaning she suffers, thinking that she might as well be dead, because what she clings to has been taken from her. As Kierkegaard notes, what she says is true but not because (as she thinks) she has lost what she clings to but because she clings to it. Moreover, in keeping with her craven identification with something outside her, this act of despair is not equivalent to reflecting upon who she truly is; instead "the despair is nothing more than a submitting."[24]

However, even when a person becomes more self-reflective, she may nonetheless despair because she recoils from some difficulty or imperfection within herself, a self that, it bears recalling, is the active synthesis of her soul and body as well as her freedom and necessity. In the immediate form of earthly despair just glossed (α1a), despair takes the form of submitting to external "misfortune," something that happens to a person. By contrast, the very act of reflecting upon herself both liberates her from that immediate form of despair and brings about the next (mediated) form of earthly despair (α1b). A person who despairs in this way does not want to be someone else (as can be the case in the immediate form of earthly despair just glossed), and, with an inkling of something eternal in her, she begins to distance herself from the surrounding world, events, and the more immediate aspects of her life. But she does so, Kierkegaard cautions, "only to a certain degree," halfheartedly, in bad faith, as it were, and the result is the mediated form of earthly despair over her lot (*SUD,* 54/188).[25]

This despair continues to be an expression of weakness and an inability or unwillingness to come to terms, in a sustained way, with oneself and, indeed, precisely in the sense identified by Kierkegaard at the outset of *The Sickness unto Death.*[26] Instead the person despairing in this way represses how she differs from the very soul and body (on which she also depends), hoping that the forbidding challenge that this difference presents her with will go away. When it does not, she gathers up all her capacities and throws herself hopelessly into a purely active life, desperately trying to escape her self. Ignoring and ultimately forgetting the source of this despair, she comes in the course of the years to feel that such despair is frivolous and that she is "over" it (*SUD,* 56–58/190–92).

We become more free, more reflective about ourselves, more empowered and less constrained, as we cross the threshold separating unconscious from conscious despair and the threshold separating despair over a setback to one's earthly fortunes from despair over an earthly imperfection. The next stage of conscious despair, still within the ambit of despairing over oneself by way of not willing to be oneself, reveals a further level of self-reflection and freedom, as the despair is directed, not at this or that particular earthly reality, but at the earthly as such. This form of despair, Kierkegaard notes, is rare (*SUD,* 63/196, 65/199). The person despairing continues to despair through an unwillingness to be herself, since she puts her stock in the earthly as such, though she is fully conscious both that she does so and that the earthly dimension cannot be what she takes it to be. "The despairer understands that it is weakness to take the earthly so much to heart, that it is weakness to despair" (*SUD,* 61/195; Lowrie translation used).

In an important twist, this despair *over* the earthly as such is equivalent to despair *of* the eternal (α2), since here despair ("not merely a suffering, but an act") is based upon investing the earthly with the quality of the eternal and despairing on account of this fraudulent investment or, more exactly, one's responsibility for it. To despair of the eternal in this way, moreover, is at the same time to despair over oneself (the formula for all despair, as discussed below). For in this despair a person is cognizant of her weakness for casting her lot with the earthly as such and that cognizance is impossible without some conception of the eternal within her. Yet not merely cognizant of this weakness, she also fixates upon it, identifying with it, and despairing over herself for it (*SUD,* 62–63/195–96). Hers is a bunker-mentality despair, as she hunkers down in a psychological reclusiveness (*Indesluttethed*) that is, paradoxically, the expression of an utterly prideful self-deprecation—even though she is able only rarely and with considerable difficulty to admit that underlying vanity.[27] She enacts and suffers this "reclusive" despair, as we might call it, even if, or better, precisely when, she gives every appearance of being a happy soul and model citizen, that is, unless or until this despair gives way to suicide or restless, vain attempts to forget herself in "dissolute living" or "the diversion of great enterprises" (*SUD,* 63–66/196–200).

The conscious despair discussed up to this point, the *weak* forms of despair, are all marked by the suffering and action of not willing to be oneself or, in some case, to be a self at all. By contrast, *defiant* despair is a despair that coincides with willing to be oneself—albeit in the sense of choosing to be a self that refuses its dependence upon God. Yet in both forms of conscious despair, one despairs over oneself—"the formula for all despair" (*SUD,* 20/153, 60/194)—and of the eternal.[28] A person who despairs by not willing to be herself despairs over some particular finite or earthly phenomenon with which she mistakenly identifies or even over the earthly as such as the finitude in which she deems herself eternally and thus hopelessly mired. In defiant despair a person does not despair over herself for any particular earthly quality or even for her finitude as such. Instead, she chooses to be herself precisely as something infinite or, at least, infinitely detached from everything, capable of making herself what she wills herself to be, despite her concrete, finite form.

In comparison with the other forms of despair, defiant despair is marked by the strongest consciousness of itself as an act. Moreover, while the weak despair over oneself is preoccupied with its eternal finitude alone (and not the eternal within it), defiant despair has, by contrast, a consciousness of the self's infinite character. However, it is conscious of that character only in the most abstract, purely imaginary form. It is precisely this abstract form, this sense of itself in contrast to all its concrete qualities, that makes defiant despair possible. Here the freedom exercised is unambiguously self-reflective freedom but, nevertheless, a freedom that duplicates the indeterminist's fantasy of being free from all constraints (or, being completely in control).

Kierkegaard elaborates this phenomenon on two levels, the self acting in such despair and being acted upon. In the former, more obvious case, the self relates to itself "only by way of imaginary constructions," recognizing no power over itself, and for that very reason both takes itself too seriously and exemplifies its utter lack of seriousness and any real foundation. In this despair, Kierkegaard writes, "the self wants to enjoy the total satisfaction of making itself into itself, of developing itself, of being itself; it wants to have the honor of this poetic, masterly construction, the way it has understood itself" (*SUD*, 69/203). In contrast to the unwillingness to be oneself that characterizes the more passive, weak forms of despair, defiant despair is a deliberate act of willing to be oneself.

Acting in defiant despair, acting under the delusiveness indicated above, obviously proves in short order to be pointless and ludicrous. When it does and the person in this defiant despair finds herself to be not the cause but the effect of things and, indeed, the object of misfortune, she does a kind of dialectical about-face. To be sure, she continues defiantly to will to be herself and to despair precisely by doing so, but she no longer wills a self with an unconstrained capacity for self-determination and self-mastery. Instead, out of spite she wills to be precisely her concrete, all-too-tormented self. She enacts and suffers a "spiteful, self-absorbed despair," as we might characterize it, utterly closed up within herself (*Indelukke*), eternally without hope of help from anyone else, let alone God—indeed, so much so that she regards this very act of desperate, hopeless defiance as evidence of her abandonment by God. As with the reclusive despair, a person's secret pride is her own worst enemy when it comes to freeing herself from this spiteful, self-absorbed despair. For it is pride that prevents her from admitting the possibility of hope, from humbling herself before others, from dying to herself so that she might live.[29]

We are now in a position to recapitulate how the forms of freedom and despair intersect. Whereas unconscious despair embodies prereflective and reflective forms of freedom, we free ourselves from such despair through an exercise of self-reflective freedom. For its part, self-reflective forms of freedom generate and progressively transcend all but the final stages of conscious despair.[30] While the power of self-reflection can help us liberate ourselves from mediated and repressive forms of despair that linger a lifetime, it is unable to overcome the rarer forms of despair that are at once the most oppressive and promising. As we have just noted, the ultimate forms of despair, both weak and defiant, are marked by a self-imposed closure, the reclusiveness that comes of not willing to be oneself or the self-absorption that comes of willing to be the ultimate loner, someone defiantly on her own and utterly left to her own devices. Both forms of despair are vain, both in the sense of being futile and in the sense of being quite narcissistic, as the despairing person closes herself off from others and ultimately from God. The only freedom from these forms of despair is the exercise and experience of benevolent freedom.

If there is a common thread to the movement of freedom through the prospects of despairing, it is that despair in each case is respectively disempowering while freedom consists essentially in the power and exercise and experience of the power of overcoming despair. Here, as promised at the outset of this study, is what I take to be Kierkegaard's considered conception of properly human freedom. Even in defiant despair, the counterpart to the weakness of not willing to be oneself, despair is indicative of a recognized infirmity and potential for empowering freedom. To be sure, it is not merely the recognition of one's infirmity, but the spiteful, self-absorbed insistence upon that infirm existence or, what is the same, an ultimately childish defiance of any possibility of solidarity with the enabling power of another (see 1 Cor. 13:11). Properly human freedom is, by contrast, epitomized by the empowerment that can only come from the manifestation of such solidarity in acts of benevolent freedom.

Perhaps the simplest and most powerful insight of twentieth-century phenomenology is the realization that, at least for human perception or existence, forms of hiddenness and absence are essential to the makeup of whatever is. Whether it be the relative absence of hidden profiles and horizons of a perceived object, the enabling recessive character of implements, or the projection of death as the absence from the world altogether (or, in Heidegger's later thought, being's abandonment of beings, including ourselves), what is concealed exercises a constant, unrelenting pull on what is unconcealed. Phenomenology is bent on disclosing the essences of things precisely by attending to and articulating these operative, hidden dimensions.

In Kierkegaard's phenomenology of human freedom, progressively realized through stages of despair, one finds the same effort to disclose the essence of the respective despair and freedom that, as it were, lurks hidden but operative in the existence of the person despairing. Indeed, his analysis begins with despair that is unconscious, the potentially most dangerous form of despair that "can be so hidden in a man that he himself does not know it!" (*SUD,* 27/160; Lowrie translation used; see also *SUD,* 29–30/162–63). But conscious despair, too, is unmasked as an unwillingness to be who we are or a willingness to be less than we are out of a failure to accept who we are (and can be). Each form of despair is the hidden work of human freedom that imposes a constraint on us (our existence, our freedom, our powers) and thus calls for overcoming in an exercise of freedom at a higher register. But the highest form of freedom—its ever hidden, absent but constitutive trajectory—is shared and discursive, a prayerful faith in divine benevolence.

Appendix

An outline of the forms of freedom and despair in part 1 of *The Sickness unto Death:*

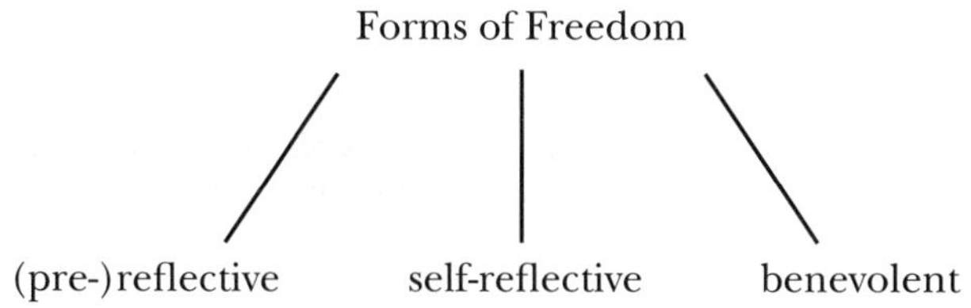

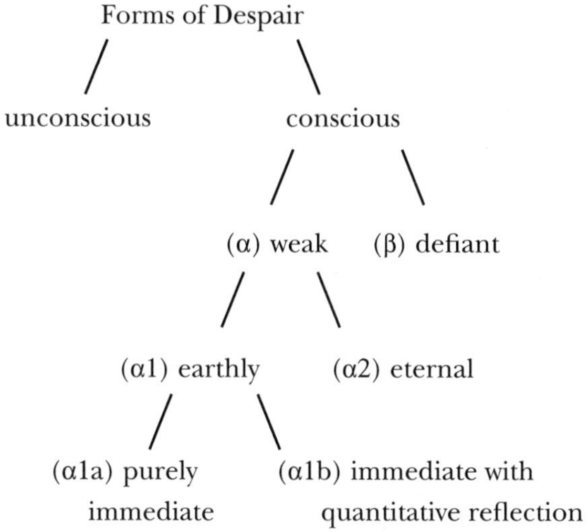

Notes

1. The following studies have been helpful in this undertaking: Heiko Schulz, "To Believe Is to Be: Reflections on Kierkegaard's Phenomenology of (Un-)Freedom in *The Sickness unto Death,*" in *Kierkegaard Studies. Yearbook* 1996, ed. Niels Jørgen Cappelørn and Hermann Deuser (Berlin: W. de Gruyter, 1996), 164–85 (hereafter cited as *KSYB* 1996); John J. Davenport, "Kierkegaard, Anxiety, and the Will," in *Kierkegaard Studies. Yearbook* 2001, ed. Niels Jørgen Cappelørn, Hermann Deuser, and Jon Stewart (Berlin: W. de Gruyter, 2001), 158–81; the essays in *Kierkegaard and Freedom,* ed. James Giles (New York: Routledge,

2000); and Jörg Disse, *Kierkegaards Phänomenologie der Freiheitserfahrung* (Freiburg: Alber, 1991).

2. See, for example, Daniel Dennett, *Consciousness Explained* (Boston: Little, Brown,1991), 45 and chap. 4, "A Method for Phenomenology," 66–98.

3. For a discussion of the connection between the analyses in *The Sickness unto Death* with Hegelian phenomenology, see Arne Grøn, "Kierkegaards Phänomenologie?" in *KSYB* 1996, 91–116; Jon Stewart, "Kierkegaard's Phenomenology of Despair in *The Sickness unto Death*," in *Kierkegaard Studies. Yearbook* 1997, ed. Niels Jørgen Cappelørn and Hermann Deuser (Berlin: W. de Gruyter, 1997), 117–43 (hereafter cited as *KSYB* 1997). See also the chapter by the same title in his *Kierkegaard's Relations to Hegel Reconsidered* (Cambridge: Cambridge University Press, 2003), 550–95; in connection with interpreting Kierkegaard, Hermann Deuser introduces multiple senses of "phenomenology" in his "Kierkegaards Phänomenologie der humanen Existenzverhältnisse," in *KSYB* 1997, 270–81.

4. Husserl's phenomenology is a reflection on consciousness (entailing analyses of its nonfoundational and, more important, its irreducibly foundational acts, contents, senses, and objects); Heidegger's phenomenology is hermeneutic, an interpretation of existence (entailing analyses of its fundamental, self-disclosing performances or enactments, what Heidegger calls "existentials," including discursiveness). Kierkegaard's understanding of the prayerful dimension of freedom, discussed briefly at the conclusion of this paper, suggests a deep affinity with the discursive existentialism of this hermeneutical phenomenology.

5. All references to *The Sickness unto Death* are cited as *SUD,* followed first by the pages of the translation by Howard V. Hong and Edna H. Hong (Princeton, N.J.: Princeton University Press, 1980) and, separated by a diagonal slash, the pages of the translation by Walter Lowrie, *"Fear and Trembling" and "The Sickness unto Death"* (Garden City, N.Y.: Doubleday, 1941). References to the *Supplement* included in the Hongs' volume are cited as *Supplement,* followed by the page number.

6. *SUD,* 29/162–63, 35/168; Pindar's second Pythian ode is typically translated as "become who you are."

7. For the difference between the senselessness (*Unsinn*) of a phrase such as "a the or gives" and the contradictoriness or absurdity (*Widersinn*) of a phrase such as "a square circle," see Edmund Husserl, *Logische Untersuchungen* (Tübingen: Niemeyer, 1968), bk. 4, §12, 326–27.

8. *SUD,* 15/147–48, 57/191; Lowrie translation used. In this connection, Kierkegaard alleges that the forms of despair as forms of the sickness unto death are open only to Christians. Later he appears to contradict this claim, as he asserts that there is no one outside of Christendom and no one in Christendom who is not in despair (*SUD,* 22/155). These discrepancies can be removed by differentiating forms of despair.

9. *SUD,* 15/148.

10. *SUD,* 14/147; see also *SUD,* 29–30/162–63, 49/182. Precisely as an "infinitizing reflection," imagination is essential to despair and to freedom from despair (becoming oneself *transparently*) (*SUD,* 31/163–64, 86/217); for an illuminating account of the roles of imagination, see M. Jamie Ferreira, "Imagination and the Despair of Sin," in *KSYB* 1997, 16–34.

11. In this respect at least Kierkegaard's phenomenology of freedom resists incorporation in contemporary compatibilist theories of freedom. By locating choices within causal chains of necessity, compatibilism argues for the reconcilability of the experience of freedom with natural necessity or a super-nature conceived in a way analogous to that natural necessity. Kierkegaard explicitly addresses the latter in the form of the "god" of the fatalists (*SUD,* 40/173).

12. Heiko Schulz notes that "possibility" here replaces the use of "freedom" in an earlier draft; see Schulz, "To Believe Is to Be," 166n7. In my gloss here I assume that "personality" and "self" are not synonyms, though it is not clear to me whether and, if so, how Kierkegaard construes a relationship between them.

13. See §24, "Das Prinzip aller Prinzipien," in E. Husserl, *Ideen zu einer reinen Phänomenologie und phänomenologischen Philosophie* (Tübingen: Niemeyer, 1922), 43–44.

14. Ferreira, "Imagination," 21: "The failure to *become* oneself, which is 'precisely despair,' is thus ultimately a failure of imagination."

15. Determinists as well as indeterminists despair, but the despair of necessity and the despair of possibility are alike practical denials of the actual phenomena as they present themselves in the human situation. Or, to paraphrase Kierkegaard, determinism and indeterminism represent a loss of self in mirrors of necessity and possibility, respectively (*SUD,* 36–37/169–70).

16. Despite an occasional reference to metaphysical perspectives, Kierkegaard "usually prefers the *phenomenological* viewpoint," as Heiko Schulz puts it; see Schulz, "To Believe Is to Be," 165; also 171–72, 179, 184–85. However, given the traditionally metaphysical viewpoint on the themes at issue, the question presents itself whether Kierkegaard or anyone else can drop the metaphysical viewpoint without being in historical bad faith of some sort.

17. The effort to consider the self-reflectedness or reflexive synthesis as such (including its relation to truth) also anticipates what Husserl regards as the phenomenological attitude in contrast to the natural attitude (the parallel of which is the prereflexive synthesis of soul and body); see Husserl, *Ideen,* 1–6.

18. For examples of Kierkegaard's rejection of a sheer indeterminist account of freedom, see *SUD,* 49/182 and the references cited in Schulz, "To Believe Is to Be," 174n45.

19. Here I differ with Schulz's view that this self-relating requires "an ideal of oneself" (Schulz, "To Believe Is to Be," 167). Without denying that self-relating can suppose such an ideal, I take it (a) that there are quite elementary forms of self-relating that do not and (b) that there is no sufficient reason to restrict the meaning of Kierkegaard's sense of self-relating in this way.

20. Of course, no one always or even typically exercises this freedom deliberately or consciously. But the great value of existentialist thought is to remind us that we are exercising this freedom, even if we do so by conforming to the status quo. What Kierkegaard and other existentialists remind us is that, whether we conform or not, we are responsible for doing so.

21. Augustine of Hippo, *Opera Omnia,* vol. 38, *Sermo II,* "De tentatione Abrahae a Deo," 3.3, in *Patrologia Latina,* ed. J. P. Migne (Paris: Garnier, 1958), 29: "Nescit se homo, nisi in tentatione discat se."

22. *SUD,* 14/147, 26/159, 30/163, 56–57/190–91. Similarly, he observes that "to will to be the self that he is in truth is the very opposite of despair," whereas, by contrast, what the person despairing wants is "to tear his self away from the power that established it" (*SUD,* 20/153). In this same context he speaks of the despairing person having "dreamed up" (*SUD,* 20/153) or "chanced to choose" (*SUD,* 20/153) a self that requires getting rid of the self that he is. This choosing and willing is, however, obviously not the exercise of the freedom of his true self.

23. For an outline of the forms of despair discussed in *The Sickness unto Death,* see the appendix to this paper. For the distinction between despair over the earthly and despair over something earthly as well as the role of this distinction as a springboard to despair over the eternal, see *SUD,* 60/194–95.

24. *SUD,* 51/184. Also, in this connection he identifies three progressively lower stages of this form of despair, from not willing to be oneself, to not willing to be a self, to the willing to be someone else, anyone else than oneself (*SUD,* 52–53/186). The lowest of these stages is ludicrous, Kierkegaard points out, since the realization of willing to be someone else would presumably eliminate the possibility of recognizing the fact that the aim had been achieved.

25. The development from (α1a) to (α1b) is, accordingly, a move from a lower to a higher level of self-reflective freedom.

26. Kierkegaard locates this stage of despair in someone with "a dim idea that there may even be something eternal in the self," though he lacks "consciousness of a self that is won by infinite abstraction from every externality, this naked abstract self, which, compared with immediacy's fully dressed self, is the first form of the infinite self and the advancing impetus in the whole process by which a self infinitely becomes responsible for its actual self with all its difficulties and advantages" (*SUD,* 55/188).

27. Thus, she admits this weakness of her self to herself and thereby despairs precisely out of pride of doing so.

28. Like despair over the earthly as such, this defiant despair is rare; it is also so inward that there are no outward marks of it (*SUD,* 72–73/206–7). Discernment of its essential character thus calls for precisely the sort of phenomenological sensibilities that Kierkegaard shares with the masters of twentieth-century phenomenology. Given the rarity of both the ultimate form of weak despair ("reclusive despair") and defiant despair ("spiteful, self-absorbed despair"), the exercise and experience of benevolent freedom is also anything but commonplace.

29. Note that her spiteful condition, supervening as it does self-reflectively on her condition, further demonstrates not only that despair is an act and despair over oneself the formula of all despair, but also that such despair is not the only possibility available to her; once again, the possibility of despair (in this case, defiant despair) is constitutive of a stage of freedom.

30. This diagnosis is arguably tenuous, to be sure, in the case of (α1a), the most immediate form of weak, earthly, conscious despair since the level of self-reflectiveness is minimal, as it barely or, perhaps, only infrequently transcends unconscious despair.

Self-Givenness and Self-Understanding: Kierkegaard and the Question of Phenomenology

Arne Grøn

Phenomenology?

How to make sense of the question: Kierkegaard and phenomenology? What is it about? It is, of course, about reading Kierkegaard, but it is also about asking the question: what is phenomenology? Instead of taking our point of departure in some established idea of phenomenology, we should look at the motive in calling what one is doing phenomenology. This approach is in line with how phenomenology begins or establishes itself. Positions labeling themselves phenomenological are in search for the meaning of phenomenology. Therefore, to be discussed in the following is: Kierkegaard and *the question of* phenomenology.

Where to begin then? Following a phenomenological approach, let us begin by reflecting on the phenomenological project and the problem of beginning. If we do so, we are likely to stumble over the strange, nonnatural character of this project. If we define phenomenology as the attempt to go back to the phenomena, we must ask ourselves: What is the point of going back to that which shows itself? Isn't it too obvious that we should begin with the phenomena? Does this require a move on its own?

Making a method out of this move (going back to the phenomena) only makes sense if something has come in between, so that we are not simply dealing with the phenomena. But what comes in between? It cannot just be something interfering from outside. Rather, it must have to do with our own ways of approaching the phenomena. We are not just dealing with the phenomena, but are doing so in the form of traditions, opinions, or fossilized interpretations and ideas about what the phenomena in question are. This means that the question about what the phenomena are is not really a question to us.

Phenomenology is not just "reading off" the phenomena. Rather, as *logos,* phenomenology is a countermove, directed against that which comes in between. But this leaves a phenomenological approach with the problem: how to account for what comes in between? Let us call this the problem of *negativity.* If phenomenology claims to show that we are already "out there," in contact with that which shows itself to us, why are we in need of phenomenology as a countermove?

Let us first look at the reflective method of going back to that which is already given to us. The project of phenomenology is radical. It is a search for the beginning. This is odd, inasmuch as we have already begun, taking part in traditions that have begun before us. That which is given to us is already interpreted, and we have already begun interpreting it without really being aware of what we are doing. The only way to begin again, then, is to ask the *question* of beginning. The claim of phenomenology to be a radical, that is, philosophical method lies in reclaiming the idea that philosophy begins in questioning. It is reflective in questioning our preconceived interpretations, and this is only possible by going back to *die Sachen selbst* ("the things themselves"). But this reflective move itself is provoked by the problem of negativity. Phenomenology as a radical quest is made possible because we do not simply deal with the phenomena.

In order to understand for ourselves the motive of phenomenology we must therefore make a double claim: phenomenology is the search for the beginning in going back to *die Sachen selbst,* but we cannot simply or directly begin with *die Sachen selbst* because we have already begun. What comes in between is not only traditions already operative in our ways of seeing, established opinions, or unquestioned interpretations. There is not only something we do not see and something still to be seen, but also the tendency to overlook, ignore, or forget that which we see or know.

The second part of the claim constitutes the difficulty that phenomenology itself faces. Can we reach the beginning except through that which has come in between, that is, by questioning our own interpretations? In a first move phenomenology appears to be antihermeneutical. It is "against interpretation" in pointing out that we are not just caught up in traditions. In a second move, however, phenomenology itself must become hermeneutical. In order for us to come to ask the questions where philosophy begins, we have to critically appropriate traditions that both disclose and close these questions.

What I have presented here as a systematic outline of the motive and the project of phenomenology is itself a reflection on the history of phenomenology. It points back primarily to Heidegger's *Sein und Zeit* (and lecture courses leading up to *Sein und Zeit*) where we can find both the motive of beginning anew, in a search for the beginning of questioning, and the difficulty facing this beginning. What is the connection between the two, the motive and the difficulty? The hermeneutical turn of phenomenology applies to both: to the question of beginning (in the sense of appropriating a sense of questioning), and to the countermove that must not only look once more, as it were, into *die Sachen selbst,* but can only do so by rereading traditions having formed us. In the hermeneutical turn of phenomenology, there is a double critical insight at work. First, as Heidegger points out, a phenomenon in a distinctive sense, in need of an explicit exhibiting (*Aufweisung*), is "something that proximally and for the most part does *not* show itself." What in this sense shows itself only "in disguise [*verstellt*]" is the *Being* of entities (*das Sein des Seienden*).[1] Second, we tend to overlook what is closest to us, our subjectivity (anticipating our reading of Kierkegaard). We do not ask what it is, or if we do, it is difficult for us to understand. We know what we are in being ourselves, and yet, we turn out to be *terra difficultatis* (land of trouble)[2] to ourselves when we try to understand ourselves.[3] The critical motive of negativity (in the form of forgetting and overlooking or ignoring) inheres in the project of phenomenology itself. Phenomenology is a sort of reminder. It is about seeing once more, because we can, and indeed tend to, overlook and forget what we know.

In Heidegger's rereading of tradition, in the genesis of *Sein und Zeit,*[4] Aristotle and Kierkegaard are of particular importance, also in terms of method. Aristotle's insight is that it takes something to reach the beginning of the problem, the question or the issue ("Sache"). There are two beginnings: the first is where we are beginning our search, the second where *die Sache selbst* begins. Kierkegaard's thought is also a search for beginning, and it is so in rereading tradition. Furthermore, it is also about how to think about our own existence. In question is human existence that is both our own and common. This puts remarkable constraints on our thinking. Reflecting on the conditions for existential communication, Kierkegaard points to what (in anticipating Heidegger) could be called the issue of formal indication. Interpersonal communication about issues concerning human existence depends on the participants understanding for themselves what the communication is about.[5]

A Passing Glance: Reading Kierkegaard

Let us now make a second start: how to read Kierkegaard? Let us begin by observing a remarkable feature in Kierkegaard's texts. Almost in passing, Vigilius Haufniensis (the vigilant observer of life in Copenhagen and the pseudonymous author of *The Concept of Anxiety*) mentions "the slightest touch, a passing glance, etc." that is sufficient to provoke inclosing reserve to disclose itself involuntarily, and he continues: "The disclosure may declare itself in words, as when the unhappy man ends by thrusting his concealed secret upon every one. It may declare itself in facial expression, in a glance, because there is a glance by which one involuntarily reveals what is concealed" (*CA*, 129/*SKS* 4, 430).

Kierkegaard's texts are abounding with indications like these, pointing—in passing—to what is passing by, that is: to phenomena which we live by and easily ignore. Let me take just two other passages. In a passage in *Concluding Unscientific Postscript,* Johannes Climacus, the pseudonymous author, points out that what makes communication so difficult dialectically is that the receiver is an existing person, and he continues: "To stop a man on the street and to stand still in order to speak with him is not as difficult as having to say something to a passerby in passing, without standing still oneself or delaying the other, without wanting to induce him to go the same way, but just urging him to go his own way" (*CUP,* 277/*SKS* 7, 251). Continuing this line of pointing to phenomena of communication, let me add one more passage from *The Concept of Anxiety*. Here Vigilius Haufniensis mentions "silence and the power of the eye" as a method that an inquisitor may use in order to provoke an obdurate criminal to confess: "A man with a bad conscience cannot endure silence. If placed in solitary confinement, he becomes apathetic. But this silence while the judge is present, while the clerks are ready to inscribe everything in the protocol, this silence is the most penetrating and acute questioning" (*CA*, 125/*SKS* 4, 426).

In seeking to understand what Kierkegaard's texts are about, we encounter passages pointing to silence, touch (even the slightest), and passing glances. What do such indications and references mean? What do they tell? Should we just read them in passing? Or should we pause, halt, and come to reflect? Maybe the texts are also about what, for example, a passing glance means, as an indication of what it is to be human, situated in a world of passing glances. Describing the world in which humans live and move, the passages quoted remind us about what we tend to overlook: what it is to be thus situated. Thus, they point to human subjectivity. To be an existing subject implies being on one's way in life and, being on one's way, being exposed to encounters and glances in passing by, being in communication with others having each their way to go. It is to exist as an embodied and embedded self.

In reading Kierkegaard's texts, we encounter figures in movements, situated in a world of seeing and being seen, expression and silence, disclosure and concealment. We may come to resituate ourselves in our world, being ourselves on our ways in life and exposed to what we encounter. Reading the text, then, is a sort of reminder. It is about coming to see for ourselves. I cannot here follow this line of thought further, but just indicate what I have in mind: if we are looking for a hermeneutics of reading in Kierkegaard, it would also have phenomenological features.

Let us move one step further. In reading passages as the ones just quoted, abounding with indications of situated subjectivity, we may ourselves come to ask the pivotal question in Kierkegaard's texts: what is it to be what we are? The texts not only point to phenomena that we live by and most often overlook; they also point to the reader, in exploring features of human subjectivity. Especially one feature is accentuated: concern. It is so in a characteristic twofold manner. Kierkegaard's texts both address "their" reader as the one concerned and take concern as a key theme in investigating what it is to be a self.

Claiming that reading is about coming to understand for ourselves does not imply that it is about self-understanding in contrast to understanding the world. It is about self-discovery in the sense of being reminded of what we tend to overlook, that is, phenomena we live by and tend to overlook or ignore. In being reminded we encounter ourselves as the one overlooking. Subjectivity, however, is not only at work in overlooking. It is also what we overlook or ignore. Asking the *question* of subjectivity, then, requires a countermove. The *Postscript* in which Kierkegaard has Johannes Climacus conceptualizing existence as specifically human brings the problem of negativity into the foreground. Climacus addresses the question of subjectivity as a countermove to a culture of *forgetting* what it means to exist. In contrast to what he diagnoses as the prevailing understanding of human subjectivity, namely that it requires no effort to understand subjectivity, Climacus insists on the problem in becoming a subject and in understanding what this means.

I have deliberately begun in what appears to be the margin of Kierkegaard's texts, asking how to read in a sort of phenomenological vein, in order to come to ask the question of subjectivity. Kierkegaard's way of coining key themes such as existence, choice, and anxiety has prefigured and formed modern thought. Yet, the reception of Kierkegaard's thought often takes the form of schematic interpretations. In particular, he is seen as advocating a notion of subjectivity that lacks a sense of the body, the social, and the world. Although Kierkegaard is commonly taken as a thinker of subjectivity, there is a need to rediscover what is implied in his thought on subjectivity.

Such a rediscovery could amount to a reclaiming of the *question* of subjectivity. My argument is that it is crucial to understand how the very approach to subjectivity is complicated. Precisely because subjectivity concerns us, as a matter of what and who we are, it tends to escape our grasp. In dealing with subjectivity, subjectivity itself comes in between. We can only understand what subjectivity means if we take into account the possibility, or even tendency, of forgetting what it means to exist. We only come to understand the question of subjectivity if we realize that subjectivity is a problem to itself. In this perspective, it is important to read Kierkegaard's thought of subjectivity as a countermove, in response to possibilities of forgetting what it means to be a subject. In order to understand the question of subjectivity a phenomenological approach in reading Kierkegaard is helpful.

In the following I'll focus on the issue of subjectivity that is crucial and problematic both in phenomenology and in Kierkegaard. It is about the *problem* of subjectivity, not subjectivity as foundation for relating to the world, but subjectivity *as* relating.

Phenomenology of Subjectivity

If we take phenomenology as a search for the beginning, in the form of a countermove, how should we move on? The first step is to focus on *how* that is given which is given to us. In this first emphasis (*how*) there is a second: how it is given *to us*. The point in the second emphasis is not to reduce what is given to subjectivity, but to let subjectivity appear as already situated. Subjectivity is itself given, but how?

In focusing on *how* something appears to us, phenomenology cannot take subjectivity as just one issue among others. Subjectivity is the dative of manifestation. Furthermore, subjectivity is implied in the very project of phenomenology. The project is to begin ourselves, against preestablished ideas, opinions, or traditions that have formed us, and that we may ourselves share without actually seeing and thinking for ourselves. Phenomenology thus harbors a motive of appropriating, in questioning.

Already at this point, phenomenology faces the critical difficulty: how does subjectivity—the dative of manifestation—come to appear? How can phenomenology account for the subjectivity it presupposes, both as the dative of manifestation and as questioning? Subjectivity does not appear in the same way as that which directly appears to subjectivity. We are not given as that which is given to us. Yet, we are given to ourselves. Consciousness means that the world manifests itself, but how does consciousness itself appear?

Hegel's *Phenomenology of Spirit* is about this difficulty. To put it most briefly, consciousness relates to its object, but does not relate to itself as an object. Yet, it comes to experience itself in experiencing the world. In failing to understand that which it takes as its object, consciousness encounters its own ideas of the object and the world. But only in encountering another self-consciousness that can itself relate and reverse the perspective, consciousness comes to see itself as consciousness. Hegel's answer to the difficulty of subjectivity coming to appear to itself is *his* phenomenology, which is about experiencing experience,[6] as a long detour of self-understanding. It is about *coming to* understand ourselves. To this, we can give a phenomenological response in claiming that, in this long detour in coming to understand ourselves, we are already given to us. The process of coming to understand ourselves requires self-givenness. Although we are not given to ourselves as objects are, subjectivity implies that we are immediately given to ourselves, in being ourselves.

How to account for this self-givenness? In continuing the first step dealing with *how* the given is given to us, we can focus on how subjectivity is cogiven as the dative of manifestation. In something being given to us, we are given to ourselves. Subjectivity manifests itself in how something appears to us. That is, subjectivity lies in relating to the given, to the situation in which it is given, and to the world as horizon for understanding the situation. Still, we are not just given to ourselves. Self-givenness implied in subjectivity does not amount to the given being given *to us,* or to the mineness of my experiences. On the contrary, in order to account for my experiences being mine, I must take into account that I am the one relating to that which is given to me. I am involved in experiencing. If I experience something that changes how the world is to me, I am myself changed in that I come to see differently.[7]

If subjectivity is not given as something is given to us, but *in* something being given to us, how is it given *as subjectivity*? The answer just indicated runs: as our *relating to* that which is given to us. But this implies that subjectivity does not show itself to us as an object. Subjectivity is self-manifestation in the strong sense that it manifests *itself.* In relating it makes itself manifest. Does subjectivity as self-manifestation require that in relating, we relate to ourselves?

In seeking an answer to this question we would profit from rereading Kierkegaard. Having this one-step-further outline of the project of phenomenology in mind that emphasizes the question of subjectivity as self-givenness and as coming to appear to itself, let us briefly consider the project in Kierkegaard's *The Concept of Anxiety*.[8]

Why does Kierkegaard focus on the phenomenon (or phenomena) of anxiety, so much as to write a book about its concept? The question he asks is: what does anxiety show about being human? He answers that a human being is a synthesis that relates to itself as body and as soul. The implication is that it is given to itself as a task. But this first answer implies a second. In anxiety, a human being comes to experience itself *as a self*. The first, anthropological, answer (human being is a synthesis) interprets the second (experiencing oneself in being in anxiety). In Kierkegaard's approach, anxiety is self-experience as self-discovery in the emphatic sense of coming to see oneself *as a self*. Once this experience of oneself is made, everything is changed. We are then selves in having to carry ourselves with us in relating to the world.

Kierkegaard's approach to the phenomenon of anxiety is phenomenological in the sense that it seeks to give an account for what is to be seen in this phenomenon. Being in anxiety is a way of relating oneself, but what is it that one relates to? It is nothing, Kierkegaard says; it is not a thing or an object, but a possibility that imposes itself upon us: the possibility of freedom or spontaneity in the sense of ourselves making a beginning. What shows itself to us in anxiety, then, is subjectivity, but subjectivity only appears in that it comes to appear *to itself*. This is not a matter of choice; we do not set out to appear to ourselves; rather, it *happens* to us in anxiety. Why anxiety? Let us briefly consider the following famous passage:

> Anxiety may be compared with dizziness. He whose eye happens to look down into the yawning abyss becomes dizzy. But what is the reason for this? It is just as much in his own eye as in the abyss, for suppose he had not looked down . . . Freedom succumbs in this dizziness . . . In that very moment everything is changed, and freedom, when it again rises, sees that it is guilty. Between these two moments lies the leap, which no science has explained and which no science can explain. He who becomes guilty in anxiety becomes as ambiguously guilty as it is possible to become. (*CA*, 61/*SKS* 4, 365–66)

The ambiguity of anxiety implies the intertwinement of subjectivity as passivity and subjectivity as activity. One *becomes* dizzy or anxious, yet one relates in anxiety (this is brought out in the possibility: "suppose he had not looked down"). What one encounters in anxiety is oneself *as relating*. In anxiety we come to appear to ourselves in "standing out" from the world to which we relate. We are given to ourselves, but given *in ourselves relating*. But this implies that, although *we* relate, our relating is not something we first consider to do (to relate) and then do it (as if relating were something we enacted or executed). In an important sense we *are* relating. What anxiety discloses is that we are given to ourselves, not as an object, but *as self-relating.*

This reopens the question of self-givenness. Self-givenness not only means that we are given to ourselves (in something being given to us); it also means to be given *as a self.* In fact, the two senses go together. To experience oneself as a self changes one's life. It means to face the question: how am I to live the life that is mine? It is important to note that this question about one's decision, or what to make out of one's life, presupposes the experience of oneself as given. This brings out the implication in talking about subjectivity as self-given. As cogiven with the world, as the dative (given to us in something being given to us), subjectivity is not simply what we make out of it, or what we make ourselves into. Rather, it is implied in asking: what do we make out of ourselves?

As humans we can seek to explain how subjectivity emerges in terms of circumstances and conditions. We can claim to be what we are in virtue of circumstances and conditions. Yet, there is a limit to this explanation. Subjectivity only emerges *as subjectivity* in taking itself as subjectivity. This is the critical distinction in *The Concept of Anxiety* between sinfulness (circumstances and conditions of the world in which we come to be ourselves, and that we can use in trying to explain what we have done, especially why we have failed) and sin (that is, oneself bringing evil into the world). To come to experience oneself as a self changes the conditions upon which one lives. One now has to live with the awareness that not only can one change one's life—one also does so whether one wants to or not.

In *The Concept of Anxiety* the point is made in terms of history. Humans are embedded beings. Not only according to Hannah Arendt, but also according to Søren Kierkegaard, humans are born in order to begin, but it is only possible to begin in a history in which one has already begun. It is only possible to lead a life that is already one's own in the sense that one is the one to live this life. Yet, we are ourselves to begin in this history. We are to live this life of ours. The decisive moment referred to in the passage about dizziness is not a moment in which one makes a decision, but the moment one comes to realize that one is a self to make decisions and to carry the weight of what one does and thinks. In this moment, Kierkegaard states, one's history begins. We *come to have* a history of our own, but only in experiencing that we have already begun, being ourselves embedded in a historical context. The question implied—how to begin having already begun—grows out of the problem: how do we come to appear to ourselves?

What is described and analyzed in *The Concept of Anxiety,* then, is human subjectivity coming to itself, as selfhood. The analysis of anxiety can be read as a phenomenology of subjectivity. Arguing along this line, I have not only Hegel's phenomenology in mind. What is important is *the problem* that a phenomenology of subjectivity thus understood addresses. It is a problem inherent in the project of phenomenology: how is subjectivity given to itself? The point is that subjectivity *coming to* appear to itself is a matter of subjectivity. The problem in understanding how subjectivity can be given (because as subjectivity it is not given as that which is given to subjectivity) pertains to subjectivity. It is about the difficulty of self-consciousness. Human subjectivity only appears as self-consciousness to others, if it relates to itself, and it only relates to itself as self-relation: being given to itself as self, having to lead a life of its own. This is self-manifestation in a strong sense. Subjectivity is not only cogiven in something being given to subjectivity; it manifests *itself,* and it does so because it appears *to itself.* In an intensified sense subjectivity manifests itself in relating to itself, facing the question: what do I make out of myself? Self manifests itself as self-relating.

The Concept of Anxiety deals with the phenomenon of anxiety in asking: what does anxiety show? What shows itself in anxiety is the possibility of freedom. But in anxiety one can also relate in such a way that one becomes unfree. This is brought out in chapter 4 of the book on anxiety about evil and anxiety about the good. Following Kierkegaard's suggestion we can read the book as a treatise on situated freedom and the positions that a human subject can take in relating to the world, to others, and in this to itself.

Both insights—on self-relating and on negativity—point to Kierkegaard's *The Sickness unto Death.* Before following this lead, let us briefly review where this interpretation of a phenomenology of subjectivity in *The Concept of Anxiety* brings us. A first point is that coming to appear as subjectivity means to appear to oneself, and that this changes one's history: one comes to have a history of one's own to live, in taking part in a history in which one already has begun. What is accentuated here is that human subjectivity is embodied and embedded *as* subjectivity.[9] The task is to spell out what being embodied and embedded means in terms of subjectivity. Second, self-givenness is open in the sense that one is given to oneself as a self, that is, one is to live *as oneself,* also when one changes.

Phenomenology of Despair

The Sickness unto Death opens with the famous definition of selfhood: "The self is a relation that relates itself to itself or is the relation's relating itself to itself in the relation" (*SUD,* 13/*SKS* 11, 129). This definition could be taken as if the self directly relates itself to itself, or as if self-relation amounts to self-reflection. The next move, however, argues that a self does not establish itself. Instead it is given to itself. Later, in the second part of the book, the self is defined as a self in relation to that to which it relates (*SUD*, 79/*SKS* 11, 193). Holding these two definitions together I'll suggest reformulating the definition of selfhood as follows: self is to relate (oneself) and, *in* relating (oneself), to relate *to* oneself. As a self, one does not establish oneself or one's relation to oneself. Instead, one *is* self-relation in relating.

Still, this is an opening definition. It is supposed to open up an investigation that unfolds what selfhood means. As in *The Concept of Anxiety* the argument is that such an investigation must take the form of observing and describing how a self comes to appear as a self and this implies: how it comes to appear *to itself*. But in *The Sickness unto Death* negativity is built into the form of presentation. This "development" (as Kierkegaard has Anti-Climacus put it) of the self unfolding itself now takes place through *a negative detour*. Kierkegaard's book on selfhood becomes what the title indicates: an analysis of forms and figures of despair (the sickness unto death) defined as: *not* being oneself. What is here put into the foreground is what "comes in between." This is not only ignoring or forgetting, but resistance in the sense of not wanting to be oneself. What comes in between is *oneself:* not wanting to be oneself.

Let us take a phenomenological approach to this. It is not self-evident what it means: not to want to be oneself. How does it appear? How do we want not to be ourselves, or, for that matter, how do we want to be ourselves? At least not in the same way as we want to do something, for example, go for a journey, move, educate ourselves, marry, or apply for a job. Wanting or not to be ourselves is not a separate, distinct choice we can make. Rather, it is a matter of what we are doing and wanting *in* what we are doing and wanting. It is a choice in one's choices. It is how we relate to ourselves in what we are doing.

This reflects how one is given to oneself. We are given to ourselves *as selves,* that is: *in* what we are doing, *in relating*. But this does not mean that we are transparent to ourselves. As in Hegel's phenomenology, the process of coming to understand oneself takes time. It is slow and inert. Moreover, Kierkegaard also points to a resistance in understanding oneself that makes the process negative in an intensified sense. Negativity is built into the mode of presentation, but it is not integrated into the development of self-understanding, as it seems to be in Hegel. Rather, it is the constant possibility, or even tendency, of failing, falling, or fleeing.

Defining self as self-relating implies that we are not simply what we are. We also relate to ourselves. What we are can be a problem to ourselves. It is even possible to relate to ourselves in not wanting to be ourselves. This can take forms of weakness, but it can also be more defiant, claiming to be what we construct ourselves to be. Consequently, the process of coming to understand oneself is complicated, turning self-understanding into a matter of *self-acknowledgment*. The process is twisted, but this is a twist of self-understanding. The difficulty is not just that we want not to be ourselves. It is also to acknowledge oneself as the one we already are, *also* in wanting not to be ourselves, for example, in wanting to construct ourselves differently. There is self in this difficulty. As in anxiety, we come to experience ourselves in despairing, and in both cases this does not happen in a straightforward manner. If it did we would turn into an object for ourselves. The difficulty we encounter pertains to the ways we relate, that is, our ways of seeing others and the world. But this means that in this difficulty, we come to appear not just as given to ourselves, but given in an intensified mode: as to be acknowledged. That is, the way we come to appear points back to our relating to ourselves. We also come to appear in not wanting to be ourselves.

The fact that we do not just acknowledge ourselves points to the problem implied in the question of *self-givenness and self-understanding*. We are given to ourselves, yet we do not simply understand ourselves. As indicated, the insight into the difficulty of self-understanding is not exhausted by saying that we are not simply what we are because we relate to ourselves. Rather, in the process of coming to understand oneself—even in not wanting to be oneself—*one is already oneself*. Although we must acknowledge that we are not just what we are (because we relate to what we are), in a critical sense we *are* ourselves: *being* oneself is not just a matter of *becoming* oneself. We are already the one having to become oneself, or the one wanting or not wanting to be oneself. In this sense, one is given to oneself also in the process of self-understanding, in being the one to understand oneself. Therefore, the reformulation of the definition of selfhood I gave must be further refined: *in* relating to others and to the world that we more or less share with others, we relate to ourselves (wanting, or not wanting, to be ourselves), but in this we are self-related. The fact that—even though we relate to ourselves in the form of not wanting to be ourselves—we are the one not wanting to be oneself, is reflected in the strange self-experience of not succeeding in getting rid of oneself (*SUD*, 17/*SKS* 11, 133).

What I have done so far in this section is to discuss in a systematic approach what is at stake in Kierkegaard's analysis of despair as an investigation into selfhood. I am not going into any detailed interpretation.[10] I'll only draw attention to one feature of the central part of this analysis, section C.B in the first part of *The Sickness unto Death*. This feature has to do with the question of method. How is despair to be analyzed? Kierkegaard's definition of despair reflects his definition of selfhood: despair is misrelation in the self-relation (*SUD* 14/*SKS* 11, 130). This definition tells us where to look. In despairing, something is at stake for the one in despair. What is at stake is the very relation to one's own life. Therefore, the analysis of despair must focus on the self in despair, or to be more precise, on the ways one relates in despair. That explains why this key section operates with figures (*Skikkelser*) and their movements, as Hegel's *Phenomenology* does. In Hegel, figures (*Gestalten*) of consciousness are ways of relating to the world, to others, and, in this, ways of relating to oneself. The process of coming to self-understanding turns on figures of consciousness acting and suffering, relating and experiencing themselves in relating. In Kierkegaard, figures of despair are ways of relating to what happens to oneself and, in this, they are ways of self-relating, but they are so in an intensified mode, marked by the constant negative possibility, or tendency, of failing oneself.

As mentioned, in this negative process (described in section C.B) the self also comes to appear to itself. Although it seeks to get rid of itself, it cannot. This means that the self comes to appear, not simply in coming to understand itself, but as a *self to be understood*. It comes to appear through the difficulty of self-understanding. Kierkegaard describes the negative process, "the development," as a process of self-consciousness. It is not quite clear what this means, but I think that the insight just formulated offers an answer. What comes to appear is the self that fails, or even resists, in understanding itself, but in this it is given to itself, as the self to be acknowledged. Not wanting to be oneself means not acknowledging oneself, but in not acknowledging oneself one is still given to oneself.

As in *The Concept of Anxiety* it is pointed out that subjectivity shows itself *as* subjectivity to itself, in becoming and coming to itself, but in *The Sickness unto Death* the question of negativity is intensified. Where does this leave us with the question of phenomenology? If we take it as a *question* of phenomenology, and not simply measure our reading of Kierkegaard on a preconceived idea of phenomenology, the problem of negativity is of critical importance. As a search for the beginning, phenomenology is a countermove, directed against that which comes in between. The point is that what comes in between is not just to be left out, without any significance, but must itself be a question of what is at issue (*die Sache,* or truth). The truth we reach must tell something about the untruth, through which we reach it. I'll argue that this is a critical motive in Hegel's phenomenology, as well as in Kierkegaard's *The Sickness unto Death.* Almost on a programmatic note, Anti-Climacus declares that the truth of subjectivity is to be reached only through the negative detour of forms of despair (*SUD,* 44/*SKS* 11, 159). But in this detour of self-understanding, we are already given to ourselves: as the one not being oneself. This means that the problem of self-givenness and self-understanding, which is at the core of phenomenology, is complicated. We are not just given to ourselves. We are given to understand ourselves. What we are is also how we understand ourselves, but there is a critical point to this: self-understanding requires *self-acknowledgment.* Although we are self-interpreting animals,[11] we do not just come to understand ourselves in a process of self-understanding, as Hegel seems to claim. Rather, this process is about, or makes manifest, the difficulty of self-understanding; being involved in this process, we come to face a resistance, and in this we experience ourselves. There is self in the resistance against self-understanding.

In a critical sense, then, the process of coming to understand oneself is *about* self-understanding. This is what is at stake, and not just given. Coming to understand ourselves requires that *we* come to understand differently and change how we view ourselves. However, seeing ourselves differently is not something we can do in a direct or straightforward choice. If we choose to change our view, the question still is whether we actually do so. It is a matter of changing our position or attitude toward ourselves, and this means: to change the way we relate, that is, to change (ourselves). How is this possible? The change required must, according to *The Sickness unto Death,* take the form of self-acknowledgment. This self-acknowledgment implies that we understand that we do not understand ourselves. That is: acknowledging the difficulty, and even the resistance, of self-understanding becomes part of self-understanding. But even if we, in the process of self-understanding, encounter ourselves in more enigmatic forms than in Hegel's phenomenology, we are given to ourselves in the primitive sense of being the one to acknowledge oneself.

What I have presented here is not just an exegesis of Kierkegaard. Rather, it addresses the question of phenomenology in reading Kierkegaard. It is, however, also about reading Kierkegaard's texts. A phenomenological approach in reading is about reopening the questions we encounter, in particular the question of subjectivity. In this double perspective it makes sense to operate with the idea of a negative phenomenology in reading Kierkegaard. The method in *The Sickness unto Death* is to look for what is implied in what appears, or what is hidden in what is shown.[12] It is critical toward appearances, looking for decisions at stake in what we let appear. Humans do something about appearances: we make things look. But we also come to appear, in making things appear.

Seeing—and Not Seeing

The critical approach to appearances not only deals with how we let things appear or not. It is also about seeing and not seeing. As we can make things appear, in view of others (or us) seeing, our seeing is a matter of paying attention to. The question is: What are we doing in seeing? In particular what do we not see in seeing?

I have argued for reading Kierkegaard's *Works of Love* in terms of a dialectics and an ethics of vision.[13] In seeing the other who is there to be seen, how do we see her? It is possible to see her in ways that deprive her of significance. Thus, ignoring her is a way of seeing her. But this indicates that, in seeing others in ways depriving them of significance, one can also depend on others. For example, seeing the other with the eyes of arrogance is a way of telling her how *she* should see herself: as inferior to the one seeing her. Whether one succeeds in the project of arrogance, then, depends on the other. If she resists, the project is likely to fail.

The other is given to us to be seen, and yet, in a critical sense it is up to us to see her. The question to ask oneself is what it means to see the other *as the other:* in herself, beyond our seeing her. This is, I would claim, what is at stake in seeing the other as our neighbor. Seeing the other is in an important sense about *not* identifying her. Although she is given to us, she is not to be taken as what we take her to be.

In seeing it is easy to ignore what we ourselves are doing. Yet, we also encounter ourselves. Although it is up to us to see the other and to pay significance to her, and although it takes an effort to see her, we are not free to see her as we like. In the ways we see her, we ourselves come to appear. This is brought forth in the first, opening discourse in *Works of Love.* Love is given in and through questions, first and foremost the question: does love exist? In order to find an answer we may go out in the world and see whether love is there to be found. Kierkegaard's discourse here performs a reversal of perspective: love is to see love. That is, the question is: How do *we* see when looking for love? Do we see with the eyes of love?

Works of Love is about the (in)visibility of the other, but also about love's appearing. As the title indicates, love is not to be seen as an inner emotion, but is in its deeds. If we are moved in love, we must show this in what we are doing. It is not about how love comes to appear, but how we make it appear. In this sense, a discourse on love must focus on the phenomena of love. Yet, the ambiguity just mentioned enters into the foreground. Why is love linked to questions about deceit and change? On the one hand, love must manifest itself, and, on the other, it is not simply to be judged by appearances. What is it, then? According to the answer just given, love is a matter of seeing—the other. "Love's appearing" must be qualified, but this also goes for "seeing." The question is how we show ourselves in seeing the other. In a sense, then, appearing and seeing intertwine.

Still, love cannot be reduced to what we make out of love. Seeing the other is a matter of seeing that she is beyond what we take her to be. Likewise, love cannot be measured in terms of what we do. If we try, what we do changes its nature. It is no longer a work of love. This means that it is only possible to act out of love if we see love as a gift.[14] If we would speak of love's manifestations, then, we can only do so if our ways of seeing can be called into question.

Experience and Decision

As should be clear from what I have said, my argument is not about phenomenology providing some sort of basis for what Kierkegaard says as a religious writer. However, if we want to understand Kierkegaard as a religious writer, we should reflect upon how he is so, for example, his existential approach, his ways of problematizing and questioning.

Quite often, Kierkegaard has been interpreted in terms of a schematic contrast between experience and faith, with the understanding that in experience, humans are autonomous, while faith is a decision beyond decisions we make as it were. As indicated, I'll argue that the question of self-experience in Kierkegaard is not only more complex, but undermines this schematic contrast. His analyses of anxiety and despair, for one, are dealing with experiencing oneself in the negative. Moreover, experience and decision are concepts we use in order to understand our situation. That is, we must account for how we think in terms of experience and decision, and such an account must show what we talk about. If we make a decision, what it means to us is still open. It will depend on how we live our life. In making a decision, then, we are involved not only as the subject making the decision, but also as the one living and bearing the decision. The decision one makes depends on whether one is "decided." In the activity of making a decision, there is a double passivity implied: first, in coming to make the decision; second, in carrying the decision through in one's life. What I have in mind here is that we cannot avoid a phenomenological approach if we want to account for our situation, not least in terms of experience and decision.

Faith as faith in a new beginning given as a gift relates to our history. Having already begun, we are given a new beginning that does not simply replace our own beginning. This is a paradoxical possibility in that our life is not replaced, but—as this life—made new, not as our own doing, and yet as a possibility for our own doing. In what sense, then, is faith a decision? We do not produce or establish this possibility, we cannot make it into our own, it is given to us, and yet, we are to take it as a possibility *for us,* changing our lives. The paradoxical structure means that we cannot take the possibility of faith simply as part of the life it concerns. This has to do with the way it concerns *this* life. We cannot reach or reconstruct this possibility from the life it concerns. And yet, we are to understand what it means in terms of this life.

Self-Givenness and Self-Understanding

If phenomenology is going back to that which shows itself to us, it has to give an account of that which "comes in between." In the movement back we *encounter* subjectivity, but subjectivity as *relating to* the world. This does not mean that subjectivity is simply "worldly." Subjectivity is embodied and embedded, but it is so *as* subjectivity: as relating to the world. It is in the world, relating to the world.

A phenomenological approach, however, is also a countermove to established ways of dealing with subjectivity. Often it seems to go without saying that subjectivity is "only" subjective, that is: something that can either be left out in scientific procedures or cultivated in, for example, artistic practices. While the implication of the first option seems to be that we can have approaches to the world that are without subjectivity, the second is often taken as dealing with our ways of perceiving and inhabiting the world. These various options show that subjectivity is not simply given, but can be ignored or cultivated. Where does this leave a phenomenological approach?

A first answer would be to ask: what about the subjectivity already implied in ignoring or cultivating subjectivity? A phenomenological approach must seek to give an account that points to the subjectivity implied or ignored in ways of dealing with subjectivity. As I have argued, the further implication is that, although it points to subjectivity as self-givenness, a phenomenological approach has to account for ways of dealing with subjectivity. How is it possible that human subjectivity can show itself in ignoring, forgetting, or cultivating subjectivity?

In the outlined reading of Kierkegaard's main texts on subjectivity I have focused on his *approach,* in particular on the role that the problem of negativity plays for his method. Thus, the emphatic definition in the *Postscript* of subjectivity as passion, interiority, and appropriation is a countermove to ways of dealing with subjectivity, inscribed in contemporary culture, which is diagnosed as ways of forgetting human subjectivity. In terms of both approach and account, the question is: how to account for subjectivity as self-givenness, if it is possible for us to ignore or forget what we are? I have suggested a double answer: first, the possibility of ignoring and forgetting testifies to our subjectivity; second, in forgetting, ignoring, or not wanting to be what we are, we are the ones forgetting, ignoring, or not wanting. We are given to ourselves also in the negative. But this makes the task of understanding ourselves both more pertinent and complicated. We are given to ourselves as ourselves to be understood and acknowledged. However, this implies that self-givenness is not a stable, basic feature of human subjectivity, but at stake in self-understanding. Reconsidering the project of phenomenology in reading Kierkegaard may bring us to question ideas often associated with phenomenology.

Notes

This study was funded by the Danish National Research Foundation.

1. Martin Heidegger, *Being and Time,* trans. John Macquarrie and Edward Robinson (New York: Harper and Row, 1962), 59/[35].

2. Saint Augustine, *St. Augustine's Confessions,* trans. William Watts (Cambridge, Mass.: Harvard University Press, 1970), x, 16.

3. Heidegger, *Being and Time,* 69/[43–44].

4. See Theodore Kisiel, *The Genesis of Heidegger's "Being and Time"* (Berkeley: University of California Press, 1993).

5. For a discussion of the question of beginning in Heidegger's "Natorp-Bericht" (1922) in relation to Kierkegaard, see my "Die hermeneutische Situation—die Hermeneutik der Situation," in *Heidegger und die Griechen,* ed. Michael Steinmann (Frankfurt: Klostermann, 2007), 233–60.

6. In making experiences, consciousness comes to experience itself. In German this can be described as "Erfahrung mit Erfahrung." Compare the original title of *Phenomenology of Spirit:* "Wissenschaft der Erfahrung des Bewusstseins." G. W. F. Hegel, *Phänomenologie des Geistes,* ed. Hans-Friedrich Wessels and Heinrich Clarimont (Hamburg: Felix Meiner, 1988) (pagination following *Gesammelte Werke,* vol. 9), 547–48.

7. Compare the notion of experience as reflective in Hegel's phenomenology (Hegel, *Phänomenologie des Geistes,* 66–67/*Phenomenology of Spirit,* §86).

8. See my *The Concept of Anxiety in Søren Kierkegaard,* trans. J. B. L. Knox (Macon, Ga.: Mercer University Press, 2008).

9. See my "The Embodied Self: Reformulating the Existential Difference in Kierkegaard," *Journal of Consciousness Studies* 11, nos. 10–11 (2004): 26–43.

10. I have argued elsewhere in detail for reading this section as a phenomenology of despair. See my "Kierkegaards Phänomenologie?" in *Kierkegaard Studies. Yearbook* 1996, ed. Niels Jørgen Cappelørn and Hermann Deuser (Berlin: W. de Gruyter, 1996), 91–116.

11. Charles Taylor, "Self-Interpreting Animals," in *Human Agency and Language: Philosophical Papers 1* (Cambridge: Cambridge University Press, 1985), 45–76.

12. Compare, for example, the phrase: "The externalities under which the despair conceals itself" (*SUD,* 73/SKS 11, 186).

13. See my "Ethics of Vision," in *Ethik der Liebe. Studien zu Kierkegaards "Taten der Liebe,"* ed. Ingolf U. Dalferth (Tübingen: Mohr Siebeck, 2002), 111–22.

14. Compare the last discourse in the first part of *Works of Love:* "Our Duty to Remain in Love's Debt to One Another."

Part 3

God and Experience

A Phenomenological Proof? The Challenge of Arguing for God in Kierkegaard's Pseudonymous Authorship

Heiko Schulz

Despite the extraordinary variety and richness of its pseudonymous and nonpseudonymous views, standpoints, and perspectives, Kierkegaard's authorship as a whole seems absolutely unanimous when it comes to assessing the meaning and viability of the so-called proofs for the existence of God. There can be no doubt that in Kierkegaard's opinion all pertinent attempts are and must be not only deeply flawed, but also highly dubious in terms of their ethico-religious implications—a foolish (*PF*, 39) enterprise at best, a "shameless assault" (*CUP*, 545) on God's presence and majesty at worst.

This notwithstanding, I will try in the following to show and to explain in some detail that a phenomenological reading of the pseudonymous authorship (in particular, *The Sickness unto Death*) may also—though arguably not at first sight—provide us with a fresh, original, and philosophically fruitful perspective on the problem of God in Kierkegaard. Thus, I will argue on the one hand that on a surface level there is indeed an argument for God's existence to be found in Anti-Climacus's book; however, it is neither conclusive in itself nor intended to be read as and/or believed to be conclusive by the author himself, since it turns out simply to be correct or *formally* valid, leaving the question of its being actually *true* undecided and up to the reader. On the other hand—and as a supplement to this overt and explicit, yet only formally valid argument—we do in fact find another, although indirect and genuinely phenomenological argument in *Sickness*. As such the argument is based on the assumption that it can possibly be established and justified only from the internal or "experiential" perspective of the self, more exactly: the self in despair. There has already been a number of successful attempts to reconstruct basic Kierkegaardian ideas (e.g., his notion of freedom) in a phenomenological vein,[1] and in the present paper I simply want to supplement these attempts by shedding light on the problem of God's existence.

In what follows, I will initially outline Kierkegaard's main counterarguments against the so-called proofs for the existence of God. Secondly, I will present a reconstruction of the phenomenological argument and its relation to the formal one. In this context I will also try to reconcile Kierkegaard's (more exactly: Climacus's) strictly critical, in fact at times polemical attitude toward the proof issue and my own case for an, albeit hidden, phenomenological type of proof—a proof, which as such and at first sight seems diametrically to run counter to Kierkegaard's own explicit views and intentions. In conclusion I will abandon the limits of the purely pseudonymous perspective by incorporating two pertinent journal entries. Here Kierkegaard, speaking in his own voice, does not only repeat and confirm the pseudonymous views already explained, but he also argues—persuasively, in my opinion—that for better or worse we can never have it both ways: we cannot on the one hand give a truthful account of (the ideality of) the Christian faith *and* at the same time prove the existence of God, much less of the Christian God of love. Either of these goals is and must necessarily be realized at the expense of the other, since both are strictly speaking incompatible.

Climacus's Five Ways of Arguing Against Any Attempt to Prove God's Existence

Kierkegaard's attempt to refute the purported proofs for the existence of God builds upon two main lines of argument. The first line is supposed to show, in a rather straightforward way, that existence as such and in general cannot be proved—and thus also and a fortiori the existence of God. The second line aims at showing that even if the first one would *not* obtain (namely in the sense that at least *God's* existence could be proved) such proof, or more exactly, the mere attempt of such a proof, would be a meaningless, in fact even a foolish enterprise and as such highly problematic on ethico-religious terms also. Let us take a closer look at each line of argument in turn.

The (following) subarguments supporting the *first* line turn on certain premises about the nature, scope, and limits of proofs as such and in general.[2] The meaning and function of these premises become clear once we incorporate them into a corresponding argument. Climacus writes:

> If . . . the god does not exist, then of course it is impossible to demonstrate it. But if he does exist, then it is foolishness to want to demonstrate it, since I, in the very moment the demonstration commences, would presuppose it, not as doubtful—which a presupposition cannot be, inasmuch as it is a presupposition—but as decided. (*PF,* 39)

It seems to me that a (in fact, rather counterintuitive, see below) premise about the meaning, nature, and scope of proofs in general is part and parcel of the argument presented here:

1. Any wish or intention to prove "that p" is foolish, if it has to be presupposed as decided "that p" by the subject undertaking the proof.

Adding a second premise we may then reconstruct the first and more general part of the argument as follows:

2. If X exists no attempt at proving that X exists can be made, without the subject undertaking the proof having to presuppose as decided that X exists.
3. Therefore, if X exists, any wish or intention to prove that X exists is foolish.

Since Climacus also holds that it is "*generally* a difficult matter to want to demonstrate that something exists,"[3] there seems to be in his opinion no principal difference between the attempt to prove the existence of (the) God or of any nondivine entity. If so, we may reconstruct the rest of his argument as follows:

4. There is no principal difference between proving the existence of "the god" or of any nondivine entity.
5. Therefore, if "the god" exists, any wish to prove that he exists is no less foolish than the wish to prove the existence of any nondivine entity.

Due to the focus of my paper it is not my task here to criticize this or any of the subsequent argument(s) in full detail; however, I cannot help but note in passing that the argument presented so far appears highly dubious to me. My main concern is about (1) and (2). Climacus seems to hold that "presupposing something as decided" is simply tantamount to *believing* or to be "convinced"[4] about the truth of the proposition in question (e.g., "two plus two equals four," "God exists," etc.). Now, if this is correct, a double reading seems obvious, in fact hardly avoidable with regard to the arguments Climacus actually endorses: a weaker, *psycho-*

logical, and a stronger, *epistemological* one—yet, both are equally flawed in my opinion. According to the latter, Peter *can* prove only what he already believes to be true, and in that sense any proof will be circular. Or more exactly: either the proof will fail or Peter will merely arrive at a conclusion, the truth of which has already been "presupposed by him as decided" (i.e., it has been believed by him to be true) from the very beginning.[5] And, of course, in that sense it is also true that one "*cannot* prove" (*JP* 1334; my emphasis) the existence of anything, much less the existence of God. Now, even if we admit that there is a certain—namely pragmatical—circularity here, the argument invoking it is nevertheless doubly flawed: for one thing, it is simply wrong that in order to want and try to prove something Peter has to *believe* what he wants and tries to prove beforehand. Rather, the mere *acceptance* of (that is, the—e.g., inferential—acting *as if* he believed) the respective proposition to be true is good enough and does the job perfectly.[6] Therefore, if he succeeds in proving what he wanted to prove, this success will be and will be experienced by him as a welcome corroboration and confirmation of what he surmised, tentatively assumed, or merely accepted in the first place. In this sense proving is by no means a futile or foolish enterprise, but a perfectly meaningful one with a clear epistemological function.

A second flaw is closely connected with the first: Climacus is certainly right that it is impossible to prove that "p" (here: "God exists"), if "*not* p" (here: "God does *not* exist"). Yet, this does not imply, as he seems to suggest, that Peter can and will have to presuppose as decided "that p" *only* in the case of "p." For even if "*not* p," he may simply be *ignorant* about this and thus still try to prove "that p," thereby presupposing as decided "that p," in exactly the same sense as described before. Hence the purported foolishness of the attempt to prove "that p" (provided there *is* any such foolishness) in no way turns upon the fact that "p" actually obtains.

The psychological argument does not fare any better in my opinion. According to Climacus, if Peter does not already believe in God's existence (or in any other proposition, for that matter), he will not be able to try to prove it; however, *if* he already believes it, the idea (or more exactly: the intention and/or wish) to prove it is apparently futile or even foolish, because in that case the whole project seems to lose its point. The very condition determining the possibility of an *attempt* to prove something (namely: the belief in the truth of the proposition supposed to be proved) renders the *wish* or intention to do so pointless or foolish—note well: according to Climacus, I *could* "not try to prove God's existence unless I were already convinced that God did exist";[7] however, *if* I were already convinced of his existence, "why should I [*want* to] try to prove it?"[8] This seems to me to be a strangely confused argument, and this mainly for two reasons. First, it is misleading to suppose, as we have seen already, that the attempt to prove "that p" entails the *belief* "that p," so that only the person who is already convinced "that p" may try to prove it. Why should an undecided agnostic, a skeptic, or even a devout disbeliever *not* try to demonstrate God's existence—if only with the intention in mind to arrive at the conclusion that the attempt has actually (or even necessarily) failed? Secondly, even *if* it were exclusively the believer who could want to try to undertake the proof: would such an attempt be necessarily pointless or foolish? Not at all: the attempt may still have "value for me in confirming and strengthening my belief, showing me that the belief is reasonable. Even more significantly, Climacus fails to consider the idea that such a proof may have value for other people than myself."[9]

So far, Climacus's efforts to come to terms with the arguments for God do not seem to be overly successful: both his epistemological and his psychological arguments are found wanting. But we should not jump to rash conclusions here. For there are at least "five ways" of rendering the whole demonstration-venture hopeless in Climacus, and the remaining three—namely the *ethico-religious,* the *ontological,* and (what I would call) the *manifestational*—seem to me to be much more promising.

The first one is closely connected with the psychological and/or epistemological argument(s) already explained; however, it can and does stand on its own feet, thus proving to be independent of the former and also of its shortcomings. For, according to Climacus (and I agree with him at this point), a proof for the existence of at least any *personal* entity would be highly problematic on religious and/or ethical terms, even *if* such a proof could be deemed successful. So here the issue is by no means, whether such proof *is* possible or not; the real issue is purely consequential: namely, whether the attempt to undertake such a proof could be deemed meaningful and justifiable on ethico-religious terms—that is, completely independent of the demonstration-issue as such and in principle. Climacus's answer is in the negative. In the *Postscript* he writes:

> A king's existence [*Tilværelse*] or presence [*Tilstedeværelse*] ordinarily has its own expression of subjection and submissiveness. What if one in his most majestic presence wanted to demonstrate [*bevise*] that he exists? Does one demonstrate it, then? No, one makes a fool of him, because one demonstrates his presence by the expression of submissiveness . . . And thus one also demonstrates [*beviser*] the existence of God by worship—not by demonstrations. (*CUP,* 545–46)

Note, first of all, that existence is understood here as involving presence (in fact "majestic presence"). In general we may say that according to Kierkegaard a personal being is existent—*if* it is existent—by also and simultaneously being present. Apart from other essential connotations associated with the term it is obvious, in any case, that the presence of a person has important intersubjective implications—implications, which among other things render certain ways of relating to him (or her) ethically appropriate, while at the same time excluding others as improper or inappropriate, for example, as "an attempt to make him ludicrous" (*CUP,* 545). Secondly, we should not overlook that Climacus uses the term "demonstration" (*bevis*) ambiguously here, and in *one* sense he subscribes to the view that a "demonstration" of God's existence *is* in fact possible: if only by way of "worship" (*CUP,* 546).[10] Finally, it is noteworthy that the viability of the argument defended by Climacus turns on the crucial premise that God actually *exists*—or at least: that we cannot exclude the *possibility* that he does exist.[11] Sure enough, if he did *not* exist, it would not be possible to prove *that* he does (see above). And yet, it would still make perfect sense at least to try to prove his *non*existence. Furthermore, the ethico-religious argument would lose its whole point, if he did not exist—note well: *and* if we could actually know this to be the case. It goes without saying that Climacus is fully aware of this; and of course he also and correctly presupposes that—at least thus far—our "epistemic situation" as finite human beings has it that we simply do *not* know whether God exists or not. Hence his whole point is purely consequential again: *given* that God actually exists; and given also that for the time being we cannot know for sure that he does *not* exist; finally, provided that his existence is coextensive with his (omni-)presence as a divine majesty, the ethico-religious argument obtains—it may as such be summed up as follows:

6. If some personal being X actually exists, and if no human being can definitely exclude that he does, then any human attempt to prove that he exists "is an attempt to make him ludicrous" (*CUP,* 545).
7. Any attempt to make a personal being ludicrous excludes the possibility of properly relating to him.
8. God is a personal being.
9. Therefore, if God actually exists, and if no human being can definitely exclude that he does, then any human attempt to prove that he exists excludes the possibility of properly relating to him.
10. Any attitude, conduct, or behavior, which excludes the possibility of properly relating to a personal being, is inappropriate on ethico-religious terms.

11. Therefore, any attempt to prove that God exists is inappropriate on ethico-religious terms.

The second argument draws on Kierkegaard's ontology, more exactly his distinction between factual and ideal being. Ideal being qualifies the essence or "essence-determinants" [*Vaesens-Bestemmelser*] (*PF,* 41n) of an entity, judgments like X "is a stone" or "is perfect." Factual being or existence—both of which are used synonymously in Kierkegaard and also in Climacus[12]—refer to the (a) spatio-temporal being of X as (b) an individual and as such (c) a unity between ideality and contingency.[13] Thus, when I say that X exists I am saying in effect that X is an individual and as such a spatio-temporally determined unity of ideality and contingency.[14] Now, according to Climacus, proofs are possible only with regard to the former, that is with regard to the realm of ideal being, but not as a demonstration of existence: "I do not demonstrate that a stone exists but that something which exists is a stone" (*PF,* 40).[15] The corresponding argument runs as follows:

12. Proofs are possible only if what is supposed to be proved belongs to the realm of ideal being alone.
13. Existence does not belong to the realm of ideal being alone.
14. Therefore, existence cannot be proved.

In addition to the Kantian idea that existence is not a real predicate (an idea that Kierkegaard himself invokes in *JP* 1057), the ontological argument, as I prefer to call it, is also reminiscent of the "Humean claim that only 'relations of ideas' are subject to demonstrative proof"[16]—and thus conceived the argument seems to me to be sound.

The final, in my own term "manifestational" and in effect antiteleological, argument builds upon and is closely connected with the ontological argument just explained. It starts where the latter left off, so to speak. Due to the relation between ideal and factual being we can, according to Climacus, prove at best that some factual being X is a manifestation of an ideal being Y (for instance: X "is a stone" or "is perfect"). However, we can never prove that X exists. If we arrive at the (overt) belief that X exists, this belief has either (if tacitly) already been there or we arrive at it thanks to a volitional act of conscious and deliberate acceptance.[17] In either case the existence of X has not and cannot be proved. This notwithstanding, one might hit upon the idea to argue the other way round, namely by starting with some ideal being Y and then try to deduce X from it, as the actually or even necessarily existing bearer of Y. Thus, within the human world, we might want to prove Napoleon's existence by demonstrating it "from Napoleon's works" (*PF,* 40)—in which case these works represent the realm of ideality and as such are supposed to function as the "manifestational" starting point and premise of the proof. However, according to the author of the *Fragments,* we run into a serious dilemma here: For either

> if I call the works Napoleon's works, then the demonstration is superfluous, since I have already mentioned his name. If I ignore this, I can never demonstrate from the works that they are Napoleon's but demonstrate (purely ideally) that such works are the works of a great general etc. (*PF,* 41)

The dilemma is obvious: either the purported proof is circular, or it is doomed to prove something other than what was supposed to be proved in the first place. Now, at least one way of escaping the dilemma[18] is considered by Climacus himself, namely pointing to what he calls an "absolute relation" (*PF,* 41) between an entity and its manifestations. Such a relation obtains, where- and whenever a manifestation is capable of unambiguously referring to and identifying its bearer—if, in other words, its extension is precisely one. Thus, if, for instance, we want to deduce Napoleon's existence from some given act (or more exactly, from its empirically accessible consequences or manifestations), this would be possible, but only if we knew beforehand that the act in question could have been done by Napoleon, and in fact by Napoleon alone. Yet, as we have seen already, there does not exist anything like an absolute relation in the sense described between Napoleon's acts and himself, so that the purported "proof" of his existence by way of pointing to those purportedly identifying acts is bound to fail. Not so in the case of God, for between him "and his works there *is* an absolute relation" (*PF,* 341; my emphasis). In other words: God does (in fact he *can* only do) what *only* God can do (see *PF,* 41). And yet, according to Climacus, a corresponding dilemma looms large: for what is the extension of or "what are the god's works?" (*PF,* 42). These works, namely, from which—as genuinely divine works—we want to demonstrate God's existence, "do not immediately and directly exist" (*PF,* 42). This is due, in particular, to the radical ambiguity in which they appear to us within the bounds of human experience: the "wisdom in nature and the goodness or wisdom in Governance"—as essential properties of God—are never "right in front of our noses" (*PF,* 42); that is, they are not and can never be unambiguously present in what we "immediately" take to be and perceive as meaningful and teleologically structured or preordained, so that, by becoming aware of this, we may, on the contrary, "encounter the most terrible spiritual trials here" (*PF,* 42).

Summing up, we may say that we are confronted with two corresponding dilemmas: In the case of finite agents we are able to imagine or directly identify ideal manifestations of an entity such as the agent in question; however, these manifestations can never strictly and unambiguously fulfill their referential or identificatory function with regard to the agent himself, the existence of whom we want to prove by referring to them. By contrast, in the case of (the) God those manifestations would indeed be capable of doing the job—however, we cannot sort out the proper candidates, at least not "directly and immediately." Hence, the corresponding argument directed against any "manifestational" attempt to derive the existence of a (finite or divine) agent from his works may be summed up as follows:

15. Proving the existence of something by referring to its manifestations is possible only if (a) there is an absolute relation between the entity in question and its manifestations, and (b) the manifestations referred to can be identified as unambiguous and exclusive manifestations of the entity in question.
16. All finite beings violate (a).
17. God violates (b).
18. Therefore, it is impossible to prove the existence of either God or any finite being by referring to their manifestations, respectively.

Is There Any Necessary and/or Actual Disagreement Between Climacus and Anti-Climacus on the Proof Issue?

Despite the explicit refusal by one of Kierkegaard's pseudonymous authors to seriously consider, much less to accept any (actual and/or possible) attempt to prove the existence of God; and, furthermore, despite the fact that Kierkegaard himself has repeatedly followed suit in this refusal,[19] there are Kierkegaard scholars who nevertheless insist that at least in fact (if not intentionally) there is something like a proof for the existence of God to be found in Kierkegaard's, and here, in particular, in the pseudonymous authorship. One of them is Louis Pojman.[20] Drawing mostly on some pertinent passages in *The Sickness unto Death, The Concept of Anxiety,* and *Fear and Trembling,* Pojman claims to have discovered traces of both a cosmological "argument from contingency"[21] and a genuinely teleological argument[22] in Kierkegaard. The first one is more important for our present purposes, therefore I will dwell on it for a moment.

The backbone of Pojman's argument is a famous passage in the opening section of *Sickness*. Here, after having introduced the tricky notion of a (human) self as a synthesis of dialectically opposed relata (finite/infinite, temporal/eternal, necessity/freedom: see *SUD,* 13), relating to itself and as such simultaneously admitting of despair as a misrelation within a self thus structured, Kierkegaard's pseudonym Anti-Climacus provides Pojman with the crucial argumentational move:

> The human self is . . . a derived, established relation, a relation that relates itself to itself and in relating itself to itself relates itself to another. This is why there can be two forms of despair in the strict sense. If a human self had itself established itself, then there could be only one form: not to will to be oneself, to will to do away with oneself, but there could not be the form: in despair to will to be oneself. This second formulation is specifically the expression for the complete dependence of the relation (of the self), the expression for the inability of the self to arrive at or to be in equilibrium and rest by itself, but only, in relating itself to itself, by relating itself to that which has established the entire relation. (*SUD,* 13–14)

Since Anti-Climacus himself, as arguing from a religious, in fact Christian perspective (see *JP* 6433), is quick to admit that it is "*God,* who constituted man a relation" (*SUD,* 16; my emphasis), Pojman's conclusion seems prima facie justified: the fact that (particularly by desperately wanting to be oneself) one "cannot succeed in . . . attaining authentic selfhood" is, according to the author of *Sickness,* a straightforward piece of "evidence for a higher being, a God, who must have established our being in the first place."[23] Pojman spells out the underlying argument as follows:

1. Man must either be constituted by another (superior to himself) or be self-constituted.
2. If he has been self-constituted, he will not be in despair over trying to attain selfhood.
3. But he *is* in despair over willing to be a self.
4. Therefore (by 2 and 3), man cannot have constituted himself.
5. Therefore (by 1 and 4), man must have been constituted by a superior power.[24]

There are several formal and/or hermeneutical inaccuracies in Pojman's paraphrase. I will only mention one of them: Anti-Climacus's argument does in no way depend upon claiming a universal and/or particular *facticity* of despair over willing to be a self (as suggested in Pojman's premise 3); rather, assuming the mere real and/or logical *possibility* of such a despair suffices, fulfills its argumentational function perfectly and is as such also brought to bear by Anti-Climacus (see line 4 and 5 of my quotation from *Sickness* above). A more accurate, formally abbreviated, and more condensed version of the argument runs as follows:

19. Desperately wanting to be oneself is possible only if God exists.
20. Desperately wanting to be oneself is possible.
21. Therefore, God exists.

Now, at this point we are obviously faced with a serious hermeneutical problem: for whether or not we do in fact disagree with one or both of the premises (19) and (20), we cannot apparently help but admit that the argument in toto seems to be a truthful rendition of Anti-Climacus's actual standpoint. Yet, how does this mesh with our previous account and thus, in particular, with Kierkegaard's and/or Climacus's repeatedly inculcated warning not only not to *accept* any attempt to prove God's existence, but, furthermore, to even resist the temptation to *undertake* such an attempt in the first place? There are, in my opinion, at least three strategies to solve the problem. The first and most obvious is the idea that what prima facie appears to be a truthful account of the position Anti-Climacus advocates, turns out to be a misreading upon closer scrutiny. This view, again, may take different directions. According to the strongest variant the quoted passage neither gives us any hint that Anti-Climacus actually wanted us to read his text as a more or less overt expression of his *intention and/or belief* that his typology of despair might among other things also function as the basis for some kind of (anthropological) proof for the existence of God, nor that the latter is *actually* the case—whether Anti-Climacus himself intended and/or believed it to be so or not. A weaker version might argue as follows: perhaps Anti-Climacus himself was not aware of the hidden potential of his analysis (and a fortiori he did not intend to make it explicit), but this does not rule out the possibility beforehand that we, his readers, do in fact understand him, the author, better than he understood himself—namely in discovering and making use of this hidden potential by spelling out its implications in terms of an argument for God.

According to the second approach Pojman's account *is* in fact truthful and thus at least in principle correct—however, upon closer inspection this does *not* compel us to admit severe hermeneutical problems as a consequence; for the view Anti-Climacus subscribes to is actually not (much less necessarily) at variance with the standpoint of Kierkegaard's other pseudonyms, especially Climacus. For instance, one might hold that the latter simply did not know about the possibility of proving God's existence anthropologically. Had he known about it, he would have probably agreed with Anti-Climacus and thus restricted the scope of his own critical observations. Anti-Climacus, on the other hand, by being confronted with the critical insights of the earlier pseudonym, might have actually felt enriched by these insights, for instance, by arriving at the conclusion that except for the anthropological approach any other attempt to prove God's existence is not only doomed to fail, but also ethically problematic.

More radical, if also contextually more promising, is a third strategy. Like the second (and unlike the first) it is also based on the assumption that Pojman's account is hermeneutically more or less adequate: there is, at least in fact, if not necessarily in terms of the author's (reader-addressed) intention and/or belief, an anthropological argument to be found in *Sickness,* an argument that lends itself to being interpreted as a formally valid demonstration of God's existence. However, this conviction is supplemented by yet another, according to which such a view (whether it be attributable to Anti-Climacus himself or not) is actually *incompatible* with the standpoint of other Kierkegaardian pseudonyms, Climacus in particular. Someone who favors this approach will then presumably seek refuge in the additional explanation that the different pseudonyms represent different—and at times apparently also incompatible—views and standpoints, so that, given the latter obtains in the present case, three questions remain: How can the differences be adequately accounted for? Where does Kierkegaard himself stand? Which of the opposing views is correct?

I am not going to answer any of these questions, because I do not need to, since I myself take sides with the second reading, which in my opinion makes most sense. Of course, not in the form presented above. For somebody defending this view would simply ignore the fact that the objections raised by Climacus against the attempt to prove the existence of God are in fact objections raised against *any* such attempt. In other words: Climacus makes a universal claim, so that from his standpoint any purported exception (like that of an anthropological proof, for instance) would make no sense at all. This seems to render a decision between the first and the third alternative unavoidable. However, both of them are equally flawed, if I am not mistaken: the first one, because, judging from the textual evidence, there does not seem to be any reason to deny that Pojman is essentially right in his reading of the text; the third one, because it seems to me that it construes an unnecessary tension between Climacus and Anti-Climacus. Let me briefly dwell on the latter point, in order to explain and justify my inclination to defending (a corrected version of) the second strategy.

The first and most important thing to note seems almost trivial: we must distinguish between the correctness or formal validity and the truth of an argument.[25] As is well known, in order to be more than just formally valid, arguments or syllogisms have to meet the additional requirement that both of their respective premises (in our case: 19 and 20, see above) are true. Now, without any doubt the argument Anti-Climacus endorses (or the argument, which may at least be extracted from his text, whether the author himself intended and/or took it to function as such or not) is correct, in the sense of being deductively or formally valid. However, this does not imply per se that it is true also—or, for that matter, that Anti-Climacus himself believed it to be true—and thus conclusive *as* an argument. Sure enough, as a Christian and as a Christian psychologist, Anti-Climacus in all probability *believed* both premises to be true. He believed, in other words, that there is (the possibility of) a particular form of despair, which he labeled the despair of wanting to be oneself; furthermore, he took it for granted that God exists and that, by establishing the human self as a self-relating synthesis, also and necessarily conditions the possibility of despair in general, plus the despair of wanting to be oneself, in particular. This notwithstanding, the conclusion that he also considered it possible to *demonstrate* or at least to provide sufficient empirical evidence for the truth of one or both of these premises would be rash, to say the least. And if I am not mistaken, he would just as little be prepared to defend the claim that one or both of these premises are self-evident.

Now, *why* would Anti-Climacus believe these propositions without holding them capable of being demonstrated? The answer is easy, once we keep in mind that he is writing as a devout Christian (see *JP* 6433). Kierkegaard himself formulates the decisive point in a journal entry: "That I exist [*er til*] was the eternal presupposition of the ancient world; that I am a sinner is the new spontaneity of the Christian consciousness; the one can be demonstrated no more than the other" (*JP* 1032). In other words: (1) Existence can just as little be proved as (the facticity of) sin—even in a first-person perspective; rather, both have to be believed or chosen or held fast to by virtue of a conscious act of acceptance.[26] (2) Just as existence is the starting point and axiomatic presupposition of the secular mind, so it is, *per analogiam,* with sin on the part of the Christian.

Now, even though sin—just like the despair of wanting to be oneself—is possible only if God exists (since it is by definition guilt in relation to God), this does not permit us to jump to the conclusion that sin itself is possible, much less necessary or at least (universally) actual. Anti-Climacus is well aware of this: for unlike despair, which functions, in his opinion, as a necessary (albeit "negativistic"[27]) key to the understanding of the self and its underlying structure, sin can only be considered a sufficient, but not per se as a necessary condition of despair. Sure enough, the notion of sin makes the Christian explanation of despair appear coherent and at least possibly true; yet, as such it merely enables, but it does not compel us to agree with it. But if that is the case, then something similar holds for premise (20). For granted even that (19) obtains—in other words: the despair of wanting to be oneself presupposes or entails the existence of God in order to be possible, it will not do to derive from it that the despair in question is itself possible. Such a conclusion would only be justified, if it were possible to prove the actuality and/or possibility of sin—a requirement that, according to both Kierkegaard and Anti-Climacus, cannot be met objectively and/or be established by discursive reasoning. In short: if being able to desperately want to be oneself depends upon the reality of God; and if the reality of God cannot be proved, then, a fortiori, the former cannot be proved either.

Now, if this reading does justice both to the text and to Anti-Climacus's underlying attitude toward his own purported argument for the existence of God within this text, we may actually have it both ways: On the one hand we may still admit that Pojman's reconstruction of the argument on the basis of textual evidence from *Sickness* is, at least in principle, correct. On the other hand, we are equally free to deny that discovering a *formally* valid argument for the existence of God in the text compels us to exclude the possibility of any agreement, at this point, between Anti-Climacus and Climacus. Rather, on my reading, the devout Christian Anti-Climacus would—or at least he could in principle—share the substantial reservations against all alleged proofs for the existence of God, which are so eloquently put forward and defended by the subjective thinker Climacus from a non-Christian and purely philosophical standpoint.

How a Phenomenological Rereading of *Sickness* May Bear upon the Proof Issue

Anti-Climacus and Climacus are in full agreement, as far as their refusal to accept any purported proof for the existence of God is concerned; yet, there are passages in the opening paragraph of *Sickness* that may nonetheless be considered a *formally* valid argument for God—even if it was not taken or intended to be so or to be read in this way by the author of the book. For some readers this conclusion may sound somewhat too conciliatory or harmonious to be truly convincing. For despite (or even because of) the fact that Climacus and Anti-Climacus can be read as being in mutual agreement about the meaning, use, and viability of these alleged proofs, it can hardly be denied that the former would still be inclined to criticize the latter for not having been more outspoken in trying to prevent even the *impression* to arise that eventually there may be a strategy left at our disposal to prove God's existence.

Heeding this somewhat critical reminder I will in the following and concluding section of my paper outline yet another, in fact a supplementary—or more precisely: a phenomenological—rereading of the text. Being no more than supplementary this reading is, of course, not meant to suggest that I intend to withdraw or distance myself from my earlier interpretation, or that I am even aiming at a radical alternative supposed completely to do away with the former. If this were the case I would clearly torpedo my own hermeneutical project, according to which the second of the three possible readings of Anti-Climacus sketched above—that is, roughly, Pojman's reading—is, at least in principle, correct and thus to be preferred in direct comparison to reading one and three. I would torpedo or at least jeopardize it, since now it would seem like I wanted to unravel the "real intentions" of Anti-Climacus, thereby implying that in his book he merely "expressed himself infelicitously" and thus obscured these intentions, at least to some degree. Such a claim would have me unwittingly return to reading number one. But I am careful not to make any such claim. What I want to argue instead is that, although Anti-Climacus clearly *believed* in propositions (19) to (21),[28] his primary *interest* as an author lay elsewhere. To my understanding it did not lie in communicating and elaborating on the former beliefs and/or his own account of their mutual (logical, epistemical, ontological) relation; he was interested, rather, in establishing a full-fledged typology and phenomenology of the (desperate) self in its various relational dimensions, forms, and stages.

Now, it is well known that neither Kierkegaard himself nor his pseudonyms can be considered phenomenologists in any stricter, namely programmatical, conceptual, and/or methodological sense. They do not provide us with a theory of intentionality and they do not discuss the principles of *epoché* or of eidetic reduction, in particular. This notwithstanding, one may say that they are phenomenologists in practice. That is, they actually, if nonexplicitly, follow and apply rules and principles of what Husserl and others later described as phenomenology. For one thing, they share the basic conviction that consciousness is structurally intentional and thus directed toward (something as) an object: we do not just feel, perceive, know, desire, and want *simpliciter,* but we feel, perceive, know, desire, and want *something,* and this in a variety of modes and variations. More specifically and in terms of what was later referred to as eidetic reduction, the author of *Sickness* develops an ontology of the self qua phenomenology: a detailed description of (the different modes and stages of) *being* a self, and this precisely by pointing out the different ways of consciously or subconsciously *relating to* something as (one's own) self. Thus conceived, the question What *is* a self? is being transformed into a genuinely phenomenological one: What are the essential forms, stages, and modes, in which a self—and in particular: a self in despair—is *given to* itself, as such, within conscious experience? How, in other words, does a (desperate) self present or become manifest to itself within self-consciousness or within the actual awareness of something *as* a (desperate) self?[29] In addition, Kierkegaard's analyses repeatedly call attention to the impact of the subconscious, subliminal, or prereflexive level of consciousness within the life of the human mind and of the self, respectively. Finally and in terms of what, for the sake of the argument, may be called quasi-suspension (*epoché*), these analyses lead us to suspending and releasing us from the notorious question as to whether what is "experienced as" is in fact real—or is in any case identical with what it is taken to be within this very experience. The self is *real*—and is *what* it is: a self (or at least a preliminary, imperfect, and at times desperately distorted form and expression of it), inasmuch as something is experienced and interpreted to that effect, if, in other words, it is considered, by the experiencing subject, an expression or manifestation of his or her own self, as such.[30]

Now, in which sense might a phenomenological rereading of Anti-Climacus contribute to a deeper understanding of Kierkegaard's attitude toward the project of trying to prove the existence of God? The answer is: because the concept of God itself is (also, though not exclusively) invoked in *Sickness* in a phenomenological manner. According to Anti-Climacus, God is real, precisely if, to the extent and as soon as someone refers to something or someone as God. And as we have seen, it is in his opinion part and parcel of the nature and actuality of the self to establish and permanently, though often reluctantly and via despair, to uphold and cultivate such a relation, if at first only on a subliminal or prereflexive level.

This being said, we can now reformulate our original syllogism (19–21) in a weaker and epistemically less ambitious, yet phenomenologically more accurate form, which hopefully does not only do justice to Anti-Climacus's overall intentions, but also highlights them more pointedly:

22. Desperately wanting to be oneself is possible only if a person being subject to this form of despair takes God to be real.

23. Desperately wanting to be oneself is possible.[31]

24. Therefore, a person desperately wanting to be him- or herself takes God to be real.

Of course, on a purely *genetical or descriptive* level much more could and should be said about "taking God to be real," but I only mention some details in passing, for instance: that the "thought of God emerges with a leap" (*JP* 2349); that its emergence goes hand in hand with the emergence of reflexive self-consciousness; that what emerges is not to be confused with the idea of God's existence *simpliciter,* but is the perception of a *particular* God, a God with certain properties, challenging among other things one's own self-understanding; that the experience of such a God is initially dominated by (pretended) indifference, reluctance, or even hatred, before under specific appropriate circumstances it may eventually be transformed into love or trust; that education and parental authority play an instrumental role in "axiomatically" establishing, consolidating, and stabilizing the idea of a loving God to emerge and to be held fast to (see *JP* 1163, 2341, and 3453), et cetera.

Instead of the genetical I would like to treat the *epistemical* aspect in some more detail. It seems justified to maintain, first of all (as Anti-Climacus in fact does—and here I largely agree with him), that as soon as we imply an actual reference to (something as) God within the conscious or subconscious experience of a human being, it would be *phenomenologically* misleading, in fact deeply flawed, to give a description of that experience, which actually ignores or at least methodically abstracts from the reference in question. Other than its "explanatory" sibling any "descriptive reductionism," which as such may be defined as the failure to identify an emotion, practice, or experience under the description by which the subject (at times unwittingly) identifies it, must be deemed phenomenologically illegitimate.[32] Perhaps Peter erroneously believes that what he defiantly struggles with in his attempt, desperately to be oneself, is in fact *God;* but he does not and cannot erroneously believe that he actually refers to it *as* God.

It goes without saying that a prima facie justified quest for a phenomenology qua descriptive nonreductionism does not exclude the possibility—in fact the need, for the sake of sincerity and epistemological integrity—of an unbiased assessment of the reductionist issue in its explanatory dimension. And as we have seen, there can be no doubt as to Kierkegaard's own preferences concerning the alleged conclusiveness and cogency of existing and/or imaginable attempts "to go further" than what is available on a strictly phenomenological basis. Interestingly enough, though, there is, to the best of my knowledge, at least one single passage to be found in the authorship, where Kierkegaard himself seems to "jump," as it were, from the genuinely descriptive or phenomenological to the epistemical level, thus apparently drawing an all too rash conclusion from a certain *experience* of (something as) God to the latter's *existence.* We should note beforehand, however, that the passage in question is a mere quotation, and although I do believe that Kierkegaard himself would actually subscribe to its basic point, this does not admit of any conclusions as to a possible wavering in his own standpoint within the proof-debate. The text itself, quoted in the Greek language—it is actually an excerpt from a dialogue between Demosthenes and Nicias in Aristophanes' play *The Knights*—is part of the "Diapsalmata" in *Either/Or I* and only half ironically introduced by the author as "yet another demonstration of the existence of God that has hitherto been overlooked" (*EO I,* 36). In translation the "neglected argument" (to borrow a term from C. S. Peirce) reads as follows:

> DE. What, do you really think [t]hat there *are* gods?
> NIC. I know it.
> DE. Know it! How?
> NIC. I'm such a wretched god-detested chap.
> DE. Well urged indeed. (*EO I,* 37)

If there is hatred or detestation, there must be someone who hates or detests—at least, so it seems. And yet, even though this may very well be true in principle, it remains an indisputable fact that we can never know for sure (in any case not in a third-person perspective) whether the former requirement is actually met in a given case or not, and therefore we must also abstain from any conclusion as to the latter claim—not to speak of the right to identify the allegedly hate-inflicting subject with God.

A second aspect concerning the epistemical implications of Kierkegaard's phenomenology can and needs to be tackled at this point. *If* Anti-Climacus is right in assuming that (a) *all* human beings outside of Christian faith are in a state of despair[33] and that (b) no despair is possible without (at least a grain of) wanting to be oneself,[34] we may extend his argument presented so far as follows:

25. Desperately trying to be oneself is an essential element in all forms of despair.
26. All human beings outside of Christian faith are in a state of despair.
27. Therefore, all human beings outside of Christian faith take God to be real.
28. No Christian does *not* take God to be real.
29. Therefore, all human beings take God to be real.

Of course, it would be tempting to extend the argument in its present form again, for instance as follows:

> **30.** God cannot be taken to be real by all human beings unless he actually exists.
> **31.** Therefore, God exists.

Such an extension might be tempting, since it would seem both logically compelling and epistemically justified now to draw a conclusion, which renders the so-called proof *e consensu gentium* ("from general consent") resuscitated, as it were, and fully rehabilitated. But, hardly surprising, this will not do—neither (as I suspect) on purely philosophical grounds, nor, and in particular, in terms of a truthful Kierkegaard exegesis.[35]

Some Further Kierkegaardian Considerations on the Proof Issue

Is this Kierkegaard's final word as to the epistemology of and the arguments for God? Not really. As far as I see, he considers, if somewhat experimentally, at least two further options to "demonstrate" the truth of Christianity, or more exactly, certain Christian and/or religious truth-claims. The first is closer to the Climacus discussion, thereby remaining this side of the genuinely phenomenological context. Here Kierkegaard probes a version of a "proof by authority": "Actually, the best proof for the immortality of the soul, that there is a God, and the like, is the impression one has of this from his childhood, and therefore this proof . . . could be stated thus: It is absolutely certain, for my father told me" (*JP* 1170). A few pages earlier something similar is being considered with regard to the central Christian idea that God is love:

> Here . . . everything depends upon a religious upbringing, on the *apriority* which is thereby won, so that it is absolutely settled from the very beginning for a person that God is love. This, the proof that God is love on the basis of an inexplicable impression, an impression which from the beginning is fused with one's whole being, this is really the most important. (*JP* 1163)

Tying together both entries we may say that, according to Kierkegaard, a "proof" for the existence and/or the nature of God qua love is possible—and in fact also convincing—if only on the basis of an a priori[36] and as such "inexplicable impression" of those ideas, as they are imprinted, as it were, into the mind of a child, so that the whole issue is "settled" from the very beginning.[37] For this impression to arise, a religious upbringing of the child is mandatory, and here, in particular, the acceptance, on the part of the latter, of the unconditional and unquestionable authority of the father, testifying to the truth of the respective idea. It goes without saying that in order to take this approach seriously we (or Kierkegaard himself) would have to be prepared to accept a *metabasis eis allo genos*—an unwarranted leap from the genetical to the epistemological realm, namely by arguing: "X is *true,* because and inasmuch as X is (or has come, via parental authority and education, to be) *certain.*" Any such argument would only pass as conclusive, if by definition the propositions in question ("God exists," "God is love") could not be certain without actually being true. However, Kierkegaard does not provide any, much less any sufficient reason as to (a) the truth of such claim, and (b) the possible certainty of (either of) the propositions in question. And yet, it can hardly be denied that he himself was fully aware of this, so that here again the term "proof" must be taken with a grain of salt.

With a second and final remark I want to call attention to a journal entry, in which Kierkegaard ponders the idea of a subjectively based proof—however, not a proof for the existence of God, but rather for the truth of Christianity in comparison to that of a purely philosophical worldview (and also, I guess, to that of other religions). The "proof" is based on the observation that quite often the "most zealous enemies" of Christianity "have become its most zealous defenders" (*JP* 455).[38] This purely genetical or descriptive observation is put into service by Kierkegaard for epistemical purposes, in that he claims that this "double relationship in Christianity," in other words, the fact that the latter "goads just as intensely as it attracts" is "the very thing that demonstrates its absolute truth" (*JP* 455).[39] By contrast, any "objective" apology must, in his opinion, prove deeply flawed for pragmatical or "subjective" reasons already: it makes things seem all too easy, thus apparently releasing its addressee from the burdensome task inherent to the life of faith, as the latter is based on ideas, which can only be held fast by permanently overcoming the (subjective and objective) offense invariably going along with them. Only a religion, which attracts *by means of* "frightening away" and vice versa, might be called "absolutely," namely both objectively and subjectively true—and that is precisely the achievement of Christianity (as being rooted in the idea of the God-man), and in fact of Christianity alone. Now, one might argue that even *if* we could demonstrate that a religion, in order to be "absolutely true," would have to meet the double requirement just stated; and, moreover, if we were also capable of showing that it is Christianity alone, which actually and/or possibly meets this requirement, we would still be in charge of justifying the claim that Christianity (more exactly, the God-man as the fundamental idea that it rests upon) is *itself* possible. For, trivially enough, that A is possible only if B does not prove B to be possible.

Despite appearances this objection need not worry us much—nor Kierkegaard, for that matter. The simple reason is that it cannot even function as a proper objection, since it unwittingly repeats a point made by Kierkegaard himself:[40] any straightforward, apologetically motivated recommendation of Christianity is impossible, since Christianity is built upon the idea of the paradox, or more exactly, a number of closely related paradoxes—one Christological (the God-man), one hamartiological (sin), and one soteriological (the forgiveness of sins) in nature.[41] As such, these paradoxes defy any rational explanation and appropriation—for instance, by lending themselves to being demonstrated. Now, it is not my task here to assess the truth and/or justifiability of this claim. Suffice it to say that on strictly consequential grounds one can hardly help but admit that Kierkegaard is basically right: *if* the paradoxical premise obtains, any possibility of proving that Christianity can and has to be considered the "absolute truth" (in the sense described above), would in fact be incompatible with the project of giving a true account of Christianity. More formally speaking, the possibility of *proving* Christianity to be a, in fact the sole manifestation of an "absolute truth" would be sufficient for the impossibility of *being* any such manifestation. In turn, the *impossibility* of demonstrating Christianity to be absolutely true must itself be deemed necessary for the former's absolute truth to be possible. So, once more we have to take the term "proof" with a grain of salt: it is used by Kierkegaard in a purely consequential or "coherentistic" way, and it should have become obvious by now that he (knew he) would contradict himself and have his arguments run counter to their own fundamental premises, if this were otherwise.

Conclusion

The present article has fulfilled its purpose if it has succeeded in explaining and arguing persuasively for the following claims:

1. There is a fundamental unity, continuity, and unanimity in Kierkegaard's authorship as regards the actual and/or imaginable attempts to argue for the existence of God: none of these attempts is, in fact none of them can be, successful, and this for various reasons; more-

over, any such attempt proves highly problematic on ethico-religious grounds already.

2. In particular, Kierkegaard and/or Climacus try to come to terms with the so-called proofs by employing at least five arguments supposed to refute them: a psychological, an epistemological, an ontological, an ethico-religious, and a manifestational one. Some of these arguments seem to be sound, others are found wanting.

3. Despite appearances, Anti-Climacus is no exception among the pseudonyms as regards the proof issue: what appears, at first sight, to be a full-fledged argument for the existence of God in *The Sickness unto Death,* turns out, upon closer inspection, merely to be a correct and formally valid syllogism, the truth of which remains undecided for the time being. Although Anti-Climacus himself obviously believes in these premises (and thus also in the conclusion deduced from them), he knows full well and in fact welcomes without reservation that the argument in toto cannot be persuasive, since the truth of its premises depends on fundamental Christian ideas (sin, in particular), which in turn cannot be justified outside of faith and as such already presuppose the existence of God in order possibly to be true.

4. Anti-Climacus at least implicitly accepts that readers may take the pertinent passages of *Sickness* to contain and also to be intended as an attempt to argue for the existence of God—and he does so in spite of Climacus's explicit warning against the deplorable consequences of any such impression to arise. Whatever reason he may have had for this acceptance, the main intention of his text lies elsewhere, in any case: it is a phenomenologically exhaustive typology and description of the different forms and stages of despair—a description, which in turn functions as a "negativistic" index and illumination of the (structure, content, and purpose of the) human self, Christianly conceived. This description may indeed take the form of a formally valid proof for the existence of God; however, Anti-Climacus is quick to admit—and rightly so—that (a) the experience of something as God can still be erring, even if such an experience is universal (the *consensus gentium* may rest on a mistake); and (b) the theistic ideas or premises on which the phenomenological argument is based (God and sin, in particular) provide sufficient, but they obviously do not and cannot provide necessary conditions for the understanding of despair to be possible; at least it cannot be demonstrated objectively that they do.

5. Additional and supplementary considerations concerning these and related issues are to be found throughout Kierkegaard's journals; however, the journals do not (and in fact they do not intend to) provide radically different views about the matter. In particular, they undergird

the hypothesis that Kierkegaard deemed it impossible, both to give a truthful account of (the ideality of) Christianity *and* to prove the existence of God (in particular, the Christian God of love). Either the latter is possible or the former—*tertium non datur.*

Notes

1. See, for instance: Jörg Disse, *Kierkegaards Phänomenologie der Freiheitserfahrung* (Freiburg: Alber, 1991); Wolfgang Janke, "Kierkegaards Phänomenologie des subjektiven Geistes," in *Sein und Geschichtlichkeit. Festschrift für K. H. Volkmann-Schluck,* ed. W. Janke (Frankfurt: Klostermann, 1974), 103–13; Heiko Schulz, "To Believe Is to Be: Reflections on Kierkegaard's Phenomenology of (Un-)Freedom in *The Sickness unto Death,*" in *Kierkegaard Studies. Yearbook* 1996, ed. Niels Jørgen Cappelørn and Hermann Deuser (Berlin: W. de Gruyter, 1996), 164–85; Heiko Schulz, "Philosophie als Existenzwissenschaft: Empirismuskritik und Wissenschaftsklassifikation bei Sören Kierkegaard," *Theologie und Philosophie* 71 (1996): 205–23; and in a certain sense (phenomenology as hermeneutical ontology) also Klaus Schäfer, *Hermeneutische Ontologie in den Climacus-Schriften Sören Kierkegaards* (Munich: Kösel, 1968).

2. As to the scope and limits of proving in general (in Kierkegaard), see also Alastair Hannay, *Kierkegaard,* 2nd ed. (London: Routledge, 1993), 138–39. For a brief, yet concise and informative account of Kierkegaard's (and in particular Climacus's) critique of arguments for God, see C. Stephen Evans, *Passionate Reason: Making Sense of Kierkegaard's "Philosophical Fragments"* (Bloomington: Indiana University Press, 1992). See also Evans, "Kant and Kierkegaard on the Possibility of Metaphysics," in *Kant and Kierkegaard on Religion,* ed. D. Z. Phillips and Timothy Tessin (Houndmills: Macmillan Press, 2000), 3–24, for an updated version.

3. *PF,* 40; my emphasis. I will return to this generalized claim shortly.

4. Evans, *Passionate Reason,* 65.

5. See also *JP* 2341, where Kierkegaard maintains that all *deductive* conclusions "are essentially tautological."

6. As to the similarities and differences between a believing and an accepting attitude (plus the important epistemological and psychological role that the latter plays inside and outside of science), see Jonathan L. Cohen, *Belief and Acceptance,* 2nd ed. (Oxford: Oxford University Press, 1995), especially chap. 1.

7. Evans, *Passionate Reason,* 65.

8. Ibid.

9. Evans, *Passionate Reason,* 65. And of course, the same would apply with regard to the attempt to prove that God does *not* exist—given *that* he in fact does not exist.

10. Compare Kierkegaard's critical note on Anselm in *JP* 20: "Anselm prays in all inwardness that he might succeed in proving God's existence. He thinks he has succeeded, and he flings himself down in adoration to thank God. Amaz-

ing. He does not notice that this prayer and this expression of thanksgiving are infinitely more proof of God's existence than—the proof."

11. See *JP* 1342, where Kierkegaard is more explicit on this presupposition, while drawing on the same God-king-analogy as used by Climacus: "If the subjects of a country where a king is on the throne were to set about investigating whether or not it is right to have a king, he would become enraged. This is the way man acts toward God—he forgets *that God exists* [*er til*] and ponders whether it is proper, acceptable, to have a God" (my emphasis).

12. See *PF,* 41n: "Factual being [*Den faktiske Væren*] is indifferent to the differentiation of all essence-determinants, and everything that exists [*er til*] participates without petty jealousy in being and participates just as much."

13. As to this idea in context, see Schulz, "Philosophie als Existenzwissenschaft," 210–11. Kierkegaard admits that as a *concept* existence is also "an ideality" (*JP* 1057), and as such it has "concept-existence, ideal existence" (*JP* 1057) only. However, existence is as such never "*absorbed* in the concept" (*JP* 1057; my emphasis), and this is due, in particular, to the individuality (and thus also, contingency; see *JP* 3652) of the existing entity in question. See also Evans, *Passionate Reason,* 66.

14. Which leads to the conclusion that, according to Climacus, we may speak of ideality without having to refer to existence—but not vice versa. Thus, for instance, we may refer to the ideality of a unicorn, knowing full well that such a thing does not or even cannot actually exist. On the other hand, we cannot speak about Peter's existence without having to imply at least some concept of his ideality: as a person, as an individual, and as such as having specific properties.

15. Unfortunately, Climacus is semantically ambiguous here. A few lines prior to the quotation above he writes: "If . . . I interpret the expression 'to demonstrate the existence . . . of the god' to mean that I want to demonstrate that the unknown, which exists, is the god, then I do not express myself very felicitously, for then I *demonstrate nothing,* least of all an existence, but I develop the definition of a concept" (*PF,* 39–40; my emphasis). The former quotation has us believe that proofs are possible, if only within the realm of ideal being. The latter suggests a stronger and more radical reading, since it even denies this restricted possibility. My reconstruction of the argument builds upon the former, weaker claim.

16. Evans, *Passionate Reason,* 66.

17. In the latter case Kierkegaard speaks of conviction (*overbevisning*); alluding to the two root elements of the word in Danish (*over*=above; *bevis*=proof), he writes: A "man of conviction . . . has made a resolution and voluntarily raises himself higher than the dialectics of proofs and is convinced [*overbeviist*]" (*JP* 2296). Thus conceived conviction (or more exactly the acquisition of conviction) corresponds to the leap [*spring*] as a "pathos-filled transition" (*JP* 2340) from possibility to actuality. Applying this latter notion to the genesis of a (purported) proof for the existence of God, he writes: "The results (*resultare,* to leap backward) in the proofs for the existence of God occur with a leap" (*JP* 2349; see also *PF,* 42–43).

18. And Climacus does not tell us whether in his opinion it is in fact the only way.

19. See, for instance, *JP* 20, 1032, 1033, 1334, 1342, 1881, 2296, 2341.

20. Louis J. Pojman, *The Logic of Subjectivity: Kierkegaard's Philosophy of Religion* (Tuscaloosa: University of Alabama Press, 1984). See especially p. 14. For a somewhat different and in fact critical account of what he takes to be Kierkegaard's "existential/pragmatic argument for God" (169), see Peter J. Mehl, "Despair's Demand: An Appraisal of Kierkegaard's Argument for God," *International Journal for Philosophy of Religion* 32 (1992): 167–82.

21. Ibid., 15.

22. Ibid.

23. Ibid., 14.

24. Ibid., 15.

25. A simple example may suffice to prove my point: "1. All Indians wear plaits. 2. Karl Lagerfeld is an Indian. 3. Therefore Karl Lagerfeld wears a plait." Formally speaking this syllogism is impeccable; furthermore, its conclusion is both valid and true. Nevertheless it is flawed, since both of its premises are wrong.

26. As regards the latter we should not forget, however, that Kierkegaard—as a *Protestant* Christian—was of the opinion that this act of choice or acceptance is only and justifiably deemed possible within the realm of a non- or pre-Christian form of religiousness. By contrast, both the act of faith and of sin-consciousness (as an integral element of the former) in a strictly Christian sense are not within the power of the human subject acquiring it. See, for instance, *PF*, 62–63; *CUP*, 583.

27. To borrow a term from Theunissen. See Michael Theunissen, *Der Begriff Verzweiflung. Korrekturen an Kierkegaard* (Frankfurt: Suhrkamp, 1993), 16.

28. And also in the truth of the corresponding syllogism, of which they are a part—though, as we have seen, under the axiomatic and thus indemonstrable presupposition of sin.

29. See also my "To Believe Is to Be" as an attempt to show how the "existence" of freedom—in other words: its experience and actualization by virtue of aesthetically, ethically, or religiously relating to something *as* (an expression of) freedom—is in fact conceived of in the authorship as part and parcel of its own "essence." Thus Kierkegaard favors what I would label a "categorical" understanding of freedom, according to which the latter is possible (and actual) only *as such.* The different forms and stages of freedom, thus conceived, primarily (though of course not exclusively) call for being tackled phenomenologically, and this is precisely what Kierkegaard and his pseudonyms regularly do.

30. As seen in this light one might also trace Kierkegaard's understanding and practice of phenomenology back to Hegel's notion of the term, according to which it refers to the description, analysis, and dialectical critique of the various forms and stages within the (self-)experience of consciousness. See Mark C. Taylor, *Journeys to Selfhood: Hegel and Kierkegaard* (Berkeley: University of California Press, 1980), and in a more recent version, *After God* (Chicago: University of Chicago Press, 2007), 184–85, 195, for an attempt to come to terms both with

the apparent proximity and the radical distance between Kierkegaard and Hegel in this respect.

31. For simplicity's sake I renounce a reformulation of this second premise in equally phenomenological fashion. As such it would read as follows: desperately wanting to be oneself is experienced and/or tacitly implied as possible by the person desperately wanting to be him- or herself.

32. I owe this distinction to Wayne Proudfoot. See Wayne Proudfoot, *Religious Experience* (Berkeley: University of California Press, 1985), 196.

33. See *SUD*, 26: The "common view that despair is a rarity is entirely wrong; on the contrary, it is universal." I presume Anti-Climacus would justify his claim primarily by drawing on the idea of (hereditary) sin; see the following footnote.

34. See *SUD*, 14: The despair to will to be oneself "is so far from designating merely a distinctive kind of despair that, on the contrary, all despair ultimately can be traced back to and be resolved in it." I take this to be a theologically (instead of just phenomenologically) motivated claim on Anti-Climacus's part; as such it is apparently based upon the—note well: paradoxical—idea of sin as ultimately being rooted not in error, but in a conscious preference or choice for evil: see *SUD*, 87–96, especially 93. Thus conceived, both claims (as to the first, see the previous footnote) function as quasi-axioms or ultimate premises admitting of no evidence other than the truth of certain dogmatical ideas—and of course Anti-Climacus both knows, confirms, and welcomes this.

35. As to the latter, see, for instance, Climacus's polemic against the purported "evidence of the centuries for the truth of Christianity" (*CUP*, 46–49).

36. Kierkegaard uses the term rather loosely or metaphorically here. Alternatively he states, in another journal entry, that the highest degree of conviction (here: concerning the idea that God is love) is attained whenever the latter is not conceived of as "a dogma which [as such] always requires proof but *has become my axiom,* which [as such] never needs proof" (*JP* 3453; my emphasis).

37. The idea of an issue being "settled" from the outset reminds us, hardly by accident, of Climacus's urging that any attempt to prove the existence of (an actually existing) God proves foolish, since in order to begin one always already has to presuppose the very existence one sets out to prove, and this "not as doubtful . . . but as decided" (*PF*, 39; see above).

38. An observation that not by accident alludes to the "neglected argument" explained before.

39. See also *JP* 4897: "This is the proof that Christ is the God-man, for in willing to win all, unconditionally, he frightens everybody away."

40. That is also the reason why I think that Peter Mehl's (otherwise instructive) critique of Anti-Climacus misses the point. Mehl argues that there is sort of a pragmatical argument for God to be found in *Sickness:* God exists, because and inasmuch as the infinite quest or "demand," inherent to all forms of despair, for fully authentic selfhood and moral integrity can as such only be thought of as being met by God—and in fact the despairing person him- or herself perceives things to be so. In Mehl's opinion, the argument is flawed, however: it tacitly presupposes what is supposed yet to be proved, God, and this, because "despair's demand" or inherent disease, in its being "infiltrated by Christian theism" (Mehl,

"Despair's Demand," 179), is all too quickly taken to be infinite, so that not only the corresponding cure must consist of nothing less but *fully* authentic selfhood and *complete* moral integrity, in order to meet the demand, but that, furthermore, the source, being able to provide the cure, must be conceived of as equally infinite, thus divine (see Mehl, 169, 171, 173–74, 179–80). Once we give up Kierkegaard's religiously infected and as such unnecessarily strong "ideal of humanness" (179)—and Kierkegaard himself provides sufficient reason to do just that (180)—the argument for God derived from it loses its force, and rightly so. Mehl fails to note, however, that the claim that it is God and God alone who can actually satisfy the desire for fully authentic selfhood and thus heal the "sickness unto death," cannot, as ultimately unwarranted (because of its tacitly being present already in the diagnosis of despair's disease), be turned against Anti-Climacus, simply because this is precisely what he himself, as a devout Christian, presupposes and affirms as a final axiomatic premise of his own analysis, a premise, which as such (and also and especially because of its paradoxical implications) defies rational explanation and appropriation.

41. See, for instance, *PF,* chap. 3, esp. 44–48; *CUP,* 204–34, 578–81, 583; and *SUD,* 92–93.

Kierkegaard and the Phenomenology of Temptation

Brian Gregor

As a topic of phenomenological inquiry, temptation is a particularly intriguing theme: in temptation, an enticing project, a possible course of action, is given, and at the same time I am aware of an obligation to resist its solicitations. Because of this interplay between enticement and conviction, temptation is phenomenally very rich. But it is also a very challenging phenomenon insofar as it implicates so many different facets of the self.[1] A complete phenomenology of temptation would also need to include phenomenologies of desire and affectivity, solicitude, freedom, memory, ethical conviction, deliberation, decision, and action. My goal in this paper is not, however, to work out a comprehensive phenomenology of temptation. Instead, I want to show what Søren Kierkegaard can contribute to such a task. Kierkegaard may not qualify as a classical or pure phenomenologist, just as some critics want to deny that he really qualifies as a philosopher. Yet this predilection for contamination is part of what makes Kierkegaard so thought-provoking, and one of the wagers of the present volume is that there is much to be gained by reading Kierkegaard as a phenomenologist—even if as a phenomenologist of a different variety.

In what follows, I begin with a clarifying analysis that distinguishes temptation from two related phenomena: spiritual trial on the one hand, and anxiety on the other. Part 2 then takes on the more descriptive work, with a particular eye to the place of imagination in temptation. Kierkegaard's Anti-Climacus writings are important here, since they help us establish a working definition of temptation as being enticed by the lower. Part 3 then sketches, in conclusion, some remarks on the role of memory and forgetting in responding to temptation.

1. Kierkegaard on Spiritual Trial, Anxiety, and Temptation

In order to benefit from Kierkegaard's understanding of temptation, we need to start by distinguishing it from two closely related phenomena: spiritual trial [*Anfægtelse*] and anxiety [*Angest*]. Kierkegaard often comments on temptation while discussing spiritual trial and anxiety because these three phenomena are often interwoven, and at times even seem to coincide. On some occasions Kierkegaard writes of spiritual trial as though it is a type of temptation, or conversely, that temptation can be the occasion for spiritual trial (*JP* 4374). Similarly, he suggests that anxiety can arise over temptation (*JP* 4748) as well as spiritual trial (*JP* 4370). On another occasion, he refers to anxiety as "the most terrible kind of spiritual trial" (*JP* 1401). With the complex interweavings of temptation, anxiety, and spiritual trial, we are dealing with variables that can be related in a variety of possible combinations. What we must do in this section, then, is sketch out the general differences between these distinct yet related phenomena.[2]

Temptation and Spiritual Trial

Throughout his authorship—pseudonymous and veronymous writings alike—Kierkegaard locates spiritual trial [*Anfægtelse*] as a defining feature of genuine religiousness. But Kierkegaard believes that spiritual trial had become a rarity in his time, just as true Christianity had been abolished by the spiritlessness of Christendom. Christian faith had become something to be taken in moderation and with a grain of salt. In *Concluding Unscientific Postscript,* Johannes Climacus complains that the category of spiritual trial had fallen into disrepair. One symptom of this is the fact that people no longer know how to distinguish it from such phenomena as temptation and adversity (*CUP,* 458). In response, the *Postscript* provides one of the clearest distinctions between spiritual trial and temptation to appear in the Kierkegaardian corpus.

According to Climacus, temptation is a more common experience than spiritual trial, since it confronts everyone who tries to live ethically. From the ethical point of view, temptation is the highest danger one must confront. Ethical temptation gives the possibility of transgressing the universal—a move that would undermine the constituting principle of one's selfhood, as well as the social and political order. The self is tempted by the lower, which targets us in moments of weakness. Structurally speaking,[3] the "lower" refers to that which is lower than what one ought to choose in a particular situation. Thus it can refer to typical forms of sensate indulgence and vice, as we might expect. But perhaps more interesting, from a religious point of view, it is possible for the ethical itself to become a temptation. This is why *Fear and Trembling* describes Abraham as being tempted by the ethical. While he is being tested[4] by God's command to sacrifice Isaac (*FT,* 60, 115), the ethical would be tempting for Abraham because it is the universal (*FT,* 54, 68, 82) and thus the means by which he could be mediated—that is, communicate his situation and make himself understood.

Unlike temptation, spiritual trial is a strictly religious category. According to Climacus, it is a religious counterpart to the ethical concept of temptation. This is not to deny that there are temptations that only arise in the religious; the case of Abraham's temptation by the ethical is one example, as is the spiritlessness of Christendom.[5] Rather, the point is that while temptation is the highest difficulty in the ethical, an even more intense challenge appears in the religious. In temptation, the lower tries to draw the individual to itself by appealing to inclination; but in spiritual trial, the higher, "seemingly envious of the individual, wants to frighten him back" (*CUP,* 459). Spiritual trial concerns the individual's relation to the absolute telos. A central challenge of Christian faith, as Climacus describes it, is to relate absolutely to the absolute telos, and relatively to all relative ends (*CUP,* 458, 460–61). Spiritual trial is the boundary that confronts the self when it tries to relate itself absolutely to the absolute. Consequently, while temptation subsists on moments of weakness, spiritual trial confronts the self in those moments when the absolute relation to the absolute is most intense. Spiritual trial arises further along the pathway of the religious, and it "increases in proportion to the religiousness" (*CUP,* 459).

Another notable difference is that temptation arises in some degree of continuity with the self's ethical constitution; thus the specific temptations that solicit one will be related to one's habits, practices, and desires.[6] By contrast, spiritual trial has no continuity with the self; it does not emerge from any immanent potentiality of the self but rather arises from the absolute, which is the source of resistance (*CUP,* 459).

The question is, why would the absolute offer this resistance? Or to put a finer point on it, are we to suppose that God resists the individual—as if to "frighten him back"—when he is advancing along the religious? In a journal entry from 1848, Kierkegaard describes a case in which a man struggles with evil thoughts and is unable to put them out of his mind. In this particular situation, these besetting thoughts amount to a spiritual trial. This trial is not without purpose; "it is, to define it teleologically, an educational torture which, whatever else, is intended to break all self-centered willfulness" (*JP* 4370). The goal of this education is that the self learns to submit to God, to become nothing before God, to surrender its claim to be able to stand before God on its own terms.

Becoming nothing before God does not mean that the self is obliterated, as though God is for some reason jealous of human agency per se. Instead, spiritual trial helps to rid the self of its delusions so that it can at some point along this religious pathway earn God's favor—that any merit could suffice to justify oneself, to be worthy of God's favor. Kierkegaard is too psychologically astute (and also too Lutheran)[7] not to recognize what is at stake in this struggle: rather than taking consciousness at face value, he digs deeper to observe that if the sufferer were able to rid himself of these evil thoughts, or perhaps suppress them through praying or thinking pious thoughts, he might think he had staked out a corner in his life—however minuscule—in which he is worthy of God's favor. In that domain, he is no longer a sinner. Thus, Kierkegaard argues that the man must stop trying to flee the evil thoughts; he must stop fearing that those thoughts are decisive for determining God's favor or his judgment. Rather than fleeing, he must stand fast. He must push forward and be honest before God:

> His salvation lies right here, in his acquiring the frankness to think these evil thoughts together with God before God—in order to dispose of them. His salvation lies in his getting a Savior or in his Savior's coming to exist for him so that he dares say to him: These evil thoughts haunt and hound me, not letting himself be frightened by the notion that naming these is the same as having them again.

Through this honesty, Kierkegaard observes, the concept of "the Savior" acquires a new level of meaning for the self (*JP* 4370). Only through this honesty can the self appreciate the full radicality of grace and the promise that one is justified precisely while one is yet a sinner. It is correct then to say that God uses spiritual trial to frighten the self back, but the purpose here is to reveal the true basis on which anyone is able to proceed through the religious: namely, grace.

Perhaps most trying of all, the self must continue to wait on grace, in the religious task of hoping that God will remove this trial. The temptation here is to seek the premature resolution in which the self can resign himself to the conclusion that this suffering is meaningless. Difficult as this may be, this closure would allow him to settle into the task of bearing his burden with patience and humility. But there is still some self-centered willfulness here, because this resolution allows the self to retain a degree of sovereignty over the meaning of the situation. This egocentricity can only be finally rooted out when the self allows itself to be suspended in the unresolved tension of hope—in expectation of the moment [*Øieblikke*] when hope will be brought to fruition (*JP* 4378).[8]

To put it mildly, spiritual trial resists us; it moves against our inclination. In this way it differs from temptation, which moves *with* our inclinations. Thus these phenomena call for opposite tactics: the appropriate response to temptation is to "shun the danger," to flee the source of temptation. Flight from temptation runs counter to our inclinations, and might be very difficult, but it is the wisest way to escape the lure of the tempting. In facing spiritual trial, however, flight itself becomes the temptation, since it is the very thing to which we incline. Spiritual trial strikes terror into us, it fills us with anxiety, so we would naturally like to flee, to retreat into the lower. But it is precisely at this point that we must move toward it—indeed, go *through* it (*JP* 4367, 4023, 4382).[9] This, Kierkegaard writes, is the course of faith.[10]

Temptation and Anxiety

If it is difficult to distinguish between anxiety and temptation, it is because they often appear in such close proximity to each other. But even if the two phenomena are closely connected, they are distinct because they intend different things. In *The Concept of Anxiety,* Vigilius Haufniensis writes that the prohibition against a certain tree awakens Adam to the possibility of freedom, and thereby induces anxiety in him (*CA*, 44). But this new awareness of possibility is not yet temptation. The prohibition precedes the temptation, which comes later. Furthermore, what emerges from the prohibition is not temptation, but an awareness of the possibility of freedom.

Adam's anxiety does not, however, emerge from an abstractly free will deliberating between good and evil.[11] Adam "has no conception of what he is able to do." His anxiety has no object; it refers to nothing. Instead, he has "the anxious possibility of *being able*" (*CA,* 44–45). This is the fundamental difference between anxiety and fear: while fear refers to a definite something, anxiety is the actuality of freedom "as the possibility of possibility" (*CA,* 42). Like fear, temptation differs from anxiety because it has a more determinate object; it intends a particular thing that we could choose.

Anxiety is so disquieting precisely because of this indeterminacy; it aims at nothing but the possibility of freedom (*CA,* 61). Things become more complicated, however, after the leap into sin. With this leap the particular possibility of freedom is actualized,[12] yet neither possibility nor anxiety is annulled. Because the self is now aware of the distinction between good and evil, anxiety becomes increasingly more reflective, such that "the nothing that is the object of anxiety becomes, as it were, more and more a something" (*CA*, 61). Now the self can be anxious over the possibility of evil. The self becomes anxious over this "unwarranted actuality"—the unfreedom of sin. The self also becomes anxious over the future—the possibility that "no matter how deep an individual has sunk, he can still sink deeper" (*CA*, 113).[13] And so the self becomes anxious over the possibility of an even deeper unfreedom.

At this point anxiety appears closest to temptation, with its sympathetic antipathy and antipathetic sympathy toward *evil*. Now anxiety has a more determinate object. But it is still different from temptation, because it regards a different type and degree of determinacy. Anxiety arises with, but most importantly *over*, temptation. This is why Kierkegaard can write that temptation "has frightful power for making one anxious" (*JP* 4748). In anxiety over temptation, I become terribly anxious over what might happen with regard to the choice that confronts me—namely, the possibility that I might *freely* leap into deeper *un*freedom. Anxiety is both drawn and repulsed by the possibility of a deeper unfreedom. Therefore, I become anxious over the temptation but not over the determinate tempting object itself.

We must also note that this postlapsarian anxiety can take the form of anxiety over the *good*, in a form of anxiety that Haufniensis calls the *demonic* (*CA*, 118). In his account the good signifies salvation, or redemption, or "the restoration of freedom" (*CA*, 119). Here the unfree self is in anxiety over the possibility of freedom (*CA*, 123); one is drawn, yet repulsed, by the possibility that the good might open it up to freedom.[14] And so the self closes in on itself, shutting itself off in a demonic isolation that Haufniensis deems "inclosing reserve" [*Indesluttethed*] (*CA*, 123). The fact that we can be anxious before the good is also an important point of distinction between anxiety and temptation; we cannot, after all, properly speak of being tempted by the good.[15]

Finally, anxiety demands a different response than temptation. We have already seen that Kierkegaard commends flight as the wise response to temptation. Like spiritual trial, however, anxiety calls for *faith* rather than flight. In the conclusion to *The Concept of Anxiety,* Haufniensis writes of learning how to be anxious—of being educated by anxiety (*CA*, 155). Anxiety provides the occasion for us to clarify our priorities by prompting us to be honest with ourselves, by making each of us ask, in what does my life consist? No matter what finite end we might cling to, it is not safe from anxiety. Anything is possible, and even more troubling is the fact that things can always get worse (*CA*, 158). In the characteristically profound words of Bob Dylan, "When you think that you lost everything, you find out you can always lose a little more."[16] With this insight, anxiety exposes the deceptiveness of finite ends and possibilities, whether terrible or joyful (*CA,* 155). There is no finite end that can support the self completely, since the self is spirit—a synthesis of finite and infinite. Haufniensis is therefore commending something similar to Johannes Climacus: that one must relate relatively to relative ends, and absolutely to the absolute. Thus a merely finite sagacity—whether Stoic resignation or Heideggerian resoluteness—cannot enable the self to become a true "disciple of possibility." By relating infinitely to the infinite, one receives infinity, but she also receives the finite back (*CA,* 158) by allowing finite ends to be what they are—finite. Thus "whoever has truly learned how to be anxious will dance when the anxieties of finitude strike up the music and when the apprentices of finitude lose their minds and courage" (*CA,* 161–62). This, Haufniensis suggests, is what faith looks like.

2. Temptation as Being Drawn Downward Through Deception

Now that we have gained some clarity regarding the differences between temptation, spiritual trial, and anxiety, I want to focus on Kierkegaard's treatment of the phenomenon of "being drawn" and its import for thinking about temptation. We therefore need to focus on the Anti-Climacus writings (*The Sickness unto Death* and *Practice in Christianity*), which distinguish between being drawn by the higher and being enticed to the lower.

Imagination and Being Drawn

> *Thoughts that try the spirit* are related . . . to the imagination—pure rationalists do not know about such things. (*JP* 4383)

Anti-Climacus discusses the phenomenon of "being drawn" in *Practice in Christianity,* in his third series of meditations on Christ's words in John 12:32: "And I, when I am lifted up from the earth, will draw all to myself." "What does it mean," Anti-Climacus asks, for something "to draw to itself?" First of all, one has to determine what is doing the drawing. Anti-Climacus claims that only that which is "in itself"—or later, "in and for itself"—can properly draw to itself (*PC,* 158, 159). Only that which is a self can draw to itself. Being drawn is fundamentally intersubjective; it is a relation between selves. This means, secondly, that in order for something to be capable of being drawn, it must also be a self. Only that which is also a self can be *drawn,* in the true sense of being drawn. But Anti-Climacus argues further that the self must be constituted as a self in order to be drawn. The self must be helped "truly to become itself"—the one doing the drawing must "make the self . . . to be itself." How does this helping occur? Precisely through the drawing. The self is constituted in and through being drawn (*PC,* 159).

In outlining the structure of this event, Anti-Climacus is primarily concerned with the way that Christ draws to himself. Although Christ uses a great variety of ways and means in order to draw to himself, these manifold ways "converge at one point: the consciousness of sin" (*PC,* 155). We therefore come to ourselves through repentance, through taking responsibility for our sin, and in this way we are constituted as selves capable of being drawn (*PC,* 157, 160).[17]

If one needs to be a self in order to be drawn, this means that one has to be a free being. For this reason, the imagination has an important role to play in being drawn, because the imagination is the medium through which possibility is given. Through the imagination we anticipate possible choices, projects, and consequences; without imagination, freedom—and thus the self—is inconceivable. This is why Anti-Climacus argues that imagination is "the first condition for what becomes of a person" (the *will* being the second and decisive condition) (*PC,* 186). It is not surprising, then, that God would engage the imagination in order to draw the self out into faithful existence. Anti-Climacus illustrates this with a story about a young man becoming a Christian. The youth starts out with his imagination charged with a vision of Christ, and even though this path becomes more difficult than he could have anticipated, God uses the imagination to draw him out, to help him persevere, and to transform the young person "little by little" (*PC,* 192–93). Through the imagination, Christ draws unto himself from on high.[18] This is how truth—the higher—draws to itself. But it is another matter with the lower.

Imagination and Temptation

Anti-Climacus writes that there are many things that seek to draw us to themselves—the seductive power of pleasure, the multiplicity of distractions, the concerns of the moment, busyness, as well as careless light-mindedness and brooding heavy-mindedness (*PC,* 158). But that which is not in itself—in other words, emptiness, nothingness, and vanity—can only entice through deception. All of these things trade in deception, and ultimately draw us away from ourselves; they aim to destroy rather than constitute the self. And if something draws (*drage*) to itself deceptively (*bedragende*), or draws only in order to deceive, then it does not truly draw to itself (*PC,* 157). Anti-Climacus does not deny that the seductive exhibits a quasi-drawing effect, noting that when the lower deceives, it "does not draw, it draws *downward*" (*PC,* 159).[19]

It is easier than we think to be deceived in this way. Anti-Climacus describes the danger of lingering in the moment of intrigue, of walking alongside the seduction for just a little longer. The peril of this situation cannot be overestimated, because when one lingers before the seductive, even giving a little finger is dangerous—it can easily take the whole hand (*PC,* 158). This can happen very quickly and easily: a temptation might flash into my horizon, far off in the distance. I catch the glimmer of a possibility in the periphery of my vision. Perhaps I begin to cherish the prospect. Or perhaps it fills me with pride—after all, I have developed a remarkable ability to withstand that temptation. It may be that I have not wrestled with it for some time; maybe I have even conquered it. That temptation seems to appeal to another me, in another lifetime. I once was weak; now I am strong.[20] Even better, maybe this particular temptation has never really held any appeal for me. Whatever my posture, this distance is deceptive; in an instant the temptation can traverse the distance and be standing on my doorstep. And once it has arrived, temptation has a stunning power to arrest and to fascinate. As Kierkegaard observes, the power of temptation lies in the moment: "It has frightful power for making one anxious and, as it were, for concentrating everything in a moment." But then, the very next moment the temptation is impotent (*JP* 4748). In the words of Dietrich Bonhoeffer, temptation "juts out" from the flow of our everyday awareness. We do not live in a constant state of temptation, but rather experience it as something that stands out. In terms reminiscent of Kierkegaard, Bonhoeffer describes temptation as the "sudden."[21]

Temptation often appears abruptly—accosting us, seemingly, out of nowhere. But it can also be given with less urgency and more ambiguity, such that the possibility shows itself with great subtlety: What precisely is it that is tempting me? What exactly do I find enticing? It can be difficult to articulate the temptation, to explicate precisely what attracts me. And in many cases, the temptation might barely reach beyond the threshold of my awareness. In cases like this, temptation draws me downward through the intrigue. It lurks in the periphery of my horizon; rather than striking out in a flash of attraction, it persists, pervading me like a pulse. In these subtler manifestations, temptation is like a dull ache, a discomfort, a slight troubling of the water. Yet this can also build over time. In its most intense forms, temptation appears with an urgency that fills the horizon. In the moments of its ascendance, it occludes everything else, clouding my perception, refusing to let me see beyond the possibility it discloses. At its highest pitch, temptation is given as though it were the only thing of significance. Everything else in my horizon seems to lose its capacity to appeal or call to me; every other object, concern, and responsibility retreats into a mundane flatness.

In short, temptation can advance with subtlety, as well as by laying siege with a full-frontal assault. In either case, it works on the imagination, enticing with seductive possibilities. As Paul Ricoeur observes, imagination presents the termination of need, the satisfaction of desire or impulse, without actually giving it.[22] Temptation is like an "advance emissary" of sin, announcing something that is neither fully present nor wholly absent. In temptation we are given a foretaste of sin in sketch form.[23] Imagination opens a field of possibilities already implicitly loaded with valuation, and which call for further evaluation, leading me to consider the legitimacy of my project.[24] In temptation, I imagine a possibility—not a neutral possibility, but a possibility in some way forbidden, over which I feel some compunction. And since I am not tempted by that which I perceive as impossible for me, temptation engages me and reveals me to myself as an "I can."

The sources, degrees, and objects of temptation obviously vary from person to person, but what is common to all these variations is the fact that the tempting possibility is given imaginatively. We have seen that the higher engages the imagination in order to draw to itself. But the lower also engages the imagination in order to "draw downward" to itself, using a fraudulent form of drawing to seduce the self downward into sin.

The Genesis of Temptation

Does temptation originate from outside or from within the subject? Is it exterior or interior? On the one hand, the variability of temptation from moment to moment, and from person to person, would suggest that temptation is not simply an objective property of external realities. On the other hand, the tempting objects seem to require certain attributes rather than others if they are to entice us, and if they are to sustain the seduction. For instance, I will probably not be tempted to gluttony by food that is stale or rotting.

In temptation, the intending subject plays an indispensable role in constituting the tempting object. The source of the temptation comes from within; the temptation is not self-generating, but draws its strength from the subject it tempts. Vigilius Haufniensis makes this point regarding the figure of the serpent in the temptation of Adam and Eve: Haufniensis rejects the interpretation that the serpent is an external source of the temptation, for as the epistle of James declares, "Each person is tempted by himself" (*CA*, 48). In the words of James, "One is tempted by one's own desire, being lured and enticed by it" (James 1:14).

That said, we cannot deny that we do experience temptation as something external, as something drawing us down to itself. In *The Symbolism of Evil,* Ricoeur notes that the symbol of the serpent is not exhausted by reducing temptation to the constituting subject. The serpent dramatizes something that is quite important in the phenomenon of temptation—namely, a sort of "quasi-externality." The serpent is external and already there. This indicates that the subject is not the absolute origin of evil, but that we experience temptation as an external seduction, which "lays siege" to us at the deepest levels, and to which we are tempted to yield.[25] In this regard, we find ourselves constituted as tempted subjects. Furthermore, Ricoeur also sees the serpent as showing that "every individual finds evil *already there;* nobody begins it absolutely." The serpent does not explain the origins of evil, but rather indicates that I experience evil as anterior to my particular temptation, as a phenomenon that precedes me, and afflicts human existence in general.[26]

This anteriority is evident when temptation arises intersubjectively—when one person tempts another, or prompts her on toward evil. Augustine recounts this experience in his theft from the pear tree: "Had I been alone," Augustine confesses, "I would not have done it." Others can prompt us on toward evil, even leading us to things that we would not normally look for on our own.[27] Yet temptation also often has an individualizing or even isolating effect, cutting oneself off from others. The first-person perspective of temptation makes me feel as though my own temptation is unique, that I am the exception; I start to resent my responsibilities to others. Yet there is a deep vanity in this delusion, which flatters itself with the supposed originality of one's tempting situation. Who, after all, can claim to have originated a new sin? Phenomenologically, once one overcomes the egocentricity of one's own particular temptation, what is striking about temptation is just how predictable it is. As the apostle Paul writes to the church in Corinth, "No temptation has seized you except what is common to humanity" (1 Cor. 10:13). If there is anything like a phenomenological buttress for the theological doctrine of original sin, it is this.

At any rate, we must keep in mind that while the concrete particulars of temptation vary between persons, the common feature among these variations is that the tempting possibility is given in and through the imagination. While the higher engages the imagination in order to draw to itself (a crucial point to remember, lest we denigrate the imagination per se as the source of temptation), the lower also engages the imagination, using a fraudulent form of drawing to seduce the self downward into sin.

Temptation as Deception

Temptation draws to itself by appealing to the imagination. Strictly speaking, however, Anti-Climacus does not allow that the lower can truly draw to itself. Instead, it deceives. Yet if temptation seduces through deception, should we conclude that sin is therefore a deficiency of knowledge? Anti-Climacus does not want to argue that ignorance is the fundamental reason that one succumbs to temptation. In fact, in *The Sickness unto Death* he explicitly rejects the view that sin is ignorance, which is the "Socratic definition."[28]

Anti-Climacus agrees that in a certain sense, sin is ignorance (*SUD,* 88). But he wants to dig deeper, to go back further in order to ask where ignorance comes from. The deficiency of the Socratic definition is its ambiguity about the origin of ignorance: Is ignorance original, such that one has never known or been capable of knowing? Or is ignorance a later acquisition? If ignorance is not original, then we need to ask how it was acquired. More pointedly, Anti-Climacus wants us to consider the possibility that the ignorance was self-inflicted. Was the person fully cognizant or not "when he started to obscure his knowing"? If not, then there was already a degree of ignorance at work, and we have to ask where that ignorance came from. But then the question simply returns, leading into an infinite regression. However, if the person *was* aware of the original suppression of his knowledge, then the issue of sin is not primarily a matter of knowledge but of *willing* (*SUD,* 88). The Socratic definition will not recognize the possibility that the self could willfully defy the truth it understands. According to Anti-Climacus this defiance can take the form of outright refusal, or it can take the more passive form of evasion and procrastination. As he observes, "the lower nature's power lies in stretching things out" (*SUD,* 94). Either way, there is a disruption in the transition from understanding to doing, and what the Socratic definition lacks is "a dialectical determinant" that is appropriate to dealing with this transition: namely, the will (*SUD,* 93).

In sum, while Anti-Climacus agrees that sin and evil have epistemic or cognitive effects, he does not locate their origin in epistemic deficiency. The epistemic effects of sin originate in the will. This leads directly into his claim that sin is not a negation—it is not the "merely negative," such as weakness, sensuousness, finitude, or ignorance (*SUD,* 96). Instead, sin is a position that one willfully takes against the truth. Anti-

Climacus is therefore correct to argue that being drawn by the lower is a matter of deception; to succumb to temptation is to say, falsely, "this is good."[29] But behind his concept of deception is the view that epistemic failure has deeper roots in the sinful will. Temptation is so effective in its deceptions because it draws its power from the subject's sinful propensity for *self*-deception. I can be deceived by temptation because at some level I want to be deceived.

This has methodological implications for a phenomenology of temptation. Anti-Climacus emphasizes the fact that "sin has its roots in willing, not in knowing, and this corruption of willing affects the individual's consciousness" (*SUD,* 95). If the ignorance of sin is at some level a matter of self-deception, this means that the subject's consciousness in the experience of temptation cannot be taken at face value. We cannot understand the experience of temptation directly, because we have to contend with the problem of *false* consciousness. For this reason, any phenomenology of temptation will need to recruit, as its indispensable ally, a hermeneutic of suspicion.[30]

There is another reason why a phenomenology of temptation must be hermeneutical, which emerges when we consider Anti-Climacus's claim that particular sins presuppose hereditary, or original, sin. Anti-Climacus describes hereditary sin as "the *prius* [antecedent state] in which sin presupposes itself" (*SUD,* 89). The particular individual's willed ignorance is not a new occurrence in the history of humanity; rather, there is a self-afflicted ignorance that precedes my own sin and obtains at the level of human existence in general (*SUD,* 93). Anti-Climacus does not undertake a deeper investigation of the doctrine of hereditary sin but instead proceeds up to its border.[31] He does not attempt to give a foundational proof for the doctrine of hereditary sin; after all, the reason Socrates lacked this presupposition is because "there has to be a revelation from God to show what sin is" (*SUD,* 89).[32] Once we broach the topic of revelation, though, we reach the limits of the phenomenology of temptation.

If, that is, we subscribe to the ideal of phenomenology as a rigorous science with no presuppositions. But what if the presupposition of revelation opens up new forms or aspects of phenomenality? This is what Anti-Climacus argues in *The Sickness unto Death*—namely, that self-consciousness is fundamentally altered by the revelation that one exists as a sinner before God and is responsible for one's decision regarding Christ (*SUD,* 113–14). Should we follow Ricoeur and think of this as a hermeneutical phenomenology, which recognizes that it begins in the hermeneutical circle and cannot avoid detours through the doctrines, symbols, images, and narratives that figure our understanding of sin and evil? Or perhaps Kierkegaard's texts themselves provide a model: in the introduction to *The Concept of Anxiety,* Haufniensis speaks of "a new science," a "second philosophy," and a "second ethics," which proceed from the dogmatic presupposition of sin. The first science is the speculative, immanent science that begins with metaphysics and trades in ideal possibilities (*CA,* 20–21, 23). For just this reason, however, it cannot explain the actuality of sin, because sin is a category that concerns the concrete, existing individual. And since the first ethics is "shipwrecked on the sinfulness of the single individual," it effectively "ignores sin" (*CA,* 20, 22).

By contrast, the second ethics begins by presupposing the actuality of sin in order to explain the sin of the single individual. It continues to aim for ideality in its account of sin, but whereas the first ethics starts from above and moves downward (from ideal possibility to actuality), the second ethics starts from below and moves upward (from existing actuality to ideality).

Can we speak, analogously, of a *second phenomenology*? This phenomenology would, I believe, have a distinctly hermeneutical orientation. Beginning one's investigation with explicit presuppositions does not entail a vicious circularity, but enables a virtuous hermeneutical circularity. Haufniensis recognizes something like this, arguing that the second ethics does not presuppose dogmatics simply to reiterate it, but to "complete it" such that "the presupposition is brought out" (*CA,* 24). There is a productive gain in understanding involved.

It is crucial to recognize, however, that this hermeneutical-phenomenological understanding would be fundamentally *interested.* It would not be the disengaged cognition of a transcendental ego, but the understanding of the concrete, existential thinker. As Anti-Climacus argues, citing another basic Socratic principle, there is a difference between understanding and *understanding.* "When someone does not do what is right, then neither has he understood what is right" (*SUD,* 92).[33] For Kierkegaard, then, genuine hermeneutical-phenomenological understanding is inescapably ethical; understanding is inseparable from *doing.* This helps explain why Haufniensis claims, a few pages earlier, that "sin does not properly belong in any science, but it is the subject of the sermon, in which the single individual speaks as the single individual to the single individual" (*CA,* 16). The sermon confronts the self here and now, in the middle of concrete existence; it does not supply disinterested knowledge but an exhortation to action. Understanding cannot be divorced from the question of the edifying, because truth is not true unless it is the truth *for me.*

With the question of the edifying, then, we again confront the question of phenomenology's limits. Kierkegaard rarely undertakes any sort of description without an eye to the prescriptive. Thus our inquiry into temptation can hardly be Kierkegaardian if we fail to consider the edifying in his remarks on temptation. Of course, Kierkegaard's edifying insights into temptation also contain much of phenomenological interest—particularly regarding the role of memory and forgetting in responding to temptation. In conclusion, then, I would like to suggest a few Kierkegaardian points on the importance of learning how to remember and forget properly in response to temptation.

3. Concluding Upbuilding Fragments: Temptation, Remembering, and Forgetting

We have already seen that Kierkegaard advises flight as the proper response to temptation. Like Joseph fleeing the seduction of Potiphar's wife, one must even leave his coat behind, hanging in temptation's hand, if necessary. This is rarely an easy thing to do, especially when temptation promises a familiar pleasure.[34] But the difficulty of flight becomes particularly apparent in the case of temptations that we cannot physically flee. Certain types of temptation—such as the temptation to hate, to bear a grudge, to be proud, and so on—are not location-specific. Resisting temptations of this sort is not an action that one can simply execute and be done with. Resisting these temptations feels more like treading water than leaving a room, because there is no change in the situation unless one stops struggling and drowns in the temptation.[35]

In this case, the challenge of fleeing is best understood as one of forgetting. But this too is a difficult achievement. How do you put something out of your mind? Deliberately trying to forget simply fixes a thought more firmly in view.[36] According to Anti-Climacus, the way to forget is to *remember* something else (*PC,* 152). Specifically, he advises the remembrance of Christ. Remembering Christ is part of being drawn to Christ, and it is intriguing to observe how Anti-Climacus ties this remembering to communion: the sacramental remembrance of eating the bread and drinking the wine exemplifies the way one ought to remember Christ and forget that which ought to be forgotten. This progresses as one is drawn more fully to Christ, and it informs every mundane undertaking. Equally intriguing is Anti-Climacus's metaphor of learning (and forgetting) a language: in being drawn to Christ, one will become "as forgetful as someone who in a foreign country has forgotten his mother tongue and makes no sense in speaking it" (*PC,* 153). As one is drawn to Christ, the grammar and vocabulary of one's existence is transformed.

The path of this transformation is a difficult one, since it is one of following after (*Efterfølgelse*) and imitating Christ. Imitation goes hand in hand with suffering, including the suffering of temptation. But the example of Christ is also encouraging when we remember that Christ was tempted in all things, and yet was without sin (Heb. 4:15). This is encouraging because Christ understands, from a first-person perspective, what temptation is like. In Christ, God possesses lived experience of temptation. Commenting on this passage, Kierkegaard asks: "Where in the world does one find this deep sympathy? . . . This is a sympathy of greater worth than all the sensitivities in the world" (*JP* 4745). Remembering this sympathy is part of the imitation of Christ.

Of course, the *theologia crucis* ("theology of the cross") implied in Kierkegaard's category of imitation could very easily become a *theologia gloriae* ("theology of glory") if imitation were a matter of heroically performing a repertoire of Christlike actions. Christ is the prototype, but he is also the Savior. Thus grace is crucial because we continue to give in to temptation, and we need forgiveness. Here again we confront the difficulty of becoming nothing before God. *The Sickness unto Death* gives a profound description of someone in despair after having given in to temptation: he loudly proclaims that he will never forgive himself, as though this is a sign of a deep spirit. But it is merely subterfuge. What he cannot bear is the wound to his pride. We would like to be proud of ourselves, to be self-sufficient, and the source of our own continuity in the good (*SUD,* 111–12). We would like to be able to withstand temptation, to be great-souled selves who have no need of forgiveness. This is why, in the moment of remorse that follows the sin, we would like to encounter the temptation again: disappointed with ourselves, we pray *lead us into temptation!*—so that we can prove ourselves stronger the next time around.[37] In remembering Christ, we remember that we are forgiven; but by remembering that we are human beings—fallen, fallible, and frail—we carry around with us the recognition that we are prone to succumb to temptation.[38] And remembering that is a crucial step in learning how to flee.

By concluding with these edifying reflections, we find ourselves in a rather interesting position: to paraphrase the opening lines of *The Sickness unto Death,* these recommendations are too rigorously phenomenological to be upbuilding, and too upbuilding to be rigorously phenomenological. The same might be said of Kierkegaard's authorship as a whole. But having said that, Kierkegaard's writings go a long way in showing that this intersection of the phenomenological and the edifying is a very productive place to think.

Notes

1. Adding to the complexity is the fact that "temptation" is said in different senses. In everyday language we speak of being "tempted" in a nonmoral sense. For instance, I might say that I am "tempted" to walk home rather than take the train. In other words, I am deliberating over whether this is the best decision. (See Paul M. Hughes, "The Logic of Temptation," *Philosophia* 29 [May 2002]: 91). Another sense of temptation concerns being *tested* or *tried;* thus certain translations of Gen. 22:1 speak of God "tempting" Abraham (see note 4 below). Our primary concern in the present paper, however, will be the most common sense of temptation: namely, the event of being enticed or solicited to sin or commit moral evil.

2. For a thematic overview of spiritual trial that examines many of the passages we discuss here, see Louise Caroll Keeley, "Spiritual Trial in the Thought of Kierkegaard," in *International Kierkegaard Commentary* 12: *Concluding Unscientific Postscript to "Philosophical Fragments,"* ed. Robert L. Perkins (Macon, Ga.: Mercer University Press, 1997), 307–28.

3. On a strictly formal level it is possible to describe temptation as being enticed by the lower, without being committed to a theology or ontology that determines what the lower and higher actually are. Thus, the Nietzschean could recognize the religious as a tempting lowness, while the Christian would see it as the higher.

4. It is intriguing to observe that de Silentio also writes of God "tempting" Abraham. In *Fear and Trembling,* the term "temptation" works in two different ways. First, Johannes de Silentio writes of God tempting Abraham (*FT,* 9, 10, 19, 71, 77). The Hongs note that *Fear and Trembling* uses four closely related terms to speak of the way God tests Abraham by commanding him to sacrifice Isaac. These words are "to tempt," "temptation" (*friste, Fristelse*) (21), "to test," "test" (*prove, Prøve*) (31), "to try" (*forsøge*) (32), and "ordeal" (*Prøvelse*) (22). (See *FT,* 341n2.) Second, however, de Silentio also writes of the ethical as a temptation, as the lower appealing to Abraham during his ordeal.

5. Christendom is a temptation by the lower because it allows the self to benefit from the appearance of religiosity, while avoiding the unpleasant consequences and demands of following Christ. This sort of spiritless existence is the surest way to avoid the struggles of spiritual trial (*CA,* 117). Not surprisingly, in Christendom the absence of spiritual trial is taken for a sure indication of progress and maturity (*JP* 4382).

6. For instance, earlier in the *Postscript* Climacus notes that some individuals become so bound by evil habits that the transition from thinking to acting, from possibility to actuality, becomes so quick as to be undetectable (*CUP,* 340). In keeping with this, we might add that just as one's response to temptation can

become habitual, the particular temptations that afflict different selves also arise in continuity with habit and practice. But we should also keep in mind Kierkegaard's category of the sudden, since temptation has a way of jutting out, and taking one out of the flow of everyday life.

7. For an illuminating comparison of *Anfechtung* in Luther and spiritual trial in Kierkegaard, see Craig Hinkson, "Luther and Kierkegaard: Theologians of the Cross," *International Journal of Systematic Theology* 3, no. 1 (March 2001): 27–45. Also see "The Lightning and the Earthquake: Kierkegaard on the *Anfechtung* of Luther," *Heythrop Journal* 47, no. 4 (October 2006): 562–78.

8. Kierkegaard does believe that this moment will come: "When this will come to fruition for him or this will be granted to him, no man can say. One thing is sure, and every man of experience knows this, that grace too has its time and its times, that there comes a moment [*Øieblikke*] when that which a man has sought after year in and year out suddenly is granted and comes to fruition" (*JP* 4370). What is important, however, is for the self to recognize that this moment does not lie within the scope of its power or possibilities.

9. For instance, this is the appropriate response when the Christian is undergoing spiritual trial in the form of anxiety over the possibility of going to communion. Haufniensis discusses the communion scenario in *The Concept of Anxiety,* where it increases in complexity because of his analysis of the sympathetic and antipathetic moments that characterize anxiety; the complexity is compounded by the fact that he is also discussing the demonic or anxiety before the good: "Whoever is in a religious spiritual trial wants to go on to that from which the spiritual trial would keep him away, while the demonic, according to his stronger will (the will of unfreedom), wants to get away from it, while the weaker will in him wants to go on to it" (*CA,* 143).

10. "Spiritual trial can be fought only with the rashness of faith, which charges head-on" (*JP* 4378). Likewise: "If it is spiritual trial, go straight toward it, trusting in God and Christ" (*JP* 4023). The relation between faith and spiritual trial is more enigmatic in *Fear and Trembling,* where Johannes de Silentio seems to define spiritual trial differently, as being drawn beyond the limits of the universal into ineffable singularity, interiority, and hiddenness. On one level this resembles Abraham, or the knight of faith, but de Silentio wants to avoid calling Abraham's story a spiritual trial (see *FT,* 31, 54, 56). He suggests that the singularity of spiritual trial is not genuine—it is not from God, and thus cannot truly claim to be absolute, nor can it entail a true teleological suspension of the ethical (*FT,* 70, 115).

11. Vigilius Haufniensis is highly critical of the notion of an abstract *liberum arbitrium,* a liberty of indifference that is unimpeded or unconditioned by antecedent factors (*CA,* 49, 112, 236n58). In his journals, Kierkegaard writes that "a perfectly disinterested will (*equilibrium*) is a nothing, a chimera" (*JP* 1241, 1249).

12. That said, Haufniensis also notes that in another sense freedom is already actualized as soon as it is possible. Freedom is like God in that sense: as soon as it is possible, it is actual (*CA,* 22).

13. "As unfree, the individual in the bondage of sin exists in dis-integration,

and his anxiety is about a deeper unfreedom and a deeper dis-integration." Ronald L. Hall, "Language and Freedom: Kierkegaard's Analysis of the Demonic in *The Concept of Anxiety*," in *International Kierkegaard Commentary* 8: *"The Concept of Anxiety,"* ed. Robert L. Perkins (Macon, Ga.: Mercer University Press, 1985), 159.

14. See Anti-Climacus's description of the demonic in *The Sickness unto Death:* "What demonic madness—the thought that most infuriates him is that eternity could get the notion to deprive him of his misery" (*SUD,* 72).

15. Which is not to deny that we can be tempted to commit the good for the wrong reasons; for instance, I might tell the truth with malicious intent. But this is not properly an instance of doing the good thing. See Hughes, "Logic of Temptation," 99, 101. Moreover, we have already noted that some translations of the Bible speak of God tempting Abraham, in the sense of *trying* him. But this has a different sense than that of being tempted to commit the good—that is, being inclined to commit the good, but having scruples that it is wrong.

16. "Tryin' to Get to Heaven," from the album *Time Out of Mind.* I like to think that this line is a response to the lyric from "Like a Rolling Stone," which proposes that "when you got nothing, you got nothing to lose."

17. This account of the constitution of the self reveals the interplay between divine and human freedom: since, according to Anti-Climacus, to be a self is to be free, it is important that Christ's drawing not simply overpower freedom; instead, it posits a choice—namely, the choice to take up responsibility for oneself in repentance (*PC,* 159). At the same time, we are able to take up responsibility in this way because Christ, in drawing us, enables us to repent and respond. With this model, Anti-Climacus manages to describe the interplay between divine and human freedom without depicting it in competitive terms, as though human freedom increases at the expense of divine freedom or vice versa. Moreover, it is also crucial that the event of being drawn not abolish the selfhood of that which is drawn. Anti-Climacus rejects the idea that the self loses "all its own existence [*Bestaaen*] by being drawn into that which drew it to itself" (*PC,* 159). Christ does not draw to himself in order to obliterate the self, but with the desire to constitute the self in all its fullness.

18. But paradoxically, through lowliness and abasement.

19. My emphasis.

20. Dietrich Bonhoeffer notes that when Scripture speaks of temptation, it "does not have to do with the testing of my strength, for it is the very essence of temptation in the Bible that all my strength—to my horror, and without my being able to do anything about it—is turned against me . . . Before there can be any testing of my powers, I have been robbed of them." "Temptation," in *Creation and Fall/Temptation: Two Biblical Studies,* trans. John C. Fletcher (New York: Touchstone, 1983), 112.

21. Ibid., 112–13; and *CA,* 129–32.

22. Paul Ricoeur, *Freedom and Nature: The Voluntary and the Involuntary,* trans. Erazim V. Kohák (Evanston, Ill.: Northwestern University Press, 1966), 96.

23. The preceding is adapted from Ricoeur's *Freedom and Nature,* 101, which deals more broadly with the role of the imagination in anticipating pleasure.

24. Ibid., 73.

25. Paul Ricoeur, *The Symbolism of Evil,* trans. Emerson Buchanan (Boston: Beacon Press, 1967), 256.

26. Ibid., 257.

27. Saint Augustine, *Confessions* (bk. 2, viii, 16), trans. Henry Chadwick (Oxford: Oxford University Press, 1991), 33. As Paul M. Hughes notes, the social and cultural influences that give shape to particular temptations is an important consideration in its own right ("Logic of Temptation," 96, 102).

28. The identification of sin and ignorance is the flip side of the Socratic view that identifies knowledge and virtue (*SUD,* 179n23).

29. Compare *Freedom and Nature,* 102, where Ricoeur uses this phrase more broadly to describe our affirmation of an anticipated pleasure.

30. On the hermeneutics of suspicion, see Ricoeur, "The Critique of Religion," in *The Philosophy of Paul Ricoeur: An Anthology of His Work,* ed. Charles E. Reagan and David Stewart (Boston: Beacon Press, 1978). Also his "The Conflict of Interpretations," in *Freud and Philosophy: An Essay on Interpretation,* trans. Denis Savage (New Haven, Conn.: Yale University Press, 1970). Other helpful developments of this theme are Garrett Green, *Theology, Hermeneutics, and Imagination: The Crisis of Interpretation at the End of Modernity* (Cambridge: Cambridge University Press, 2000); and Merold Westphal, *Suspicion and Faith: The Religious Uses of Modern Atheism* (New York: Fordham University Press, 1998).

31. I believe he makes this move for fear of sidetracking his discussion; Anti-Climacus has surely read *The Concept of Anxiety,* and knows the endless complexities of the problem of hereditary sin. I do not think he avoids the topic because of strict scruples about preserving philosophical purity or maintaining theological neutrality.

32. Thus Anti-Climacus does not stage a *battle royale* between the Christian doctrine of sin and its competitors. One could argue, as Socrates does in the *Phaedo* (75d–e), that we forget our knowledge of the form at the moment of our birth. One might also go further and argue that original ignorance stems from our immortal souls undergoing a "fall" into physical bodies. Alternately, one could take a sort of Manichean view, that our ignorance is not self-willed, but instead the result of an evil demiurge afflicting us with falsehood. The point is that alternate accounts of this original ignorance are possible.

33. One also finds this point stated and restated, almost ad nauseam, by Johannes Climacus in the *Postscript.*

34. Augustine provides a striking image in the *Confessions,* where he describes the way his old loves call out to him: "'Are you getting rid of us?' And 'from this moment we shall never be with you again, not for ever and ever.' And 'from this moment this and that are forbidden to you for ever and ever'" (*Confessions,* bk. 8, xi, 26).

35. This is Oscar Wilde's point in his oft-cited remark that "the only way to get rid of a temptation is to yield to it."

36. In a journal entry Kierkegaard quotes Montaigne to this effect: "Nothing fastens a thing firmer in our memory than the wish—to forget it" (*JP* 2779).

37. This is why Bonhoeffer suggests that the prayer "lead us not into temptation" cannot be prayed by the natural man, who wants to prove his strength ("Temptation," 111).

38. One vivid example of overconfidence in the face of temptation is in bk. 6 of Augustine's *Confessions.* Proudly presuming himself morally above the bloodlust of the gladiatorial games, Alypius allows his friends to drag him to the amphitheater. Alypius sees it as a challenge, in which he will demonstrate his discipline and self-control: "I shall be as one not there, and so I shall overcome both you and the games." As Brian Stock describes it, Alypius "thinks that by closing his eyes he can be present and absent at the same time." *Augustine the Reader: Meditation, Self-Knowledge, and the Ethics of Interpretation* (Cambridge, Mass.: Harvard University Press, 1996), 85. But while he keeps his eyes closed, Alypius hears the crowd roar as a man goes down; "overcome by curiosity," he opens his eyes—still presuming to be "strong enough to despise whatever he saw and to conquer it." But he is quickly taken into the frenzy and becomes a devotee of these games. According to Augustine, Alypius was vulnerable because he relied on his own fortitude rather than on God (*Confessions,* bk. 6, viii, 13). Of course, Augustine is not implying that Alypius should have attended the games but relied on God; in this case, remembering one's fallibility would be a matter of avoiding the temptation altogether—in other words, preemptive fleeing.

The Meaning of "Negative Phenomena" in Kierkegaard's Theory of Subjectivity

Darío González

In one of his earliest autobiographical notes, Kierkegaard introduces what can be considered as a programmatic principle for his whole philosophical oeuvre:

> The crucial thing is to find a truth that is truth *for me,* to find *the idea for which I am willing to live and die.* Of what use would it be to me to discover a so-called objective truth . . . Of what use would it be to me for truth to stand before me, cold and naked, not caring whether or not I acknowledged it, making me uneasy rather than trustingly receptive. I certainly do not deny that I still accept an *imperative of knowledge* and that through it men may be influenced, but *then it must come alive in me,* and *this* is what I now recognize as the most important of all. (*JP* 5100/*SKS* 17, 24)

"Only then," he adds in the margin, "does one have an inner experience" (*JP* 5100/*SKS* 17, 24). It is certainly not difficult to comprehend those sentences against the background of the opposition between objective and subjective thinking, as some of the pseudonyms define it in later writings. Another interesting way to put the same problem, however, would be to investigate how the product of a certain "imperative of knowledge," how the possible object of a general knowledge, can become the content of an "inner experience." What is true "for me," Kierkegaard seems to tell us, *must constitute itself as a truth within the sphere of an ethical relationship:* "What I really need is to get clear about *what I am to do,* not what I must know, except insofar as knowledge must precede every act. What matters is to find my purpose, to see what it really is that God wills that *I* shall do . . ." (*JP* 5100/*SKS* 17, 24).

Nine years after the redaction of this journal entry, the same motif reappears in two parallel, albeit distinct, contexts. On the one hand, at the beginning of the third series of upbuilding discourses from 1844, Kierkegaard opposes the "indifferent" character of objective truth to what he calls a "concerned truth" (*EUD,* 233/*SKS* 5, 233), that is, a truth that is addressed to a human being as an individual: a truth—we might say—that takes into account the contingency of the individual's ethical existence. On the other hand, in the section of *The Concept of Anxiety* devoted to "the demonic" or "anxiety about the good," the pseudonymous author describes the situation in which "truth" fails to constitute itself as a truth "for" the individual. After mentioning a series of attitudes towards the religious—"arbitrariness," "unbelief," "mockery of religion," "superstition," "servility," "sanctimoniousness"—he concludes: "The negative phenomena lack certitude precisely because they are in anxiety about the content" (*CA,* 139/*SKS* 4, 431).

This characterization of "*negative phenomena*" offers the interest of pointing to the ethical determination of individual life as the fundamental condition for the constitution of an existential truth. It is worth noting that, in *The Concept of Anxiety,* the very discussion of the phenomenon of the demonic takes place in the intersection of two series of philosophical questions concerning, respectively, the experience of *truth* and the experience of *freedom:* "viewed intellectually, the content of freedom is truth, and truth makes man free. For this reason, truth is the work of freedom, and in such a way that freedom constantly brings forth truth" (*CA,* 138/*SKS* 4, 439). In fact, this is one of the passages in which Kierkegaard comes closest to a determination of his theory of existence as a phenomenology of freedom. Its most important presupposition is succinctly indicated in the same paragraph: "*truth is for the particular individual only as he himself produces it in action*" (*CA,* 138/*SKS* 4, 439; my emphasis). As we will attempt to show, the thesis concerning the "negative" character of the experiences that "are in anxiety about the content" can be explained as a development of this formula on two parallel levels. Firstly, the truth that is not truth in itself but only truth "for the particular individual" is "produced" within the individual's experience of his or her own existence as *untruth.* Secondly, the "action" in which the individual experiences his or her own freedom, insofar as its "content" (i.e., its truth) can paradoxically be something other than truth, is determined as the real possibility of *unfreedom.*

1. Infinity and Inwardness

Although it is perfectly clear that negative phenomena are, generally speaking, phenomena of anxiety, the philosophical conceptualization of their "negative" character goes beyond the specific discussion of the demonic as "anxiety about the good" and even beyond the scope of *The Concept of Anxiety*. Our double development of the above-mentioned principle is in itself an anticipation of the theory of existence proposed by Kierkegaard in other texts and under other pseudonyms. As a matter of fact, the most decisive explanation of the "negativity" of existence is the one given in the *Postscript:* "The negativity that is in existence, or rather the negativity of the existing subject (which his thinking must render essentially in an adequate form), is *grounded in the subject's synthesis, in his being an existing infinite spirit*" (*CUP*, 82/*SKS* 7, 81; my emphasis).[1] As soon as we focus on the last words of this sentence, it becomes evident that our question cannot be properly developed unless it is explicitly referred to the structure of the "synthesis" that characterizes existence. Such a synthesis is determined here as a contradiction, namely the fact that *existing* spirit is at the same time *infinite* spirit, or, as it is said in the same paragraph, "the prodigious contradiction that the eternal becomes, that it comes into existence [*at det Evige vorder, at det bliver til*]" (*CUP*, 82/*SKS* 7, 81). Thus, "the existing subject is eternal, but as existing he is temporal" (*CUP*, 82/*SKS* 7, 82).[2] The description of this contradictory synthesis is a presupposition for the analysis of anxiety, which in the 1844 treatise was associated with the conception of man as both a body/soul and a time/eternity synthesis. In the *Postscript,* nevertheless, "the subject's synthesis" is more precisely the basis for a comprehension of the subject's "existing-relation to the truth." It is with respect to this relation to truth that "the existing subjective thinker is just as negative as positive" (*CUP*, 80/*SKS* 7, 80). The existing subject, in other words, can only "think" or comprehend his or her own existence by (positively) being aware of his or her (negative) relation to truth, insofar as this truth concerns or even *is* the existing subject's as such: "He, existing, is continually just as negative as positive, for his positivity consists in the continued inward deepening in which he is cognizant of the negative" (*CUP*, 84/*SKS* 7, 84). Here it is important to notice that the "negativity" of the subject's relation to his or her own truth can be understood as the *open* character of the possibilities that constitute his or her existence. The expression of each one of those possibilities is not yet the truth that the individual's existence as such *is.*

> To be continually in the process of becoming in this way is the illusiveness of the infinite in existence. It could bring a sensate person to

> despair, for one continually feels an urge to have something finished, but this urge is of evil and must be renounced. The perpetual process of becoming is the uncertainty of earthly life, in which everything is uncertain. (*CUP,* 86/*SKS* 7, 85)

The existing subject's negative relation to truth is in fact an expression of his or her *uncertainty* with respect to his or her own being. As a matter of fact, this formulation implies that "the infinite and the eternal are the only certainty" (*CUP,* 82/*SKS* 7, 81) and that, by virtue of its concrete existence in time, the infinite presents itself as something essentially "illusive" (*CUP,* 82/*SKS* 7, 81). Climacus's emphasis on the *contradictory* character of the synthesis and, as a consequence, on the existing subject's *negative* relation to the truth of that synthesis, has in itself a polemical import with respect to the attempt to comprehend existence on the basis of "positive thinking," that is, on the basis of either "sensate certainty," "historical knowledge," or "speculative" deduction (*CUP,* 81/*SKS* 7, 80–81). Applied to existence, any of these three forms of positive certainty supposes that the individual remains unaware of his or her own negative relation to truth. In that sense, "negative thinkers" have at least "the advantage that they have something positive, namely this, that they are aware of the negative . . . By being positively secured, the subject is indeed fooled" (*CUP,* 81–82/*SKS* 7, 81). Taking into account the strategic position of Climacus's writings with respect to Kierkegaard's aesthetic and religious authorship, what he calls here "negative thinking," can be referred both to Socratic irony and to Christian faith as two parallel forms of uncertainty or, in other terms, two forms of awareness of the negative. Whereas Socratic uncertainty with respect to the outer world is a condition for the discovering of subjectivity as self-relationship, the Christian view is based on the existing subject's uncertainty with respect to the effective concretization of that self-relationship. In *The Concept of Irony,* Socratic irony has precisely "nothingness" as its goal, and its result is the purely formal delimitation of subjectivity with respect to the external world. The uncertainty presupposed by Christian faith, on the contrary, does not operate on the existing subject's knowledge concerning the world but on his or her knowledge concerning him- or herself. Already in his dissertation on Socrates, Kierkegaard qualifies this last form of uncertainty as *humor,* a phenomenon understood as a "skepticism" that is essentially higher than ironic skepticism. The limit of knowledge indicated by this skeptical position is not just the limit between subjectivity and objectivity but the limit between "man" and "God-man": not the subject's "finitude" but the subject's "sinfulness"; not his or her "ignorance" with respect to the world but his or her relation to the "absurdum" of

Christian faith (*CI,* 329/*SKS* 1, 357). Climacus applies a similar topology when he presents, in the *Postscript,* irony as "the *confinium* [border territory] between the aesthetic and the ethical" and humor as "the *confinium* between the ethical and the religious" (*CUP,* 501–2/*SKS* 7, 455). This remark is important in order to clarify the relation between, on the one hand, the conception of negativity as basically related to the phenomenon of uncertainty and, on the other hand, the negativity that characterizes the experiences of anxiety and despair. By focusing on the first conception, the author of *The Concept of Irony, Philosophical Fragments,* and *Postscript* seems to describe the area in which something like a "theory of subjectivity" can be established as a particular discipline: "irony" is in this context the negative condition for subjectivity as finite self-relationship, as much as "humor" is the negative condition for subjectivity as an existing subject's relation to his or her own "infinite validity." As a matter of fact, Climacus's "humor" implies and presupposes Socrates' "irony."[3] Climacus's question concerning the task of "becoming a Christian" is explicitly addressed to a subject that, by definition, is a post-Socratic one. The exposition of the religious notions of truth and subjectivity in Climacus's writings, as the author himself points out in *Philosophical Fragments,* constitutes a sort of "experiment," guided by the question of whether those notions can be fully displayed on the basis of their comparison with the Socratic view. The result of that philosophical experiment is the conviction that, in a religious context, truth and subjectivity are determined by a negativity that is in any case deeper than the negativity of irony. In other words, the negative character of religious subjectivity does not consist in the simple contradiction between the essence and the phenomenon (*CI,* 247/*SKS* 1, 286)—which would imply the possibility of a "negative knowledge" concerning the essence—but in a negativity that affects the very constitution of the self as a phenomenon. As soon as he repeats and transcends the skepticism of irony toward the skepticism of humor, Climacus moves from the nonknowledge that constitutes the "beginning" of subjectivity to the realm of *passion,* in which subjectivity reaches its extreme manifestation: "Subjectivity culminates in passion, Christianity is paradox; paradox and passion fit each other perfectly, and paradox perfectly fits a person situated in the extremity of existence [*i Existentsens Yderste*]" (*CUP,* 230/*SKS* 7, 210). It is obvious that the parallel analyses of anxiety and despair in *The Concept of Anxiety* and *The Sickness unto Death* are descriptions of that "extremity" of existence.

The transformation of the Socratic question into a specifically religious problem ("becoming a Christian") has important consequences with regard to the possible interpretation of Kierkegaard's "theory of subjectivity" as "ethics." Not by chance the discussion of the phenomenon of anxiety in the 1844 treatise develops itself toward what the pseudonym Vigilius Haufniensis calls a "second ethics." Even if we accept Climacus's characterization of irony and humor as the "*confinia*" (border territories) between the "spheres" of existence, it is clear that the sphere that these phenomena help delimit according to his topology, namely the *ethical* sphere, is nothing but the border territory between a self-forgotten subjectivity and an existing subject that has the possibility of radically transforming him- or herself. This was the conclusion to which Kierkegaard already had arrived, under another pseudonym, at the end of the *Stages on Life's Way:*

> The ethical sphere is only a transition sphere, and therefore its highest expression is repentance as negative action. The esthetic sphere is the sphere of immediacy, the ethical the sphere of requirement (and this requirement is so infinite that the individual always goes bankrupt [*at Individet altid gaaer fallit*]), the religious the sphere of fulfillment, but, please note, not a fulfillment such as when one fills an alms box or a sack with gold, for repentance has specifically created a boundless space, and as a consequence the religious contradiction: simultaneously to be out on 70,000 fathoms of water and yet be joyful. (*SLW,* 476–77/ *SKS* 6, 439)

As *negative action,* repentance marks the point in which a purely "ethical" theory of subjectivity comes to its end. If a hypothetical "second ethics" is possible, it should start by the description of those phenomena in which "the individual always goes bankrupt." And that happens when the ethical requirement becomes "infinite," that is, when the measure of the requirement is no longer the universality of a law but the singularity of a self-relationship that is at the same time a misrelationship. The individual's bankruptcy coincides with what the author of *The Concept of Anxiety* defines as the "shipwreck" of the first ethics "on the sinfulness of the single individual" (*CA,* 20/*SKS* 4, 328). It is clear that the notion of sinfulness is here linked to a radical skepticism with respect to the self's possibility to fulfill the ethical task, as soon as the imperative "to become oneself" expresses the requirement of an *infinite* becoming.

I have advisedly suggested that the criterion or measure of the infinite ethical requirement is not the *relation to a law* but a *self-relationship.* The suspension of the individual's relation to the law has its first expression in Socratic irony, not only in the sense that Socrates himself "was unable to contract any real relationship to the established order," but also because his irony "tipped one individual after the other out of the substantial actuality of the state" (*CI,* 178/*SKS* 1, 225–26).[4] But even if this negative operation was a condition for the individual's introspective relationship to itself, the kind of subjectivity that is at issue here is still "abstract." This point has been made sufficiently clear in the treatise on irony:

> Now it is certainly true that the phrase γνῶθι σαυτόν [know yourself] can designate subjectivity in its fullness, inwardness in its utterly infinite wealth. But for Socrates this self-knowledge was not so copious; it actually contained nothing more than the separating, the singling out, of what later became the object of knowledge. The phrase "know yourself" means: separate yourself from the other [*fra Andet*]. Precisely because this self did not exist prior to Socrates, it was once again an oracular pronouncement corresponding to Socrates' consciousness that commanded him to know himself. But it was reserved for a later age to go deeply into this self-knowledge. (*CI,* 177–78/*SKS* 1, 225)

In spite of the obvious application of the Hegelian vocabulary in this passage, Kierkegaard's allusion to a "later age" and to the "utterly infinite wealth" of concrete subjectivity is not just a reference to the subject of scientific knowledge. On the contrary, he already has in mind the question concerning the difference between Socratic and Christian truth. What becomes "infinite" in this case is not the object of knowledge but the meaning of the self's relation to itself,[5] that is, in Climacus's terms, the individual's self-relationship as infinite inwardness.

But both the difference and the articulation between Socrates' and Climacus's notions of subjectivity can be explained in yet another way. Following the conception of Christianity presented in *Philosophical Fragments* and the *Postscript,* it is possible to say that the "infinite" character of concrete subjectivity consists in the fact that subjectivity now *has a history* understood as the constitution of meaning in time. In a parallel fashion, the abstractness of Socrates' ironic subjectivity is linked to its *momentary* character. In Socrates, "existence in temporality has no decisive significance" (*CUP,* 206/*SKS* 7, 188). The "ironic" separation of the individual with respect to "substantial actuality" constitutes at the same time an act of isolation with respect to the positivity of world history, and it is precisely this isolation that gives the individual the formal possibility—which in Socrates is *only* a possibility—of developing an inwardly historical relation to him- or herself. Thus, we may conclude that the very structure of the "synthesis" in which the negative character of subjectivity is grounded (*CUP,* 82/*SKS* 7, 81) depends on the role that *temporality* plays in the constitution of the individual's relation to him- or herself. Delimited by "irony" and "humor," between the empty requirement of self-knowledge and the infinitely passionate task of becoming oneself, Climacus's theory of subjectivity has to deal with *the existential experience of time* as something that, on the one hand, cannot be reduced to world history, and whose horizon, on the other hand, is determined by the representation of eternity. We can understand now in which sense "historical knowledge"—that is, strictly speaking, world historical knowledge—is one of the forms of "positive thinking" dismissed by Climacus in his "unscientific" *Postscript* (*CUP*, 81/*SKS* 7, 80).

2. The Primacy of the Future

But his critique of positive thinking is also a critique of the idealistic postulation of a thinking subject that pretends to adopt the point of view of eternity. Here again, Climacus's description of existential temporality is his best argument against abstract thinking. In the terms of the interpretation I propose, the most important premise of Kierkegaard's nonspeculative theory of subjectivity is the thesis according to which the existing person *is only related to the eternal through his or her own experience of time,* that is, not as the eternal but *as the future.* Interestingly enough, this principle is exposited both in the chapter of *The Concept of Anxiety* devoted to the human "synthesis" and in the section of the *Postscript* devoted to "actual subjectivity":

> The future in a certain sense signifies more than the present and the past, because in a certain sense the future is the whole of which the past is a part, and the future can in a certain sense signify the whole. This is because the eternal first signifies the future or because the future is the incognito in which the eternal, even though it is incommensurable with time, nevertheless preserves its association with time. (*CA*, 89/*SKS* 4, 392)

> For an existing person, is not eternity not eternity but the future, whereas eternity is eternity only for the Eternal, who is not in a process of becoming? . . . where everything is in a process of becoming, where only so much of the eternal is present that it can have a constraining effect in the passionate decision, where the *eternal* relates itself as the *future* to the *person in a process of becoming*—there the absolute disjunction belongs. (*CUP*, 306–7/*SKS* 7, 279–80)

Climacus's characterization of "actual and ethical subjectivity [*den virkelige Subjektivitet, den ethiske*]" (*CUP*, 301–3/*SKS* 7, 274–76) as the relation between a "person in a process of becoming [*den Vordende*]" and the representation of the eternal corresponds to the above-quoted allusion to "the subject's synthesis," which is his or her "being an existing infinite spirit" (*CUP*, 82/*SKS* 7, 81). The existential *inter-esse* (between-being) that, according to Climacus, contradicts the abstract identity of being and thinking (*CUP*, 314/*SKS* 7, 286) is therefore the object of an "indirect communication." From an anthropological point of view, however, the *inter-esse* of existence is the expression of a "process of becoming" (*Vorden*) articulated by the distinction between the present time, the past time, and the future time. This point of view had been particularly developed in *The Concept of Anxiety*. As soon as we admit that "the subject's synthesis" or the indirect relation between becoming and eternity, as Climacus explains it in the *Postscript*, is the ground of "the negativity of the existing subject," it seems necessary to investigate in which sense this negativity affects the "existing infinite spirit" as a *temporally determined* self-relationship.

Both in *The Concept of Anxiety* and in the *Postscript*, the exposition of the Christian notion of hereditary sin lies at the center of Kierkegaard's theories on temporality. "Hereditary sin" is presented here not only as a dogmatic issue but also as something *experienced by a historical being*. In *The Concept of Anxiety*, the "history" that begins with sin is first of all the history of the "race," but this is only true in the sense that "at every moment, the individual is both himself and the race . . . As the history of the race moves on, the individual begins constantly anew, because he is both himself and the race, and by this, in turn, the history of the race" (*CA*, 28–29/*SKS* 4, 335). Climacus replaces the concept of history with the concept of coming into existence:

> Let us now call the individual's untruth *sin*. Viewed eternally, he cannot be in sin or be presupposed to have been eternally in sin. Therefore, by coming into existence (for the beginning was that subjectivity is untruth), he becomes a sinner. He is not born as a sinner in the sense that he is presupposed to be a sinner before he is born, but he is born in sin and as a sinner. Indeed, we could call this *hereditary* sin. (*CUP*, 208/*SKS* 7, 191)

> Sin is the new existence-medium. "To exist" generally signifies only that by having come into existence the individual does exist and is becoming; now it signifies that by having come into existence he has become a sinner. (*CUP*, 583/*SKS* 7, 530)

Sin renders the individual's inwardness infinite, insofar as the consequence of sin is that the individual "is prevented from taking himself back into eternity through recollection." In other words, the individual cannot "take himself out of existence" since "the back door of recollection is forever closed" (*CUP,* 208/*SKS* 7, 191). This remark makes sense in the context of what we have characterized above as Climacus's transformation of the Socratic notion of subjectivity. Socratic irony presupposes that "there is continually the possibility of taking oneself back into eternity by recollecting, even though this possibility is continually annulled because the inward deepening in existing fills up time" (*CUP,* 206/*SKS* 7, 188). What makes Socratic inwardness possible is the fact that irony continually annuls a possibility of recollection that, on the other hand, is still given. Irony consists in a double gesture: it always has a past, but it continually loses it. Sin, on the contrary, makes recollection impossible and inwardness infinite. But the ground of this infinitude is the individual's relation to the possibilities of existence contained in his or her own *future.* Thus, whereas irony's negativity consists in the negation of a certain actuality (the negation of the actual character of the past), the consciousness of sin is consciousness of the individual's negative relation to his or her possibilities.

This shift from irony's negativity to the negativity of sin—a displacement that Climacus only performs partially, since he remains in the position of humor[6]—involves, as we have shown above, a shift from the domain of knowledge to the domain of passion. As soon as sin is concerned, the individual's "untruth" is more strictly qualified as *unfreedom.* This is, as a matter of fact, a category to which Climacus does not pay much attention in the *Postscript,* but he himself applies it in *Philosophical Fragments:* unfreedom is the condition of "the person who has imprisoned himself," who "holds himself captive" (*PF,* 17/*SKS* 4, 226). In *The Concept of Anxiety,* the notion of unfreedom defines precisely the phenomenal character of freedom, *the way freedom presents itself to itself.* Here the emphasis is put on the very structure of the human synthesis and on the negativity of the self-relationship. What is important from a phenomenological point of view, however, is not the dogmatic presupposition of hereditary sin or the revealed consciousness of it but the concrete "presence of hereditary sin in the single individual," that is, *anxiety* (*CA,* 52/*SKS* 4, 357). On this level, unfreedom is not merely the negation of freedom. The fact that unfreedom is more than a negation can be formulated as follows: *The phenomenon in which freedom shows itself to itself as unfreedom is structurally the same phenomenon in which the individual's relation to his or her possibilities is experienced as a relation to "nothing."* In these terms, "nothing" seems to correspond to the content of the experience in which "the negativity of the existing subject" can be described.

The idea that one can establish a positive relation to "nothing" is brought about in paragraph 5 of the first chapter, along with a first definition of anxiety based on the concept of "innocence." The main point here is that, in innocence, "man is not qualified as spirit but is psychically qualified in immediate unity with his natural condition," in a solitary state of "peace and repose." In this state, however,

> there is simultaneously something else that is not contention and strife, for there is indeed nothing against which to strive. What, then, is it? Nothing. But what effect does nothing have? It begets anxiety. This is the profound secret of innocence, that it is at the same time anxiety. Dreamily the spirit projects its own actuality, but this actuality is nothing, and innocence always sees this nothing outside itself. (*CA*, 41/*SKS* 4, 347)

The author assumes that a human being, as he puts it later in the same paragraph, "is a synthesis of the psychical and the physical," and that the two are united in "spirit" (*CA*, 43/*SKS* 4, 349). However, this synthesis does not yet qualify the human being in the state of innocence. We can perhaps avoid the obvious contradiction between these two statements by introducing the category that lies at the center of Kierkegaard's theory of anxiety, namely the category of *possibility*. What appears as "nothing" is precisely the "actuality" of spirit insofar as it is "projected" as a possibility: in innocence, spirit "dreams" its actuality. The innocent soul's "immediate unity" with its "natural condition" (*CA*, 41/*SKS* 4, 347) anticipates a concrete unity or spiritual synthesis, and this anticipation of spirit has to be understood as an anticipation of freedom.

My interest in applying the category of "possibility" in this phase of the investigation responds once again to the attempt to focus on the relationship between negativity and temporality. This leads us to the point at which the individual's anxiety appears as a concrete relation to the future: "The possible corresponds exactly to the future. For freedom, the possible is the future, and the future is for time the possible. To both of these corresponds anxiety in the individual life" (*CA*, 91/*SKS* 4, 394). Thus, according to a later definition, "anxiety is freedom's possibility" (*CA*, 155/*SKS* 4, 454), that is, the experience of freedom itself insofar as it is not referred to a determined act (freedom to do this or that) but to its own possibility: "The anxious possibility of *being able* [*den ængstende Mulighed af at kunne*]" (*CA*, 44/*SKS* 4, 350), "the infinite possibility of being able" [*den uendelige Mulighed af at kunne*]" (*CA*, 45/*SKS* 4, 350). The result or the effect (*Følge*) of that possibility is not "something actual" but the entire domain of freedom as the undetermined possibility of acting: "This possibility points to a possibility as its sequence" (*CA*, 45/

SKS 4, 350); "anxiety is freedom's actuality as the possibility of possibility [*som Mulighed for Muligheden*]" (*CA*, 42/*SKS* 4, 348).

In fact, Kierkegaard's use of the modal category of possibility and its explicit association with "the future" within human experience is consistent with his conception of spirit as a synthesis that, in a way, anticipates itself. The importance he attaches here to the notion of the future, however, presupposes a more complex characterization of that synthesis. In order to clarify this point, let us focus on the relation between two of the principles mentioned above, namely (a) *the future* is for time *the possible* (*CA*, 91/*SKS* 4, 394), and (b) *the eternal* is for the existing person *the future* (*CA*, 89/*SKS* 4, 392; *CUP*, 306–7/*SKS* 7, 279–80). In *The Concept of Anxiety,* this last aspect seems to be linked to the description of the state of "innocence," in which spirit experiences its actuality as "nothing": "Because in innocence spirit is qualified only as dreaming spirit, the eternal appears as the future, for this is, as has been said, the first expression of the eternal, and its incognito" (*CA*, 91/*SKS* 4, 394). "Dreaming spirit"—that is, the immediate unity of soul in its natural condition—corresponds to an experience of time in which the eternal is only given as "incognito." At this point, it becomes clear that the *concrete* synthesis of soul and body in spirit has to be requalified as "a synthesis of the temporal and the eternal" (*CA*, 85/*SKS* 4, 388).

3. Two Syntheses?

Although the author of *The Concept of Anxiety* remarks that this synthesis "is not another synthesis but is the expression of the first synthesis, according to which man is a synthesis of psyche and body that is sustained by spirit" (*CA*, 88/*SKS* 4, 392), he is aware of the fact that the articulation between the two syntheses constitutes the main problem. Only the requalification of the psyche-body synthesis as a synthesis of temporality and eternity provides the basis for the "deliberation on the dogmatic issue of hereditary sin" proposed in the subtitle of the book. As Kierkegaard himself suggests in the draft corresponding to these passages, "If men had pursued the ancient idea that man is a synthesis of soul and body, which is constituted by spirit, men would long since have thought more precisely with regard to sin and hereditary sin, its origin and its consequence" (*CA*, 195/*Pap.* V B 55:4). Here it is important to notice that the possibility of "pursuing" this idea toward the characterization of the second synthesis is not only based on the Christian notion of eternity. In fact, what the first synthesis "lacks" in order to be requalified is first of all a better comprehension of the experience of *temporality*. This is why, in his references to pagan anthropology, the author observes that the Greeks, since they did not grasp the concept of spirit, "did not in the deepest sense comprehend sensuousness and temporality" (*CA*, 87n/ *SKS* 4, 391).

Temporality is to be comprehended as the domain in which the innocent and undifferentiated "unity" of psyche and body can be broken, with the consequence that, if the synthesis is to be sustained by spirit, the temporal has to be related to the eternal. Defined in this way, temporality is the realm of the individual's possibilities, and every relation established in it is a relation between possibilities and to possibility. Spirit can only show itself to itself as a relation to its own possibilities. But that relation can assume different forms. The two aspects we have pointed out in our characterization of the negativity of the self, namely the "nothing" to which the individual is related in innocence and the experience of "unfreedom" in which freedom shows itself to itself, can be interpreted as the two extreme points in Kierkegaard's phenomenology of anxiety. In chapters 3 and 4 of the treatise on anxiety, "spiritlessness," "fate," "guilt," "anxiety about evil," and "anxiety about the good" are in fact forms of a possible self-relationship understood as the spirit's relation to its own possibilities. It is not by chance that the most complete characterization of "unfreedom" is connected to the description of anxiety about the good, "the demonic" (*CA*, 118–54/*SKS* 4, 420–53). But the negative experience of freedom is already present in the description of innocence, spiritlessness, fate, guilt, and anxiety about evil. In the same way, the "nothing" of innocence is still present beyond innocence. Vigilius Haufniensis indicates it in the case of the anxiety defined both "as fate": "In fate the anxiety of the pagan has its object, its nothing" (*CA*, 97/*SKS* 4, 400), and "as guilt": although "guilt is indeed something" when it is seen as an ethical phenomenon, "as long as guilt is the object of anxiety, it is nothing" (*CA*, 103/*SKS* 4, 405). Regarding the experience of "the demonic," the author admits it could be qualified as "the negative" on the condition that this notion is understood as "the form of nothing" (*CA*, 134/*SKS* 4, 435). The "formal" character of this nothing seems to be related to what the author also calls "the empty abstraction of inclosing reserve" (*CA*, 124/*SKS* 4, 426). Its structure is the same as that of Socratic irony, whose expression "is the abstract itself, not in the ontological sense but in the sense of what lacks content" (*CI*, 46/*SKS* 1, 107; see also *CA*, 134/*SKS* 4, 435).

The correspondence between the manifestation of "nothing" and the anticipation of "unfreedom" can be explained on the basis of their temporal constitution. Within Haufniensis's theory of temporality, the emptiness of the nonontological "nothing" of anxiety corresponds to the structure of "the moment" (*Øieblikket*). Let us remember that, in *Philosophical Fragments,* this is one of the categories through which Climacus's project "goes beyond the Socratic," insofar as "the moment" performs the function that the category of "the decision" had in Socrates (*PF,* 111/*SKS* 4, 306). In an eminent sense, the moment consists in the inadequacy between an "eternal resolution" and a temporal "occasion" (*PF,* 25/*SKS* 4, 232) as it is experienced by an individual who is *not able to "set himself free"* (*PF,* 17/*SKS* 4, 225). In *The Concept of Anxiety,* the moment is once again "that ambiguity in which time and eternity touch each other" (*CA,* 89/*SKS* 4, 392), but it also has a concrete existential signification: "In the individual life, anxiety is the moment" (*CA,* 81/*SKS* 4, 384). "The moment" is here the temporal form of the experience in which the individual's relation to the possible—that is, to the future as the incognito of the eternal—shows itself qua possibility. Such "possibility of possibility" is, as we have observed, "freedom's actuality." But the moment of anxiety is also the one at which freedom is experienced as the possibility of unfreedom. This is what Vigilius Haufniensis means when he says that "unfreedom is a phenomenon of freedom" (*CA,* 135n/*SKS* 4, 436n). Unfreedom is nothing other than this very freedom that shows itself to itself as its own possibility. That is the reason why unfreedom "cannot be explained by naturalistic categories" (*CA,* 135n/*SKS* 4, 436n). On the contrary, it can only be referred to the possibility of freedom at the very moment in which this possibility becomes manifest to itself. The same dialectical relation between freedom and unfreedom can be described in the opposite way: as a possibility that shows itself to itself in anxiety, freedom sees itself as the possibility of unfreedom. An important passage in chapter 3 points to this dialectic: "As freedom's possibility manifests itself to itself for freedom, freedom succumbs [*segner Friheden*]" (*CA,* 91/*SKS* 4, 394). The verb used in this passage, as Arne Grøn has pointed out,[7] develops the metaphor of "vertigo" or dizziness applied to subjective anxiety in chapter 2: "Hence anxiety is the dizziness of freedom, which emerges when the spirit wants to posit the synthesis and freedom looks down into its own possibility, laying hold of finiteness to support itself. Freedom succumbs [*segner Friheden*] in this dizziness" (*CA,* 61/*SKS* 4, 365). What is crucial here, however, is that the moment in which "freedom succumbs" coincides with the spirit's attempt to establish its "synthesis." The problem concerning the relation between the two "syntheses"—the unity of soul and body sustained by spirit, on the one hand, and the encounter of temporality and eternity, on the other—assumes here all its meaning. In the anxious experience of freedom's possibility, "freedom succumbs, and temporality emerges in the same way as sensuousness in its significance as sinfulness" (*CA*, 91/*SKS* 4, 394). The experience of unfreedom, then, can be characterized as the failure or the suspension of the synthesis, in the sense that one of its potential elements (temporality or sensuousness) one-sidedly emerges as the domain in which possibility develops its infinite dialectics. In other words: temporality resists the synthesis. The parallel passage in chapter 2 does not mention temporality explicitly, but the vertigo of freedom is said to take place when freedom, looking down into possibility, lays hold of *finiteness* in order to support itself (*CA*, 61/*SKS* 4, 365). Temporality, sensuousness, and finiteness characterize, on the one hand, the abyss into which spirit fears to fall down and, on the other hand, that which spirit lays hold of in its attempt to preserve itself. This is the situation Kierkegaard refers to as "the individual's ambiguous relation, sympathetic and antipathetic," a relation that, in turn, constitutes "the selfish infinity of possibility" (*CA*, 61/*SKS* 4, 365). A first description of this phenomenon can be found in earlier writings: "Anxiety is a desire for what one fears, a sympathetic antipathy" (*JP* 94/*Pap*. III A 233). The same terms are used for defining the "psychological ambiguity" of anxiety in chapter 1 of the 1844 treatise: "Anxiety is *a sympathetic antipathy* and *an antipathetic sympathy*" (*CA*, 42/*SKS* 4, 348). It is worthwhile to note that both "antipathy" and "sympathy," "fear" and "desire" are applied here to the relation of spirit to *its own possibilities*, that is, to possibilities that, even when they manifest themselves in the form of temporal, sensuous, finite phenomena, have no other ground than spirit itself.

I have suggested in the preceding paragraph that temporality is the element that *resists* the synthesis of spirit. This interpretation implies that the double synthesis that constitutes human existence contains a fundamental tension. It is to be remembered that the two syntheses, as the author himself observes, are "formed differently": In the first synthesis, "the two factors are psyche and body, and spirit is the third, yet in such a way that one can speak of a synthesis only when spirit is posited. The latter synthesis has only two factors, the temporal and the eternal" (*CA*, 85/*SKS* 4, 388).[8] Even when it is said that the temporal and the eternal meet each other in "the moment," this last concept is not the indication of a synthesis. "The moment" is, rather, the disruption of time in which the synthesis of spirit *can* take place. In this sense, the synthesis itself—the actuality of spirit—is both temporal and eternal, both a process and a fulfillment, an "act" and a "state." Paradoxically, in the "synthesis" of the temporal and the eternal it is precisely the eternal that appears as a sort of synthesis or, at least, a "totality" of time. That is why the future, as the "incognito" of the eternal, "can in a certain sense signify the whole" (*CA*, 89/*SKS* 4, 392). This is to be kept in mind when we read that the encounter of the temporal and the eternal consists in that "time constantly intersects eternity and eternity constantly pervades time" (*CA*, 89/*SKS* 4, 392), and that the moment is "the first reflection of eternity in time, its first attempt, as it were, at stopping time" (*CA*, 88/*SKS* 4, 391).

As soon as we apply these conclusions to a consideration of "the moment in the individual life," namely "anxiety," it becomes clear that anxiety is associated with the state in which the terms of the "first" synthesis—psyche and body—only constitute a *possible* unity. This is why Vigilius Haufniensis affirms that "one can speak of synthesis [between psyche and body] only when the spirit is posited" (*CA*, 85/*SKS* 4, 388). In the terms of Haufniensis's theory, however, the mere possibility of the synthesis must be preserved as a possibility even when "the spirit is posited." That is the meaning of the otherwise enigmatic formula used in chapter 1: "In the moment actuality is posited, possibility walks by its side as a nothing that entices every thoughtless man" (*CA*, 50/*SKS* 4, 355). "The moment" is precisely the indication of the possibility of the synthesis, even when the synthesis is actualized by spirit. But the persistence of that possibility is nothing other than the persistence of spirit in the realm of temporality, constituting what Climacus will later call "an existing infinite spirit" (*CUP*, 82/*SKS* 7, 81). The "nothing" that "entices" or "tempts" (*frister*) the individual corresponds to the gap between possibility and actuality in which spirit experiences its own existence *as freedom*. Considered as a fundamental structure of existence, possibility has in itself the form of temptation. It is in this experience of the possibility of the synthesis qua possibility that freedom shows itself to itself as unfreedom.

From this point of view, it is perfectly possible to justify the application of the term "negative phenomena" to the different situations in which the self's relation to itself shows itself as a "misrelationship." This is particularly true in what concerns the phenomenology of despair, taking into account that, as Grøn has indicated, the analysis of despair begins with anxiety, and anxiety (as anxiety about the good) results in despair (as despairingly wanting to be oneself).[9] In a general sense, I have proposed to identify the negative character of these phenomena on the basis of a "resistance to the dialectics of self-consciousness," parallel to the self's lack of "transparency" with respect to "its being grounded on a transcendent power."[10] It is the description of anxiety, however, that seems to define the presuppositions for a comprehension of the negativity of existence, insofar as, in anxiety, the "action" in which freedom produces its own "truth" is open to an infinite number of possibilities that includes the possibility of untruth. Both "truth" and "untruth" are to be understood here in the sense determined by the dialectics between the disclosure (*Aabenbarelse*) of the self and inclosing reserve (*Indesluttethed*), a dialectics that reaches its highest point in "anxiety about the good" or "the demonic." It is in that point, as we have seen, that freedom shows itself to itself as unfreedom. From the state of innocence to the demonic, the various forms of anxiety do not correspond to different degrees of "truth" but to a repeated and increasingly intensified collision between reserve and self-disclosure, between silence and language. The nonspeculative "nothing" of anxiety is the only positive content that those different figures have in common. But the quality of the individual's relation to this "nothing" expresses the quality of his or her relation to the future as the "incognito" of the eternal.

Notes

1. Arne Grøn pays particular attention to this principle. See, for example, *Subjektivitet og negativitet. Kierkegaard* (Copenhagen: Gyldendal, 1997), 57, 98–100.

2. This last expression comes immediately after the sentence "let us consider an example," which might suggest that the adjective "temporal" (*timeligt*) signals a more concrete reference to "becoming." The example at issue is nothing less than the possibility of death.

3. "The thesis that subjectivity, inwardness, is truth contains the Socratic wisdom, the undying merit of which is to have paid attention to the essential meaning of existing, of the knower's being an existing person. That is why, in his ignorance, Socrates was in the truth in the highest sense within paganism" (*CUP* 204).

4. Deleuze has compared irony and humor to Job's and Abraham's position with respect to the law: "Job is infinite contestation and Abraham infinite resignation, but these are one and the same thing. Job challenges the law in an ironic manner, refusing all second-hand explanations and dismissing the general in order to reach the most singular as principle or as universal. Abraham submits humorously to the law, but finds in that submission precisely the singularity of his only son whom the law commanded him to sacrifice. As Kierkegaard understands it, repetition is the transcendent correlate shared by the psychical intentions of contestation and resignation." Gilles Deleuze, *Difference and Repetition* (New York: Columbia University Press, 1994), 7. Deleuze's statement is consistent with his attempt to explain "repetition" as opposition to the generality of moral law. This move allows him to associate Kierkegaard's "suspension of ethics" to Nietzsche's doctrine of the eternal return as "a thought beyond good and evil" (6). Thus, the idea of a reposition of the good seems to be completely alien to Deleuze's radical immanentism. According to his interpretation, Kierkegaard "can invite us to go beyond all aesthetic repetition, beyond irony and even humor, all the while painfully aware that he offers us only the aesthetic, ironic and humoristic image of such a going-beyond" (11). What is particularly interesting in Deleuze's reading,

however, is that irony and humor are presented as two moments of one and the same strategy, namely that of a suspension of the ethical view understood as the domain of generality. Abraham's "humorous" position consists in submitting to the law in order to confirm (i.e., to repeat) its ironical suspension.

5. It is true that the "later age" in Kierkegaard's history of irony properly corresponds to "irony after Fichte." It is Fichte who "infinitized the *I* in *I-I*" (*CI,* 272–73/*SKS* 1, 308–9). It is here that subjectivity is "raised to the second power, a subjectivity's subjectivity, which corresponds to reflection's reflection," an "intensified subjective consciousness" (*CA,* 242/*SKS* 4, 282). But it is important to underline, on the one hand, that what is "infinitized" by Fichte is still the abstract identity of the "I" (*CI,* 273/*SKS* 1, 309), and, on the other hand, that Kierkegaard's critique of the "abstractness" of the self does not lead him to embrace the Hegelian concept of "concrete" subjectivity but rather to a discussion of the "eternal validity" of irony. This late discussion, as we have seen, is to be pursued by Climacus.

6. As it becomes clear in some of the passages quoted here, Climacus uses the expressions "sin" and "hereditary sin" only as *arbitrary names* for "untruth" and the experience of its historicity. On Climacus's "humoristic" or "humorous" position, see the appendix to the *Postscript:* "The undersigned, Johannes Climacus, who has written this book, does not make out that he is a Christian; for he is, to be sure, completely preoccupied with how difficult it must be to become one; but even less is he one who, after having been a Christian, ceases to be that by going further. He is a humorist" (*CUP,* 617/*SKS* 7, 560).

7. See Grøn, *Subjektivitet og negativitet. Kierkegaard,* 105.

8. On the idea of a two-term dialectics and the absence of the third term, see Paul Ricoeur, "Philosopher après Kierkegaard," *Les Cahiers de Philosophie* 8, no. 9 (1989), 292. See also González, "Sin, Absolute Difference," in *Kierkegaard Studies. Yearbook* 2003, ed. Niels Jørgen Cappelørn, Hermann Deuser, Jon Stewart, and Christian Fink Tolstrup (Berlin: W. de Gruyter, 2003), 381–82.

9. See Arne Grøn, *Begrebet Angst hos Søren Kierkegaard* (Copenhagen: Gyldendal, 1994), 108–9.

10. González, "Sin, Absolute Difference," 378–79.

Part 4

Conclusions and Questions

Kierkegaard: Reenchanting the *Lebenswelt*

Mark Dooley

A Kind of Phenomenologist

Is Kierkegaard a phenomenologist? If by "phenomenology" one means the method employed by Edmund Husserl, then the answer is clear: Kierkegaard is *not* a phenomenologist. That is, you will not find in Kierkegaard anything resembling Husserl's phenomenological reduction—his suspension of the so-called "natural attitude" as a way of reaching what he calls the "pure phenomena." Neither will you find any mention of the "transcendental ego," the "intentional object," or "eidetic consciousness." Indeed, the only consistent comments Kierkegaard makes regarding the nature of consciousness are to be found in his little work *De Omnibus Dubitandum Est,* where he writes: "Reality is not consciousness, ideality no more so. Yet consciousness does not exist without both, and this contradiction is the coming into existence of consciousness and its nature."[1] One could perhaps draw a comparison between such statements and Husserl's reflections on the nature of doubt and consciousness in his *Cartesian Meditations.* But that connection would be tenuous at best, and could not withstand too much scholarly scrutiny.

So what then are we to make of the fact that Husserl's most notable disciples claim Kierkegaard as a significant influence? Philosophers such as Martin Heidegger, Jean Paul Sartre, Karl Jaspers, Gabriel Marcel, Paul Ricoeur, and Jacques Derrida draw considerably from both Husserl *and* Kierkegaard. I and some others,[2] for example, have shown how Derrida was profoundly influenced by Kierkegaardian faith as a way of challenging the Hegelian system, a fact confirmed in 1994 by Derrida when he remarked:

> In some way, a philosopher without this ethico-existential pathos does not interest me very much, and basically the sense of desire and commitment I had when I read Rousseau, Nietzsche or Gide as a very young

> man is still with me. But it is Kierkegaard to whom I have been most faithful and who interests me most: absolute existence, the meaning he gives to the word subjectivity, the resistance of existence to the concept or the system—this is something I attach great importance to and feel very deeply, something I am always ready to stand up for.[3]

We could plausibly argue, in other words, that all post-Husserlian existential phenomenology owes its principal debt to Kierkegaard. Hence, while it is true to say, following Maurice Natanson, that it "should be clear to any reader of Kierkegaard and Husserl that their views of reason involve divergent conceptions of the nature of man," it should also be clear that there may be more to the Kierkegaard-phenomenology connection than is ostensibly apparent. Indeed, as Natanson points out, the obvious differences between Kierkegaard and Husserl "did not keep Husserl from appreciating Kierkegaard." In support of that contention, he cites the following remarkable account by Lev Shestov in 1962:

> Learning that I had never read Kierkegaard, Husserl began not to *ask* but to *demand*—with enigmatic insistence—that I acquaint myself with the works of the Danish thinker. How was it that a man whose whole life had been a celebration of reason should have led me to Kierkegaard's hymn to the absurd?[4]

That is a good question, but one that is not easily answered. What it does suggest, however, is that the high priest of phenomenology derived some level of influence from the writings of the anguished Dane. My aim in this chapter is not to speculate as to the precise nature of that influence. Rather, what I want to argue is that Kierkegaard can be read as *a kind of* phenomenologist. In that vein, I want to say that there is a way of interpreting this thinker as one whose principal aim is to re-enchant what Husserl called the *Lebenswelt* or the lifeworld. Like the later Husserl, Kierkegaard confronted a crisis in European society.[5] It was a crisis of faith and culture so deeply rooted and pernicious in its effects that it threatened the very soul of the age. It was a crisis that struck at the heart of the European *Lebenswelt,* destroying, in so doing, the ethical and religious vision of the human subject. And what Kierkegaard offered in response was a way of reviving and revitalizing that damaged human world.

As I read him, therefore, Kierkegaard anticipates the later Husserl as a phenomenologist of the lifeworld. It is true that their ultimate objectives diverge significantly: Kierkegaard is an ethical and religious thinker who would eschew even the watered-down transcendentalism of the older Husserl, while Husserl had little to say about what it means to live an ethical or religious life. That said they share something of the same spirit when it comes to their reflections regarding the *Lebenswelt*.

Let me give substance to what I am suggesting as follows: if the goal of Husserl's later philosophy is "to free the phenomenologist from a perspective which is implicitly and historically dominated by the results of the objective sciences," if his ambition is to uncover "the pregivenness of the lifeworld: its intentional meaning for man in his becoming in the mundane world,"[6] then the comparison with Kierkegaard begins to seem less forced. For what Kierkegaard and Husserl share is the belief, best expressed in my view by Roger Scruton, that while "science has offered us a paradigm of objective knowledge," it remains one in which "all reference to the subject of experience is to be eliminated from the description of the world." Scruton continues:

> In seeking to emulate science, the various studies, even those which have man as their primary subject-matter, have tried to abstract from what is given in human experience, to purge the human subject, so to speak, from the archive of knowledge, and to achieve a kind of Stalinist history of the world, in which all persons are unpersons. The attempt, however, is fraught with paradox. For the human subject is the starting point of enquiry, and to refine him out of our science is to lose sight of the very thing that science endeavors to explain.[7]

The attempt to purge the human subject from the archive of knowledge is responsible for the respective crises faced by Kierkegaard and Husserl. For both men, overcoming those calamities would entail an attempt to restore as the primary philosophical focus all that is given in human experience. In the case of Kierkegaard, it would involve making the human subject the sovereign starting point in all discussions relating to truth, reality, and meaning, a fact best illustrated in the first instance by focusing on what the phenomenologists call "intentional understanding."

Intentional Understanding

There are modes of understanding which, while not possessing the objectivity demanded by the natural sciences, have nonetheless a claim to what Scruton calls "another kind of objectivity, a convergence upon a common fund of superficial truth, which entitles them to their own claims to knowledge."[8] Such, to repeat, are the everyday "truths" of the *Lebenswelt,* or the world in spite of science. If science strives to explain what Plato called the "really real"—the reality underlying the appearances—the purpose of "intentional understanding" is the opposite. Intentional understanding does not seek explanations for *the way the world is* from a mind-independent standpoint. Hence it cannot be equated with causal understanding. It is, rather, a form of inquiry that refuses to deny the centrality of the human subject and those intentional meanings that our human emotions spread across the surface of the world. In other words, intentional understanding "fills the world with the meanings implicit in our aims and emotions. It tries not so much to explain the world as to be 'at home' in it, recognizing the occasions for action, the objects of sympathy, and the places of rest."[9]

Let me put the matter like this: if science strives to adopt a purely objective standpoint, intentional understanding is content to settle on the surface of the human world. For that is where the human subject must dwell, irrespective of the claims of science. It is there, in the midst of everyday things, that we must live, love, and lament. It is there that we find meaning and significance, and where our lives are judged and justified. Put simply, the truths of science tell us only *what* we are as objects. But the truths discovered through the concepts of intentional understanding tell us *who* we are as subjects. Listen again to Roger Scruton:

> The *Lebenswelt* is not a world separate from the world of science, but a world differently described—described with the concepts that designate the intentional objects of human experience. Such concepts may not, and in all probability cannot, feature in the best scientific theory of the universe. For all that, they are indispensable to us, since they describe the focus of our attention, and signal the occasion for action. It is through these concepts that the world is seen as meaningful.[10]

That, it seems to me, is precisely what Kierkegaard was saying in that most complex of statements from *Concluding Unscientific Postscript,* "Truth Is Subjectivity." The aim of that notorious passage is not to suggest, paradoxically, that all truth is subjective. It is to say, rather, that however hard it tries, "objective knowledge" will never succeed in eliminating from the description of the world all reference to the *subject* of experience—will never succeed, that is, in purging the human subject from the archive of knowledge. And that is so because, for Kierkegaard, it is simply an ineluctable fact of existence that "the human subject is the starting point of enquiry." He writes:

> All essential knowing pertains to existence, or only the knowing whose relation to existence is essential is essential knowing. Essentially viewed, the knowing that does not inwardly in the reflection of inwardness pertain to existence is accidental knowing, and its degree and scope, essentially viewed, are a matter of indifference. That essential knowing is essentially related to existence does not, however, signify the above-mentioned abstract identity between thinking and being, nor does it signify that the knowledge is objectively related to something existent as its object, but it means that the knowledge is related to the knower, who is essentially an existing person, and that all essential knowing is therefore essentially related to existence and to existing. Therefore, only ethical and ethical-religious knowing is essential knowing. But all ethical and all ethical-religious knowing is essentially a relating to the existing of the knower.[11]

What Kierkegaard calls "ethical-religious knowing" is, I want to argue, that form of intentional understanding which, as Scruton states it, does not "possess the objectivity of natural science, being derived from man's self-conception, rather than from the impersonal observation of natural processes." Despite that, it does "possess another kind of objectivity," one that forms "a vital link with reality, and without this link appropriate action and appropriate response could not emerge with the rapidity and competence that alone can ensure our happiness and survival."[12]

Ethical and religious knowledge is "essential knowing" because it arises from the realm of *value*. It does not give us technical information, nor is it of any utilitarian significance, but answers to our longing for *meaning*. It is knowledge of *how to live* and *what to do*, of how to make one's existence worthwhile and an example for others to emulate. Essential knowing is, thus, a form of understanding that answers to our needs as *persons* or free beings in an otherwise determined world. It is knowledge concerning subjectivity—the subjectivity of others and that of God, something that Kierkegaard explains to fine effect in *Judge for Yourself!*:

> Along with the growing sensibleness there is an increase in a certain kind of knowledge about human nature; information about how we human beings *are* now or *are* at this time, a natural-scientific, statistical knowledge about the human moral state as a natural product, explained by the situation, the air currents, the wind, the rainfall, the tides, etc. Whether we human beings may have degenerated from generation to generation is of no concern to this kind of knowledge

> about human nature; it merely states accurately how we *are,* the stock exchange rate, the market price—in order, through sagacious familiarity with this information, to be able both to protect oneself against and to make use of people, to score a success, to win advantages in this world, or to be able to defend and explain away one's own contemptibleness and mediocrity, or to gain permission to be suspicious, with a kind of—scientific—good conscience, if on a rare occasion something superior should show up. But about how we human beings *ought to be,* about God's requirement, about ideals—as sensibleness increases, less and less is heard about that.[13]

Sacrificing the Sacred

The problem with the "objective reflection" of science ("sensibleness"), or indeed with all those pseudosciences that have disenchanted the *Lebenswelt* of the age, is that they regard the human being as nothing more than a complex animal subject to the same mechanistic laws as all other creatures. But, as Kierkegaard and Kant taught, we are both subject *and* object, free *and* determined, finite *and* infinite. Both dimensions of the human person exist, as Scruton puts it, "in mutual interdependence, and each is nothing without the other." Kierkegaard tells us that a "human being is a synthesis of the infinite and the finite, of the temporal and the eternal, of freedom and necessity,"[14] and that any attempt to deny either side of the relation will result in despair. Hence he believes that the real crisis of the age has been caused by a systematic attempt to *depersonalize* the self and the public sphere. Objective reflection serves to strip away the subjectivity of the human being so as to render it *purely* finite, temporal, and necessary. This process of depersonalization phenomenologically transforms the *Lebenswelt,* for in the depersonalized world the "superficial truths" of ethics and religion are banished in favor of the purely "objective" truths of science and its pseudosurrogates, all of which seek to deny the sacred source of the self. In the following passage worth quoting in full, Roger Scruton describes in stark terms what happens when the sacred view of man is sacrificed on the altar of such hubris:

> The scientific worldview contains a fatal temptation: it invites us to regard the subject as a myth, and to see the world under one aspect alone, as a world of objects. And this disenchanted world is also a world of alienation. We should not forget that the attempt to re-create the human world through science has already been made. Marx's theory of

> history, and the Nazi science of race are very bad examples of science. But they licensed forms of government in which the scientific view of our condition was for the first time in power. People were seen as objects, obedient to natural laws; and their happiness was to be secured by experts, acting as the theory prescribed. The theory informed the believer that God is dead, and that with him has been extinguished the divine spark in man. Human freedom is nothing but an appearance on the face of nature; beneath it rides the same implacable causality, the same sovereign indifference, which prepares death equally and unconcernedly for all of us, and which tells us that beyond death there is nothing. The sense of the sacred warns us that there are things which cannot be touched, since to meddle with them is to open a door in the world of objects, so as to stand in the I of God. The desacralized view of the world annihilates that sense, and therefore removes the most important of our prohibitions . . . The totalitarian system, and the extermination camp which is its most sublime expression, embody the conviction that nothing is sacred. In such a system, human life is driven underground, and the ideas of freedom and responsibility—ideas without which our picture of man as a moral subject disintegrates entirely—have no public recognition, and no place in the administrative process. If it is so easy to destroy people in such a system, it is because human life enters the public world already destroyed, appearing only as an object among others, to be dealt with by experts versed in the science of man.[15]

Now, although Kierkegaard could not have envisaged the horrors of the twentieth century, he did have a profound sense of what would materialize if human freedom were seen as nothing but a "mere appearance on the face of nature." He did indeed anticipate what would happen if the human subject were ever perceived as a myth and if its sacred sense were squandered. For the process of depersonalization was already under way in his own age, that of nineteenth-century Denmark. It was an age in which objective knowledge had eliminated all reference to the subject of experience, one in which the human person had been purged and all essential knowing buried beneath the pretensions of abstract passionless reflection. Indeed, what he diagnosed was something that besets every age once it falls prey to depersonalization and desacralization.

According to Kierkegaard, the present age is demoralized, disenchanted, and "devoid of passion."[16] It is one in which all distinctions have been "leveled" and in which indolence takes the form of a virtue. The result is that commitment and engagement have been rejected in favor of apathy and perpetual adolescence. It is, he tells us, an age that "has no assets of feeling in the erotic, no assets of enthusiasm and inwardness in politics and religion, no assets of domesticity, piety, and appreciation in daily life and social life."[17] All the values, norms, and customs that characterized the traditional *Lebenswelt* have been wiped clean, only to be replaced by a stifling egalitarianism in which achievement and excellence are expunged:

> The dialectic of the present age is oriented to equality, and its most logical implementation, albeit abortive, is leveling, the negative unity of the negative mutual reciprocity of individuals. Anyone can see that leveling has its profound importance in the ascendancy of the category "generation" over the category "individuality." Whereas in antiquity the host of individuals existed, so to speak, in order to determine how much the excellent individual was worth, today the coinage standard has been changed so that about so and so many human beings uniformly make one individual; thus it is merely a matter of getting the proper number—and then one has significance. In antiquity, the individual in the crowd had no significance whatsoever; the man of excellence stood for them all. The trend today is in the direction of mathematical equality, so that in all classes about so and so many uniformly make one individual.[18]

Abstract passionless knowledge denies real and essential difference. It repudiates distinction, merit, and achievement only to reward uniformity, mediocrity, and failure. It is, as such, an ideology for an age when liberation from responsibility, sacrifice, loss, and shame is the primary goal of existence. It is an age of individual rights and egocentrism, one in which there is little room for those "assets of feeling in the erotic" such as fidelity and love, or for those "assets of domesticity" such as the vow of marriage and all the subsequent sacrifices that it entails. It is an age of boredom in which nothing is valued because everything can be obtained at bargain price. It is an age in which the idea of the human being as an object of judgment has receded. Hence, it is an age in which all forms of judgment and discernment are regarded with suspicion, and in which every opinion, however ill conceived or irrational, must be valued equally. Such is a world in which all must have prizes, and in which moral discipline and the demands of religion have all but disappeared.

The Consequences of Chatter

In such a culture of disenchantment, there is simply no space for "essential knowing." For both ethical and religious knowledge demand passionate commitment and that is precisely what is under attack in the age of adolescence where the aesthete rules supreme. But there are other forms of "knowledge" that are far easier to conquer, such as those purveyed by the public and the press, both of which herald the triumph of opinion, detachment, and disintegration. The public, Kierkegaard writes, is "all and nothing, the most dangerous of all powers and the most meaningless."[19] For not only does it seek to smother all distinction in a web of abstraction, it also, through the press, breeds a chattering culture in which "conversation will tend to become a trivial rattling and name-dropping."[20] In saying all of this, Kierkegaard was, as Hubert Dreyfus has shown, anticipating one of the central crises of our own age. He writes:

> Kierkegaard would surely have seen the Internet, with its Websites full of anonymous information from all over the world and its interest groups that anyone in the world can join without qualifications and where one can discuss any topic endlessly without consequences, the hi-tech synthesis of the worst features of the newspaper and the coffeehouse . . . In the news groups, anyone, anywhere, any time, can have an opinion on anything. All are only too eager to respond to the equally deracinated opinions of other anonymous amateurs who post their views from nowhere. Such commentators do not take a stand on the issues they speak about. Indeed, the very ubiquity of the Net tends to make any such local stand seem irrelevant. What Kierkegaard envisaged as a consequence of the press's indiscriminate and uncommitted coverage is now fully realized on the World Wide Web.[21]

The Web has transformed the face of the world and, once again, we experience those changes *phenomenologically*. It has disenchanted the *Lebenswelt* by creating virtual communities that demand no sacrifice of their members for their long-term survival, and in which the individual is sovereign. As such, the Web heralds the triumph of the "I" over the "We"—the first-person singular over the first-person plural, the minimal over the maximal self, the ego over the community. For Kierkegaard, chatter signals the erosion of culture, of genuine knowledge and a sense of *somewhere*—as distinct from the "nowhere" of public opinion. Most serious of all, however, is the fact that a person hooked on chatter can avoid real human relationships. Real relationships are founded on sacrifice and trust: I must sacrifice my sovereignty in order to earn the trust of those I would either befriend or love. And that always assumes a degree of risk, for it may be the case that my love will be spurned or my friendship shunned. Still, genuine love and friendship demand that I surrender to others both physically and emotionally. That, in short, is the price we must pay for both.

The same does not apply, however, in a chattering relationship, for in that context I am relieved of the burden and embarrassment of the face-to-face encounter. Hence the relationship remains spectral, illusory, artificial, and aimless. As Scruton writes: "There grows between us a reduced-risk encounter, in which each is aware that the other is fundamentally withheld, sovereign within his impregnable cyber-castle. I 'click on' you, as I might click on a news item or a video. You are one of the products on display; but this does not make you an object of trust, with whom my life is mingled."[22] What this engenders is an age in which the burdens of adulthood have receded in favor of the passionless and carefree culture of eternal youth. To repeat, adulthood involves risk and sacrifice; it is accepting of love and loss, and never shirks the responsibility of truly engaging with others. But in a passionless and disenchanted age, from which all risk and sacrifice have disappeared, the basis of real love collapses.

A Phenomenology of Love

Such is the reason why I believe it plausible to interpret Kierkegaard's as a *phenomenology of love.* His analysis of the aesthetic sphere of existence is nothing less than a phenomenology of personality types that are characteristic of a passionless age devoid of essential knowing. It is a world of Don Juanism, one in which authentic love is undermined by a pseudoscience of sexology. It is the world of Johannes the Seducer, a stereotypical product of the chattering age who cannot take the vital leap from virtual to real life. It is thus a world in which the solitary ego triumphs, and in which the intentionality of human desire is corrupted by those nihilistic sciences of man that proudly proclaim that the true goal of human life is physical fulfillment, and that the road to such satisfaction is not a specific person but any member of the genus. Kierkegaard explains:

> But what kind of power is it, then, by which Don Giovanni seduces? It is the energy of the desire, the energy of sensuous desire. He desires total femininity in every woman, and therein lies the sensuous, idealizing force with which he simultaneously enhances and overcomes his prey. The reflection of this immense passion enhances and develops the desired one, who blushes in heightened beauty because of its reflection. Just as the fire of the enthusiast envelops with a seductive luster even those uninvolved persons who have some relation to him, so in a far deeper sense he transfigures every girl, since his relation to her is an essential relation. This is why all the finite differences vanish for him

> in comparison with the main point: to be a woman. The old ones he rejuvenates into the beautiful middle age of womanhood; the child he almost matures in an instant; everything that is woman is his prey (*pur chè porti la gonella, voi sapete quel chè fa*).[23]

In an adolescent world of the aesthete, the aim of sexual desire is not *this or that* particular individual, but any individual willing to sate my immediate needs. Gone is the hard work of negotiation, compromise, sacrifice, and trust upon which all truly human relationships are predicated. The sole telos of the encounter is sexual gratification, and for that purpose anyone will do. Consequently, passionless love is for "completely abstract femininity," whereas real love, between real people in real relationships, is marked by "continuance in time."[24] Here is the spin that Scruton gives these pivotal Kierkegaardian insights:

> Both erotic love and friendship are directed towards the individual and regard him as irreplaceable. There is no other who would "do just as well," and to propose a substitute for the object of love or friendship is to mistake the motive of both lover and friend. Love and friendship are both "everlasting"—they die, but they are never "satisfied," since they have no goal beyond themselves . . . Finally, both love and friendship are offered and received as *gifts* and can be offered and received in no other way. (Hence there is no contract in which friendship or love is the subject matter.) Moreover, they are expressed through gifts and are manifestations of grace.[25]

For Kierkegaard, the process of reenchanting the *Lebenswelt* requires a movement from the egomania of the aesthetic sphere to that of the ethical, where "both love and friendship are offered and received as *gifts* and can be offered and received in no other way." It is a movement from the self-obsession of the age toward a responsible, engaged, and committed life. That is why, as I have always maintained, Kierkegaard is anything but a champion of isolated individualism.[26] To repeat, his principal aim is to reestablish a sense of *somewhere* in spite of the aesthete's lust for *nowhere.* He seeks to show that human beings are fundamentally characterized by their ability to love, something that is denied to all other creatures. Love, however, responds to real and concrete things; it is not attracted by the universal in the other, but by his unique and irreplaceable subjectivity. For this reason, love and friendship are not susceptible to substitution. "Purity of heart is to will one thing," Kierkegaard writes, but he could have said "purity of heart is to *intend* one thing." For that is the nature of human intentionality: to approach the other not simply as an object, but as a unique subject whose life matters to me eternally and for whom I stand ready to sacrifice everything. However, when the world is depersonalized, or when all essential knowing is resisted, it is then that friendship and love are no longer perceived as "manifestations of grace." It is then that the moral and religious *Lebenswelt* is repudiated and the "coiled springs of life-relationships, which are what they are only because of qualitatively distinguishing passion, lose their resilience."[27]

Elsewhere, Kierkegaard describes how, without the "ethical point of view," all human relationships are rendered meaningless:

> In our age the principle of association (which at best can have validity with respect to material interest) is not affirmative but negative; it is an evasion, a dissipation, an illusion, whose dialectic is as follows: as it strengthens individuals, it vitiates them; it strengthens by numbers, by sticking together, but from the ethical point of view this is a weakening. Not until the single individual has established an ethical stance despite the whole world, not until then can there be any question of genuinely uniting; otherwise it gets to be a union of people who separately are weak, a union as unbeautiful and depraved as a child-marriage.[28]

Only self-conscious subjects can take up the ethical point of view, for that is what is specific to human intentionality. Human beings judge, and are in turn judged, on the basis of the choices they make and the actions they undertake. Our capacity to make decisions is what sets us apart from the rest of creation, and is that which endows us with a moral form. Consequently, the basis of all true love is to look upon the other as a center of subjectivity, not simply defined as an organism, but as a free being "with a life of his own, which is uniquely his and which he creates through his choices."[29] This means that any rehabilitation of the *Lebenswelt* must begin by asserting that *the truth of man is his subjectivity.* It must begin by repersonalizing the world in such a way that apathy gives way to passion, adolescence to adulthood, and lust to love. For only then will the coiled springs of life-relationships be revitalized, only then will the "I" undertake to sacrifice itself in the name of the "We." Only then will the true cost of membership become apparent to those who, as Dreyfus puts it, are tempted to "live in a world of stimulating images and simulated commitments," thus leading to a "simulated life."[30]

The Meaning of Marriage

Kierkegaard asserts that "only when there is no strong communal life to give substance to the concretion will the press create this abstraction 'the public,' made up of unsubstantial individuals who are never united or never can be united in the simultaneity of any situation or organization and yet are claimed to be a whole."[31] What he calls a "strong communal life" amounts to a lifeworld founded on essential knowing. It is one comprising subjective, but not isolated individuals. Winning another's love or friendship demands appealing to his subjective "inwardness," where "inwardness" is defined as the individual's capacity for self-reflection, decision, and judgment. Such is the reason why Kierkegaard privileges marriage as the paradigmatic ethical institution, for in marriage two subjects sacrifice everything for each other and for the community. They abandon the first-person perspective of the solitary ego in favor of the third-person perspective of society. And that is because marriage signifies a surrendering of the self to the needs of what Edmund Burke called "absent generations." It binds me to family both living and dead, which is why, for Kierkegaard, marriage has an "aesthetic validity," and also why "the ethical and the religious, insofar as they seek their expression in something particular, find this best in the marriage ceremony."[32]

For Kierkegaard, as for Roger Scruton, the marriage ceremony, as a paradigm of commitment and true passion, "marks a transition from one state of existence to another." "At such moments," Scruton explains,

> man is confronted with his fragility and dependence. As at the moments of death and birth, he is beset by awe. This feeling is a recognition of the sacred, of the intrusion into the human world of obligations that cannot be created by an act of choice, and which therefore demand a transcendental meaning. The sacred is the "subjectivity of objects"—the presentation in the contours of day-to-day things, of a meaning that sees "from I to I." Out of the mute objectivity of the surrounding world, a voice suddenly calls to me, with a clear and intelligible command. It tells me who I am, and enjoins me to enter the place that has been kept for me. In marriage I "undertake" an obligation that precedes my choice, and which resides in the scheme of things. Not surprisingly, therefore, marriage is a religious "sacrament," comparable to the sacraments of baptism and extreme unction. The universal participation of religions in the marriages of believers is testimony to the shared perception of this sacred quality. And like all sacred matters, marriage presents different aspects to the participant and to the observer. The sacred is a personal concept, one that features in the intentional understanding of the person who participates in a certain social practice.[33]

The sacred *is* the subjectivity of others. It is what the lover responds to in his beloved and what the friend answers to in the other. When observed from the perspective of scientific understanding ("sensibleness"), the other person is simply part of the catalog of nature. But when understood intentionally, what you behold in the other is a subject who can say "I," and who can speak "in the first person of his acts and attitudes, and lay claim to them as his."[34]

In marriage, it is toward the mysterious depths of the beloved that you are drawn. To repeat, if it were only the biological organism that attracted you, then any other individual would indeed suffice. But human attraction, at least in its normal course, runs much deeper than that. It sees in the other a locus of freedom that is capable of defying the biological instinct, capable, in other words, of defying the "natural-scientific" sensibleness of the age. Such is the *sacred sense,* a sense that emerges in this world from the subjectivity of human beings. The sacred is a revelation of the other's freedom in the midst of the "mute contingency" of the world. This "inwardness" or subjectivity that calls to me from another more sacred sphere is richly acknowledged in and through the sacramental rites of the marriage ceremony. But it also acknowledged wherever true love between individuals shows its face, and is the basis of any genuine community existence. For it is only by cultivating what Kierkegaard calls "neighbor-love" that people can engender "strong communal life."

Neighbor-love testifies to a "world of sacred things, in which holy and indefeasible obligations stand athwart our lives and command us along certain paths, whether we will it or not."[35] And just like the love that exists between a couple bound together by the marriage vow, neighbor-love testifies to the divine spark that lies at the core of the human condition. That spark is subjectivity, and while it is tempting to see people as mere objects, "leading them to identify completely with their biological condition," it is nonetheless true that the origin of love cannot be fully explained by natural-scientific sensibleness. "Where does love come from, where does it have its origin and its source, where is the place it has its abode from which it flows?" asks Kierkegaard. For him, as for Scruton, the answer is shrouded in mystery:

> There is a place in a person's innermost being; from this place flows the life of love, for "from the heart flows life." But you cannot see this place; however deeply you penetrate, the origin eludes you in remoteness and hiddenness. Even when you have penetrated furthest in, the origin is always still a bit further in, like the source of the spring that is further away when you are closest to it. From this place flows love along many paths, but along none of these paths can you force your way into its hidden origin. Just as God dwells in a light from which flows every ray that illuminates the world, yet no one can force his way along these

> paths in order to see God, since the paths of light turn into darkness when one turns towards the light—so love dwells in hiding or is hidden in the innermost being.[36]

The present age is one from which all inwardness, and thus all genuine love has absconded. It is an age, as Kierkegaard remarks in *Fear and Trembling,* in which "the qualification of interiority," of subjectivity and the sacred have been repudiated in favor of "exteriority."[37] It is an age whose lifeworld is dominated by sensibleness, passionless reflection, and objective knowledge. It is an age, to repeat, that has recklessly squandered its "assets of domesticity, piety, and appreciation in daily life and social life." It is an age in which, as Scruton laments, we "experience a profound conflict in our feelings, a virulent desire to desecrate, to drag the human body down to its animal essentials and show it as pure object, in which the light of selfhood and freedom has been extinguished."[38] And, like Kierkegaard, he believes that we find it almost impossible to live with this "new perception of the body" without falling prey to despair. For, recalling what I said above, despair is the natural condition of those who refuse to reconcile the finite with the infinite, the temporal with the eternal, freedom with necessity. Everything in us yearns, therefore, to return to "that religious vision from which we have strayed, telling us that the human form is sacred, untouchable, and an object of awe."[39]

Faith, Hope, and Love

It was Kierkegaard who first identified the consequences for the lifeworld when faith in the sacred vision of man declines. In doing so, he recognized that faith "is not simply an addition to our repertoire of ordinary opinions," but a "transforming state of mind, a stance towards the world, rooted in our social nature and altering our perceptions, emotions and beliefs."[40] Hence, as illustrated throughout his magisterial *Works of Love,* the loss of faith is, for Kierkegaard, something that we yet again experience *phenomenologically.* For without faith in the higher life, without faith in the sacred, we are condemned to a loveless existence and are tempted "to place man upon the throne from which God was taken away for burial." It is then that we seek to extinguish the divine spark that animates all "strong communal life." For faith, when correctly construed, is not just a personal ("inward") movement toward God, but one directed toward the other person through the God-relationship. In the Kierkegaardian sense, faith involves a process of self-renunciation in favor of the neighbor. He explains:

> The matter is quite simple. A person should begin with loving the unseen, God, because then he himself will learn what it is to love. But that he actually loves the unseen will be known by his loving the brother he sees; the more he loves the unseen, the more he will love the people he sees. It is not the reverse, that the more he rejects those he sees, the more he loves the unseen, since in that case God is changed into an unreal something, a delusion. Such a thing can occur only either to a hypocrite and a deceiver, in order to find an escape, or to someone who misrepresents God, as if God were envious of himself and of being loved, instead of the blessed God's being merciful and therefore continually pointing away from himself, so to speak, and saying, "If you want to love me, then love the people you see; what you do for them, you do for me."[41]

For Kierkegaard, thus, faith is certainly not a blind leap in the dark. It is a *way of life,* a form of discipleship that regards neighbor-love as its primary objective. It is true, of course, that faith of this kind involves supreme trust in the *person* of Christ. But Kierkegaard's point is that the relationship with Christ is, as Scruton writes, "the foundation of gift-love, since it is the thing that makes it possible to give oneself without reserve." Put simply, while faith demands a "teleological suspension of the ethical" (inasmuch as it enjoins us to resign from the virtual reality of "the public" sphere), it does not stop there. The subsequent movement of faith requires us to love the subjectivity of others as a manifestation of the sacred. It is only in that way that an authentic "ethical stance" can be appropriated, one that will serve as the basis of genuine social union.

In sum, Kierkegaardian faith is anything but irrational. It does not seek to contravene reason, "but to stake a claim in territory where the writ of reason does not run."[42] To recall what I said at the beginning of this essay: natural-scientific sensibleness explains the world by pointing to causes, but faith is more like "intentional understanding" or "essential knowing." It tells us that reason is not solely the preserve of science, for we seek not only the causes of things but also their meaning. And that is what ethical-religious knowing provides: "Moral values, aesthetic tastes, yearnings and aspirations which, for want of a better word, we call 'spiritual.'" Without the transfiguring power of faith, therefore, those living in the *Lebenswelt* would lose all sense of the fact "that some things are intrinsically worthwhile, and to be pursued for their own sake—not pleasure only, but love, duty, virtue and kindness."[43]

Returning to the *Lebenswelt*

The question of how to reenchant the *Lebenswelt* must involve, therefore, resituating the human subject at the center of the archive of knowledge. It must cease giving preference to "objective reflection" over ethical-religious knowledge, for to do so is to succumb to the fatal temptation to see the subject as a myth. And when that happens, when man is perceived as a mere object to be switched on and off as his virtual master decrees, the plagues of desecration descend upon the present age, turning it into "an evasion, a dissipation, an illusion." It is then that we witness the creation of "a new kind of creature, a depersonalized human being, in which subject and object drift apart, the first into a world of helpless dreams, the second to destruction."[44]

In order to revive essential knowing, however, we must first discover the value of true education. It seems obvious to me that the human subject cannot be idealized in the mind of young people, without an education that endeavors to nurture the sacred sense. That indeed is what Kierkegaard's authorship sets out to achieve: it aspires to bring the reader from abstract, disinterested knowledge to a point where he believes that his life, as well as the lives of all those around him, matter eternally. In this way, Kierkegaard provides us with a pedagogy that, as Scruton says of Confucius's *Analects,* enjoins us to

> obey the rites, the ceremonies and the customs that lend dignity to our actions and which lift them above the natural sphere; to cultivate the heart and the tongue so that beauty is always in and around us; and to live in the condition which Wordsworth called "natural piety," acknowledging the greatness of creation, and the imponderable mystery of time. In this way, even if we have no religious beliefs, we acknowledge the existence of sacred things, and endow our gestures with a nimbus of the supernatural. Living thus we peer serenely into the eternal.[45]

Kierkegaard, as the great thinker of subjectivity, summons us to discover within ourselves the source of the sacred. He calls us to make the transition from adolescence to adulthood by overcoming sensibleness, thereby seeing the other as a fount of freedom and an object of eternal love. In so doing, we confront the fundamental truth of the human condition: we are beings ineluctably situated in time, incapable of taking the back door out of existence and into eternity. Hence, whatever redemption is available to us can be found only *in time.* For Kierkegaard, the ultimate source of that redemption is the God-man, conceived as the unconditioned ethical prototype. This means that salvation is not, for him, to be found in the serene contemplation of timeless verities. On the contrary, it involves responding to the light of subjectivity in our neighbors, which in turn amounts to "a conscious gesture of *belonging*." Such indeed is *the* work of faith and love, a work that "connects the temporal and eternity," and which "for that very reason is before everything and remains after everything is gone."[46]

Notes

1. See Søren Kierkegaard, *"Philosophical Fragments" and "Johannes Climacus,"* ed. and trans. Howard V. and Edna H. Hong (Princeton, N.J.: Princeton University Press, 1985), 168.

2. See especially Mark Dooley, *The Politics of Exodus: Søren Kierkegaard's Ethics of Responsibility* (New York: Fordham University Press, 2001) and John D. Caputo, *Radical Hermeneutics* (Bloomington: Indiana University Press, 1987).

3. Jacques Derrida and Maurizio Ferraris, *A Taste for the Secret* (Cambridge: Polity Press, 2001), 40.

4. Maurice Natanson, *Edmund Husserl: Philosopher of Infinite Tasks* (Evanston, Ill.: Northwestern University Press, 1973), 166.

5. See Edmund Husserl, *The Crisis of European Sciences and Transcendental Phenomenology* (Evanston, Ill.: Northwestern University Press, 1970).

6. Ibid., 129.

7. Roger Scruton, *The Philosopher on Dover Beach* (Manchester: Carcanet, 1990), 107. My reliance on Scruton in this chapter testifies to the fact that it was he who taught me to see Kierkegaard as a phenomenologist of the lifeworld. For more, see Mark Dooley, *Roger Scruton: The Philosopher on Dover Beach* (London: Continuum, 2009), and my introduction to *The Roger Scruton Reader,* ed. Mark Dooley, titled "A Philosophy of Love" (London: Continuum, 2009), i–xxii. In many ways, I consider Roger Scruton a Kierkegaard for our times. As he writes in one particular context: "Like his contemporaries, the philosopher saw the aesthetic as the one true path to man's redemption, the posture towards the world which preserved, as best it could, the ethical vision which makes sense of our time on earth. In dressing up the aesthetic gaze in the attributes of holiness, Kierkegaard showed us the meaning of high culture" (*Modern Culture* [London: Continuum], 54). As I argue in chap. 3 of *Roger Scruton,* the very same description could easily be applied to Scruton himself.

8. Scruton, *Philosopher on Dover Beach,* 108.

9. Ibid.

10. Ibid., 95–96.

11. *CUP,* 197–98.

12. Scruton, *Philosopher on Dover Beach,* 108.

13. Søren Kierkegaard, *Judge for Yourself!* ed. and trans. Howard V. Hong and Edna H. Hong (Princeton, N.J.: Princeton University Press, 1990), 157.

14. *SUD,* 13.

15. Roger Scruton, *Philosophy: Principles and Problems* (London: Continuum, 2005), 108–9.

16. Søren Kierkegaard, *Two Ages: The Age of Revolution and the Present Age,* ed. and trans. Howard V. Hong and Edna H. Hong (Princeton, N.J.: Princeton University Press, 1978), 68.

17. Ibid., 74.

18. Ibid., 84–85.

19. Ibid., 93.

20. Ibid., 99.

21. Hubert Dreyfus, *On the Internet* (London: Routledge, 2001), 21–22.

22. Roger Scruton, "Can Virtual Life Take Over from Real Life?" *Sunday Times,* November 16, 2008.

23. *EO I,* 100.

24. Ibid., 95.

25. Roger Scruton, *Death-Devoted Heart: Sex and the Sacred in Wagner's "Tristan and Isolde"* (Oxford: Oxford University Press, 2004), 156.

26. Such is the central contention advanced throughout *The Politics of Exodus.*

27. Kierkegaard, *Two Ages,* 78.

28. Ibid., 106.

29. Scruton, *Modern Culture,* 11.

30. Dreyfus, *On the Internet,* 88.

31. Kierkegaard, *Two Ages,* 91.

32. *EO II,* 88.

33. Roger Scruton, *Sexual Desire: A Philosophical Investigation* (London: Continuum, 2006), 357.

34. Roger Scruton, *Xanthippic Dialogues* (London: Sinclair-Stevenson, 1993), 162–63.

35. Roger Scruton, *A Political Philosophy: Arguments for Conservatism* (London: Continuum, 2006), 88.

36. *WL,* 9.

37. *FT,* 69.

38. Scruton, *Political Philosophy,* 136.

39. Ibid.

40. Roger Scruton, *Gentle Regrets: Thoughts from a Life* (London: Continuum, 2005), 220.

41. *WL,* 160.

42. Roger Scruton, "Faith, Reason and Father Giussani" (unpublished essay).

43. Ibid.

44. Scruton, *Philosophy,* 109.

45. Scruton, *Modern Culture,* 158.

46. *WL,* 6.

Kierkegaard and the Limits of Phenomenology

George Pattison

Why Kierkegaard and Phenomenology?

In considering the question of Kierkegaard and phenomenology, I should perhaps begin by specifying more closely just what I am understanding by the term "phenomenology." It would clearly go way beyond the scope of this essay to argue for the definitive status of one or the other version of phenomenology. Instead, I shall limit myself to stating what I am assuming are the features of phenomenology most relevant to the question of Kierkegaard and phenomenology. Since I read Kierkegaard as a fundamentally religious writer,[1] this will also require some comment on what I take to be the relation of phenomenology to questions of religion.

Basically, I am understanding phenomenology here in the sense defined by Heidegger in *Being and Time* where he writes, "Ontology and phenomenology are not two distinct philosophical disciplines amongst others. These terms characterize philosophy itself with regard to its object and its way of treating that object. Philosophy is universal phenomenological ontology."[2] Heidegger was, of course, an idiosyncratic, not to say rebellious heir to Husserlian phenomenology, but in *Being and Time,* as in the lectures on the *History of the Concept of Time,* in which he sets out at much greater length his understanding of phenomenology, he is still articulating his own thought in terms of phenomenological research.[3] If he is not necessarily to be taken as an entirely reliable guide to Husserl's own understanding, he is nevertheless thinking about the task in close proximity to Husserl. Indeed, the idea that phenomenology is not merely one positive science among others, but is to be the basis for all possible science is already clearly stated by Husserl. As he puts it in *Logical Investigations:* "Pure phenomenology establishes a domain of neutral research in which various sciences have their roots" and goes on to articulate this relationship as focused on psychology, understood as comprising the various disciplines relating to representation, judgment and cognition, and logic.[4] However, this statement, coming at the start of volume 2 of the *Philosophical Investigations,* clearly presumes the argument at the close of volume 1, in which logic itself is identified as that discipline in which the essential unity of all scientific endeavor is to be found. The question as to the basic character of knowledge, then, is funneled back through a sequence of ever more compressed fields of enquiry until it finds its base in phenomenological enquiry. Whether in its Heideggerian or Husserlian versions, then, phenomenology aims to provide a universal basis for all properly scientific work, that is, for work that is assured of its own nature and status as knowledge.

With specific regard to religion, this raises the peculiar question as to whether the objects of religious knowledge are of a kind that allows them to be brought into the purview of science. Nor is this question raised only from the side of those for whom the "unscientific" nature of religion provides grounds for treating religious claims with contempt. Theology itself would seem in many of its forms also to appeal to the transcendence of God in such a way as to place God outside all possible domains of knowledge. As Husserl stated in *Ideas,* God "should not only transcend the world, but obviously also the 'absolute' Consciousness. It would thus be an '*Absolute*' *in a totally different sense from the Absolute of Consciousness,* as on the other hand it would be a *transcendent in a totally different sense* from the transcendent in the sense of the world."[5] Phenomenology, however, must bracket out such a transcendent Absolute, and neither presupposes, nor argues for, nor makes denials concerning such a transcendent Absolute. It is in this sense that, as Heidegger would put it, phenomenology is atheistic.

Yet phenomenology has often taken religion as a starting point for its own investigations, not only classically in such scholars as Van der Leeuw or Ninian Smart, but also in more recent applications such as Gavin Flood's *The Ascetic Self*[6]—and, of course, Heidegger himself devoted a series of lectures to *The Phenomenology of Religious Life.*[7] And if such phenomenological approaches to religion refrain from deliberating the "reality" of the religious object, it is also possible to see a properly theological work such as Karl Rahner's *Foundations of Christian Faith* as using phenomenological method in order to set out the structure and content of Christian life and to do so in such a way that the phenomenological exposition supports the case for the normative and universal value of Christian faith for the interpretation of human life as such.[8] Rahner's claim is that the phenomenological analysis of human existence reveals it as being fundamentally open to the absolute mystery of God. To be human is always already to be oriented toward the divine, and a full description of the human will therefore illuminate the knowledge of God that is possible to human beings. This would refer also to the "absolute" God who transcends the absoluteness of consciousness and of the world, even if (from Rahner's Catholic standpoint) a knowledge of God that did not incorporate the specific beliefs of Catholic faith would remain only provisional and partial—provisional and partial, but nevertheless also true.[9]

This is not said in order to endorse Rahner's position. Rather, in opposing Rahner to Husserl we see a basic choice regarding the relationship between phenomenology and religious knowledge. This is not a choice between hostility and amity. Both positions may be formulated in suitably irenic terms, but there is a clear decision to be made regarding the character of the relationship between the divine and the human that in turn has implications for the relationship between consciousness (and not least any putative science of consciousness) and the religious object. My argument in this essay is that Kierkegaard's choice is such that while he shares with Rahner a certain theological commitment to taking the human pole of the divine-human relationship completely seriously, and therefore incorporates a descriptive analysis of human being into his theological project, his theological presuppositions are such as to render impossible the Rahnerian project of a fundamental phenomenological analysis of the human condition that might open out onto anything that might properly be called knowledge of God. But this is not said simply to draw attention to a merely *theological* difference between Rahner and Kierkegaard (a difference that might be seen as predictable in the light of their respective ecclesiastical backgrounds). More fundamentally, it registers a basic issue with regard to the limits of phenomenological enquiry vis-à-vis religion and a religious understanding of human existence.

But why bring Kierkegaard into it at all? Couldn't we just initiate a general discussion about the limits of phenomenology without getting involved with just this particular thinker, whose work is so notoriously complex, allusive, and ambiguous, and who, on his own account, set out to make the whole issue of Christianity more difficult than it seemed to most of his contemporaries? Are we not committing ourselves to an enormous detour through the labyrinth of pseudonymous voices and biographical circumstances that may indeed contribute to the "fascination" of Kierkegaard's work, but that also make it so frustrating for philosophical interpretation?

Such grounds for hesitation notwithstanding, we would seem to be directed toward Kierkegaard by his peculiar place in the history of phenomenology. For Kierkegaard seems to constitute a significant link between two of the main figures in the history of modern phenomenology: Hegel and Heidegger. Indeed, it is just this connection that is most salient in those mid-twentieth-century readings of the Danish writer that still play such a large part in shaping his philosophical heritage. In such readings, Kierkegaard appears in the history of ideas as, on the one hand, a critical transformer of Hegelian phenomenology and, on the other, as a primary source for Heidegger's subsequent critical transformation of his existentiell/religious problematic.

Of course, both Kierkegaard's relation to Hegel and Heidegger's relation to Kierkegaard can be described in terms of critical transformation—and in both cases the issue of religion seems to have been central to the "critical" moment. Thus, Kierkegaard's central challenge to Hegel concerns the competence of philosophy to deal with the "infinite qualitative difference" between God and human beings or to account for the "absolute paradox" of the Incarnation, while Heidegger's complaint is that although Kierkegaard offers the phenomenological investigator important psychological material, he does not himself treat that material in a phenomenological way, but merely as the existentiell question of, how can *I* become a Christian? On this view, Kierkegaard is of value to the project of a fundamental ontology of existence arrived at by means of phenomenology—but only insofar as he is read in a non-Kierkegaardian way.

However, even this negative portrayal of Kierkegaard's place in the history of phenomenology seems—and, arguably, seems rather strongly—to argue for his distinctive and significant place in that history. In some way—yet to be specified more closely—Kierkegaard belongs to that history and does so in such a way that a full self-accounting on the part of phenomenology would require reckoning with his role.

Kierkegaard and the Phenomenology of the God-Relationship

But the question of Kierkegaard and phenomenology may also arise on purely exegetical grounds, and there are not a few recent commentators on his work who argue that reading him as a kind of phenomenologist is fruitful on purely internal grounds such that this sort of reading accords with his own intellectual endeavors. Important examples of this approach include Jörg Disse and Arne Grøn. The title of Disse's monograph on the subject is itself telling as regards the ambitions of such a reading: *Kierkegaard's Phenomenology of the Experience of Freedom.*[10] However, Disse does not limit himself to seeing Kierkegaardian phenomenology merely as significant for a purely human or immanent experience of freedom, but also as religiously and theologically significant. As he says: "It can be shown on the basis of Kierkegaard's phenomenology of the experience of freedom that freedom cannot be separated from a God-relationship, that the experience of freedom and the God-relationship are indissolubly bound up together, and that there is no concrete freedom where this God-relationship is not sustained by a mood of trust."[11]

This claim once again raises the general question as to whether a purely phenomenological account really can show that human existence is "indissolubly bound up" with a God-relationship. Keeping that question open, I shall focus here on the narrower question of whether or how Kierkegaard himself contributes to phenomenological progress in this regard. Putting the question in either/or terms, do Kierkegaard's own "phenomenological" investigations further the cause of a fundamental phenomenology of the religious life, or could they prove the jagged rock on which the project of such a phenomenology comes to grief?

A somewhat straightforward reading of such Kierkegaardian texts as *Philosophical Fragments* and of such Kierkegaardian tropes as the "infinite qualitative difference" between God and human beings or the "absolute paradox" of the Incarnation or the "impossibility" of the object of faith would seem to bar the route from any purely immanent analysis of consciousness to any assured ontological knowledge of God. Moreover, such a conclusion would seem to fit with his repeated protest against the claims of human reason—whether purely philosophical or theological—to understand or to offer insight into either the existence or the meaning of God. It is not simply that the God-relationship is to be found in such existential attitudes as passion, worship, suffering, faith, hope, and love rather than in reason. It is also that even these phenomenal manifestations of religious existence reach their limit in the nothingness into which existence in general sinks as a condition of rebirth into the God-relationship in a positive and creative sense. Furthermore, while there may be some phenomenal manifestation of the impact of the God on a given human life (though this is not universally conceded by Kierkegaard or his pseudonyms), these are, at best, as ambiguous as the manifestation in time of the God himself, who comes incognito or, still more provocatively, as the sign of contradiction. The manifestation of God is also the self-concealment of God and, if that is so, then the meaning of faith (if faith is correct in claiming to be a God-relationship and not merely a form of self-consciousness) will itself be concealed from the eye of philosophical discernment. Neither God as the ultimate object of the religious consciousness nor any "thing-like realities" (Husserl) or other immanent data of consciousness that might be offered as intuitive manifestations of the relation to God can become visible within the general continuum of human mental life. At which point, we might recall that it was precisely a version of phenomenology (Hegel's) that provoked Kierkegaard's sharpest criticisms of philosophical attempts to deal with the God-relationship. For on a Kierkegaardian view of religion, there would seem to be no form of religion that can offer guarantees on its own behalf or that could vouch for the ontological status of the God-relationship on which it rested. Faith, worship, and witness in the world will always be ambiguous, and there will be no way of finally telling whether they are *really* expressions of a genuine God-relationship, or whether they are fake.

Of course, if God does not exist in any sense, then all forms of the religious consciousness are illusory. For Kierkegaard, however, even if God does exist, there are no external criteria by which other human beings can decide whether a given individual is or isn't in an authentic God-relationship, and perhaps it is not even knowable by that individual him- or herself. To put it religiously, the believer's life is hid with Christ in God. To put it in phenomenological terms, the intentional structure of the religious consciousness resists fundamental clarification, and both the ontological and epistemological claims implied by the phenomenon of religious belief are, on the believer's own terms, undecidable.

It would therefore seem that if the Kierkegaardian account of the religious life is to be incorporated into a phenomenology of religion, then this can occur only by (1) omitting what is most distinctive about this account, or (2) reading Kierkegaard in a sense contrary to that which he himself intended. It cannot be ruled out in advance that one or the other of these approaches might, in the end, prove most fruitful. Even if it is the practice of some Kierkegaard commentators, we are not obliged to set Kierkegaard on a pedestal and allow his own (actually sometimes contradictory) stipulations as to how he is to be read to predetermine our own reading. Like any other author, Kierkegaard may sometimes become most interesting when subjected to strong misreadings or to what Michael Theunissen called a philosophical "correction" of his work.[12]

Thus we might (for example) arrive at the position that Kierkegaard indeed shows (in the double sense of exemplifying and self-consciously demonstrating) a certain form of the religious life as a life repeatedly driven to beat against the frontiers of what it can know and what it can will, and thus a life structured as self-transcendence toward a nonassimilable limit-situation—without prejudice to the ontological status of the limits against which such a consciousness seems fated to hurl itself. Such a religious life might prove to be merely "idiotic," in the sense of the word found in Dostoevsky's eponymous novel, or it might (as a certain reading of that novel would suggest) be revelatory of the God-relationship in which alone human beings can find blessedness.

This would seem to accord with some of the most characteristic claims Kierkegaard makes about the ontological status of human beings' all-encompassing limit-situation, claims that seem to undercut any (including his own) experience-based reflections on the meaning of the religious life. For what Kierkegaard seems (often) to be saying is that there is in fact no human experience (and therewith no human thought or word) capable of grounding the faith claim that behind all provisional limit-situations lies one universal limit-situation at which the issue is determined by the presence and power of God and which, in Christian faith, is describable only in terms of the movement of creation, fall, and redemption.[13] Yet seeing our lives in terms of such a threefold movement is not something that can be read off from the more or less accidental, more or less variegated phenomena of human life itself: it is a faith-based interpretation of life that, on its own terms, comes from beyond the limit at which human thought breaks down. Without putting too much weight on the terms, we might call it a view based on a revelational a priori.[14]

To draw the issue to a point: positioned somewhat precariously between Hegel and Heidegger and their respective attempts to use phenomenology as a key to fundamental ontology or as a way of showing Being as manifest in beings and, more particularly, as manifest in beings as manifested in human consciousness, Kierkegaardian faith raises a fundamental question as to the reliability of the links between Being, manifestation, and consciousness. Translating Kierkegaard's religious language into the language of philosophy, the question goes something like this: If human being is determined in a fundamental respect by God, and if the being of God is not adequately conceivable by human beings, or is knowable only on the basis of the special kind of consciousness called "faith," then can human being itself ever be adequately manifested in the forms of human consciousness? Isn't the link between being, consciousness, and manifestation ruptured—or at the very least problematized—in a manner that renders the ambitions of phenomenology unfulfillable?

Having thus proposed a certain limit to reading Kierkegaard as a phenomenologist, I now want to step back and to see how, nevertheless, we might discern a certain phenomenological tendency in Kierkegaard's writings and then to restate in more detail and with closer reference to specific texts the case for imposing a quite severe limit on those tendencies.

Kierkegaardian Phenomenology

The common thread linking those who read Kierkegaard as a phenomenologist seems to be the prominent role of description in his writing. Now, of course, all sorts of writers describe all sorts of things in all sorts of ways, and this is not of itself enough to justify the title "phenomenology"! In the case of Kierkegaard, however, it does seem that description is being used in a consistent and methodical way, and even being applied to certain fundamental philosophical and theological questions. This is further connected with Kierkegaard's emphasis on subjectivity and psychology, such that what he appears to offer the reader might be characterized as a carefully observed descriptive account of how the religious consciousness develops in individual psychic life. Examples might include the seemingly phenomenological account of anxiety in *The Concept of Anxiety* (itself crucially affiliated to Hegelian psychology and central to the Heideggerian-existentialist appropriation of the topic); the exploration of religious subjectivity along the trajectory of pathos, suffering, and guilt in *Concluding Unscientific Postscript;* and, not least, the exposition of the forms of despair offered in *The Sickness unto Death.* And one might also look to the many upbuilding discourses written by Kierkegaard that portray manifold scenarios in which basic religious attitudes are exemplified and that seem to show how the religious life itself must appear in the forms of the self's self-relation that, according to Kierkegaard, is decisive for the "man in man" (to borrow a phrase from Dostoyevsky).

Some of the most striking examples of Kierkegaard's "phenomenology" seem to concern the prereligious life of human beings, such as the grief of the abandoned heroines discussed in the essay "Silhouettes" (in *Either/Or*), the dialectics of seduction brought to view in "The Seducer's Diary," the anxiety of Nero as described by Judge William in part 2 of *Either/Or,* or the self-tormenting aesthetic guilt of Quidam, whose self-analyzing diary constitutes a large part of *Stages on Life's Way.* But as the examples given above seem to suggest, Kierkegaard extends the same method into the domain of the properly religious, where humility, patience, and the experience of forgiveness are treated not dissimilarly to anxiety and the other "darker" mental states (although these religious phenomena have been of far less interest to Kierkegaard commentators).

We might immediately object that, nevertheless, what is most Kierkegaardian about Kierkegaard is precisely his interest in what doesn't and even in what can't show itself on the surface of human life. Phenomena like irony and grief seem to offer significant resistance to phenomenological appropriation. The point of being ironic is precisely that no one can see whether you're being ironic. Is Socrates serious? Or is he merely jesting? Does he have any opinions of his own? Or is he pure irony—infinitely negative, as young Kierkegaard put it?

Yet although such self-concealing phenomena resist appropriation, Kierkegaard does not seem to regard their resistance as insuperable. On the contrary, he himself seems to endorse the legitimacy of a phenomenological approach to such concepts as irony in the bravura opening paragraph of the thesis on just that subject:

> If there is anything that must be praised in modern philosophical endeavor in its magnificent manifestation, it certainly is the power of genius with which it seizes and holds on to the phenomenon. Now if it is fitting for the phenomenon, which as such is always *foemini generis,* to surrender to the stronger on account of its feminine nature, then in all fairness one can also demand of the philosophical knight a deferential propriety and a profound enthusiasm, in place of which one sometimes hears too much the jingling of spurs and the voice of the master. The observer . . . ought to have a sense of his own predominance—but should use it only to help the phenomenon obtain its full disclosure . . . It is still of great importance that the phenomenon remains inviolate and that the concept be seen as coming into existence through the phenomenon.[15]

Phenomenology is not to be rejected: it must simply be genuinely phenomenological and not a matter of imposing a preconceived conceptual schema onto the phenomena.

The Concept of Irony itself attempts what Kierkegaard thus proposes. However, since Kierkegaard's argument there is predominantly historical and textual, resembling Hegelian phenomenology more than his own more characteristic psychological orientation, we might usefully turn to another example, namely, the essay "Silhouettes" from *Either/Or,* where the speaker sets out to explore the phenomenon of reflective sorrow. The whole point here is that sorrow of this kind is interesting precisely because it eludes direct observation: "People pass one another in the street; one person looks just like the next, and the next one is like almost everyone else. Only the experienced observer suspects that deep within that one's head resides a lodger who has nothing to do with the world but lives out his solitary life in quiet home-industry work. The exterior, then, is indeed the object of our scrutiny but not of our interest."[16] Similarly, it is only "the experienced observer" who knows that "when one looks long and attentively at a face, sometimes another face, as it were, is discovered within the face one sees."[17] It is this "other face" that such an observer knows how to make manifest. This claim is followed by a rapturous passage, in which we are offered a program for such "phenomenological" explorations. If we are in search of "Kierkegaard the phenomenologist," then this program might itself be taken for a template for the procedure that he will develop elsewhere for exploring the properly religious phenomena of the inner God-relationship:

> It can elude our attention for a long time, but when by chance a look, a word, a sigh, a tone in the voice, a hint in the eyes, a trembling of the lips, or a blunder in the handshake treacherously betrays what has been carefully concealed—then passion is aroused, then the struggle begins. Then it is a matter of having vigilance and perseverance and sagacity, for who is as inventive as secret sorrow, but a solitary lifetime prisoner has adequate time to think up many things, and who is as swift to find concealment as secret sorrow, for no young girl can cover in greater anxiety and haste a bosom she has exposed than hidden sorrow when it is surprised. Then unshakable dauntlessness is required, for the struggle is with a Proteus, but he must give himself up if one only holds out. Even if like that sea god he assumed every shape in order to escape, such as a snake twisting in our hands, a lion terrifying us with its roaring, changed into a tree that whispers with its leaves or into roaring water or a crackling fire—at last he must nevertheless prophesy, and sorrow must disclose itself at last. See, these adventures are our delight, our diversion; to try ourselves in them is our knighthood.[18]

This seems to be a somewhat enthusiastic expression of what will later be practiced in a more cynical-seeming mode by, for example, Sartre, when he sets out to expose such everyday forms of life as being-a-good-waiter as, in reality, ways of anxiously fleeing freedom. Can we also say that this is a program for phenomenological knights of faith? Is the aesthete, wrestling with the Proteus of secret sorrow a type of Jacob, refusing to loosen his grip on the angel until the latter reveals his divine identity? Is the face turned toward God perhaps the true face of all human beings, believers and unbelievers alike? And might a suitably vigilant, unrelenting phenomenologist of religious passion be able to get to see it?

Despair and the Limits of Phenomenology

I want now to focus this question on the topic of despair. This seems both to invite an extension of what is projected in the aesthetic exploration of reflective sorrow—despair is, after all, a human state—but it also deals with a state upon which *The Sickness unto Death* bestows a decisive religious significance. These two aspects (the human and the religious) come together in the subtitle, which runs "A Christian Psychological Exposition for Upbuilding and Awakening."

The Sickness unto Death seems to be describing how the self develops through a dialectical sequence of forms of self-consciousness. These forms are seen as ever more intensely negative, as forms of self-estrangement or despair. In terms of the definition of the self given in section A.a, the person in despair is precisely not "relating itself to itself and in willing to be itself . . . [resting] transparently in the power that established it."[19] "God" in other words, is precisely not present, or does not appear "in despair." The despairing self is not transparent to God. And yet, precisely by excluding God in this way, despair must ultimately be understood theologically. And, theologically, it is sin, the refusal to believe in the possibility of forgiveness and, consequently, premised on the rejection of Christ. Despair is the sickness unto death, but "only the Christian knows what is meant by the sickness unto death."[20] This seems to be a complete tangle of psychological and theological terminology, yet Kierkegaard himself is careful not simply to conflate these two very different elements—so what exactly is the relationship between them, and why is this significant for the question of the phenomenology of the God-relationship?

Early on in *The Sickness unto Death,* Kierkegaard draws a strong distinction between unconscious and conscious forms of despair. He then gives an account of two sets of polar categories that are determinative for both conscious and unconscious despair: finitude/infinity and possibility/necessity. Conscious despair is then further subdivided into (a) despair that is ignorant of being in despair and ignorant of having a self and (b) despair that is conscious of being in despair. This latter is again subdivided into (a) the despair of not willing to be oneself and (b) the despair of willing to be oneself in an arbitrary way that is nontransparent to the transcendent ground of the self. These last two forms are also called the despair of weakness and the despair of defiance, or feminine and masculine despair respectively.

The exploration and exposition of the interpretative framework established through the systematic interweaving of these concepts and categories makes up the bulk of part 1 of the book. Strikingly, the concepts and categories used by Kierkegaard are for the most part taken from philosophy, not least from Hegelianism. Thus far, the text operates within the orbit of a general philosophical psychology, and seems to be shaping up to be a fairly standard example of Hegelian phenomenology.[21]

However, when we turn to part 2 the picture is significantly altered. We are still within the general field projected by the rubric "despair as a form of consciousness," but consciousness is now specified more closely—or as Kierkegaard puts it "potentiated"—as consciousness of God. This, in turn, is subsequently potentiated still further as consciousness of Christ, specifically Christ as bearer of the divine offer of forgiveness of sins. From the perspective established in part 2, the forms of despair classified in part 1 are given a new and more determinate content. Despair is now renamed "sin," the ultimate form of which is despair over the forgiveness of sins, the belief that forgiveness of sins just isn't possible. When and only when one has the idea of God; when and only when one believes that one's failure to be the self one could be or would wish to be is also a failure to be the self God wills one to be, a failure to be the self one "is" in the sight of the giver of all Being, and whether that despair is then weakness (inability to believe) or defiance (rejection of belief)—only then is despair truly "the sickness unto death." Part 1, in other words, gives only a formal schema of despair. Part 2 gives content to that schema—but, in the event, this content is not derived simply from the general field of the phenomena of despair (as if despair were a state one could observe). Rather, the analysis of despair is given its content by theology ("dogmatics," as Kierkegaard says), that is, by referring to factors external to the consciousness of the one despairing. Whether a given case of despair is truly and irrevocably despair depends not on where or how we locate it on the schematization of possibility/necessity, finitude/infinity, not-willing-to-be-a-self/willing-to-be-a-self (but defiantly), but on the content of the individual's God-relationship. As Michael Theunissen has put it, it is not being able to believe that God can save.[22]

Along with the move from a psychological or anthropological to a theological account of despair, there is also a change in the kind of argument being put forward. The interpretative framework proposed in part 1 is universally applicable to all human beings. Finitude and infinity, necessity and possibility, consciousness and the lack of consciousness are polarities that can be applied to any human phenomenon. However, that is not obviously the case with regard to belief in God or, as Kierkegaard puts it, "with the conception of God." In other words, whereas part 1 may indeed offer something analogous to an existential phenomenology of despair, part 2 offers something much more like a hypothetical case: *if* the idea of God is posited, *then* the nature of despair will require radical reinterpretation along the lines that Kierkegaard goes on to develop. But there is no obvious argument given as to why one might want to adopt this hypothesis. It is derived from dogma, not from philosophy, and not from scrutinizing the deliverances of human self-consciousness. Nor does what follows seem to be based, directly or indirectly, on the observation of cases. Thus, in the second paragraph of part 2A, it is stated that "there is no room or place for a psychological delineation (*Skildring*) in this part [of the book]."[23] We might quite easily imagine that Anti-Climacus had had occasion to observe some religious individuals who both believed in God and regarded their lives as failing to conform to the divinely ordained model of an optimum human life. Nor would it be hard to imagine him drawing the conclusion that such individuals would be even more despairing than nonbelievers. Whereas the despairing nonbelievers would merely regard their lives as unfulfilled in a more or less everyday kind of way, the believers would speak of themselves as "miserable sinners" or worse (see Nietzsche for further details!). But there is nothing in his account that requires us to posit the existence of any actual believers, nothing that constitutes a demonstration of the necessity of belief, nothing that argues for the reality of the God before whom the believer imagines himself living. We could even imagine that it was what another pseudonym calls a "thought-experiment," a device to draw out certain features of despair, without having recourse to the observation of actual cases. In this spirit of imagining the case of a hypothetical believer, *The Sickness unto Death* seems also to suggest that not even belief in Christ will rescue the believer from this predicament, if that belief is not further specified in such a way as to involve full acceptance of the possibility of rebirth, forgiveness, and new life. If there is a God, then despair is sin; if Christ came to save us from our sins, then lack of faith in Christ will be the ultimate potentiation of that despair or sin. The hypothesis of God makes clear what the ultimate outcome of despair will be when an alternative—namely salvation—is on offer. But where, or how, are we to see this alternative exemplified? And what might motivate us to embrace it? Why would we want to live our lives strung out between the polarities of salvation and perdition, when we could settle for more comfortable alternatives? Why gamble so recklessly with the short time we've been given? And even if "believing in God" made us feel better for a while, would we really want to commit to such belief if we had no reason to think of it as anything other than a hypothesis?

Kierkegaard apparently at one point conceived *The Sickness unto Death* as part of a larger work, which would indeed have culminated in a further part, "Thoughts That Cure Radically, Christian Healing. Christian Healing. The Atonement."[24] It is possible that some of the Christian discourses that Kierkegaard himself wrote at about the same time as and associated in terms of content with *The Sickness unto Death* perform the function that this unwritten continuation might have had. It would, in any case, be congruent with what he did write to argue that what might motivate us to embrace the hypothesis of God/Christ would be the longing for forgiveness exemplified in figures shown in these discourses, preeminently "the woman who was a sinner."[25] But, although she would seem to offer a worked example of what faith might mean, Kierkegaard (in broad agreement with Christian tradition) frequently makes clear that the desire for God is itself a gift of God. The longing for forgiveness is not a universally observable feature of human existence. On the contrary, the majority seem to walk about not imagining they are ill, not imagining they are in despair and, if asked, would deny that they were. Being in despair—in any of the forms examined in part 1—is not of itself ever going to be enough to motivate a person to move to the religious perspective of part 2. That perspective must be freely adopted, and adopted because we want to. There is no "why" and no "because." Consequently, the desire for God is not a feature of consciousness discernible on the basis of a close description of the observed features of human life as such or in general: unlike the Kierkegaardian analysis of reflective sorrow, the Heideggerian analysis of falling, or the Sartrean analysis of bad faith, it is not drawn out of experience; it is not the secret face hidden behind the public face of the average secular person, susceptible of being made visible to the appropriately empathetic observer. Far from being derived from experience, it has a certain a priori character. At various points in his authorship, Kierkegaard seems to identify this desire for God with willing the Good.[26] In true Kantian fashion, he is adamant that no one else can make us will the Good: willing the Good is something we must freely will, if we are to will it at all. Only to one wanting to will the Good and wanting to believe what Christianity teaches as divine revelation will the story of human existence be readable as a story of creation, fall, and redemption. For such a one, and for such a one only, the universal problem of despair will be dramatically heightened, and the issue will no longer be despair versus fulfillment but perdition versus salvation.

Now, if one does in fact will the Good, it might at that point be possible to introduce arguments for showing why Christian beliefs (or those of some other religion) might best underwrite such a desire (such as: that we need a view of life maximally able to represent the nonnegotiable and infinite value of the individual). But these arguments only begin to count once one has crossed a certain threshold. I have argued elsewhere, and merely repeat here, that Kierkegaard's presentation of the key religious concepts in terms of which believers understand their religious lives suggests that they are best understood on analogy with Kant's advice on how to use metaphysical ideas—regulatively only, and never constitutively.[27] Kierkegaard's own formulation that despair is sin only for those having the idea of God and using that idea as a "criterion" or "measure" of the self already suggests something of this. But freely adopting a criterion or maxim by which to direct the exercise of freedom is something different from the disclosure of a Being whose revealed will becomes determinative for the aim and conduct of life. Believers do, of course, mostly think of themselves as living in the light of the revealed will of God, but the point here is that they come to think this not on the basis of a revelation (and Kierkegaard was skeptical about the claims of some contemporaries, such as Adolph Adler, to have had direct revelations) but on the basis of a free choice to regard life in this way.

Now I am not necessarily suggesting that, as critics of Kierkegaard have argued, this choice is unmotivated or arbitrary, as in: some people just happen to think like that. Those making the choice are able to give an account of it, but they will only do so on the basis of the life view they have subsequently adopted and in which alone that account makes sense. Yet the situation that it can never be demonstrated to universal satisfaction that this is the best way to be does not mean that there is nothing to be said about why one might want to seek the will of God or why willing the Good to the point of annihilation of self might be deemed preferable to not doing so. Kierkegaard's discourses suggest that while silence is not an inappropriate manifestation of the desire for God, this desire can also be spoken of in a variety of ways and figures, whether in terms of willing the Good or, perhaps more fundamentally, in terms of love. But he also admits—indeed this is central to his representation of the religious life—that such willing and such love has a certain circularity: one can only will the Good because it is good; one can only love because the beloved inspires one's love.

This is illustrated from another angle by the contrast drawn between the Socratic and the Christian views of sin. Where the Socratic view defines sin in terms of ignorance, assuming that anyone who knows what is Good will also will it, Christianity, according to Kierkegaard, notes that ignorance is not necessarily naïve, and that behind a professed ignorance may lie a deliberate (if foggy and confused) evasion of knowledge. On the Christian view one can (and many do) know what is Good and not will it; one can defy the divine commandment to do the Good. Seen in these terms, the tipping point between unbelief and belief is concealed in the mystery of each individual's freedom, and this mystery can never be manifest to any third party.[28]

We come down, then, to the particular orientation of the concrete individual, that individual of whom Husserl said, "For phenomenology, the singular is eternally the apeiron."[29] In the mystery of the self-choice of such a groundlessly free individual, we meet the limit of what a certain Hegelian and a certain Heideggerian phenomenology might be able to achieve by developing phenomenology in the direction of a universal fundamental ontology. From the point of view of such an ontology, the Kierkegaardian religious self occupies an ontologically indeterminable position. There is nothing to show of the kind of Being in and from which such a self lives. Now whether we say that this is because the Kierkegaardian account remains stuck on the level of the purely ontic and fails to reach the level of ontology or whether we claim that Kierkegaard had already preempted some more recent thinkers in understanding the God-relationship as being "beyond" ontology seems relatively unimportant. In either case we are faced with a radical disjunction between religious (or more specifically, Christian) faith and the task of laying bare a universal fundamental ontology.

In an earlier section of this article ("Kierkegaard and the Phenomenology of the God-Relationship"), I drew attention to the obstacle that Kierkegaard's thoroughgoing insistence on the transcendence of God places on the path to a phenomenological exposition of the God-relationship. However, as the argument has developed we have already reached a halt on the human side of this relationship. In other words (and keeping to a strictly Kierkegaardian approach), the limitations of phenomenology do not first appear at the point at which an attempt is made to bring in divine transcendence as the basis of existence. Rather, they already kick in within the account of human existence itself. This will not surprise theologians, who are familiar with the intimate dialectic between sin and knowledge of God. To the extent that human beings are seen (as they are typically seen in Lutheran and Calvinist traditions) as having fallen away from their original perfection, they are also seen as having become incapable of the knowledge of God. Whereas, on a Catholic view (in this case, perhaps, typified by Rahner), a close analysis of even the most distorted forms of human life will disclose the human being's original created kinship with God, the fallen self of Protestant dogmatics (i.e., what Kierkegaard calls the despairing self) is utterly devoid of any trace of its divine origin. But if human beings as they exist in the world are indeed utterly estranged from the original ground of their being, then not even the most careful analysis of human consciousness is going to be able to ground or explain the reasons for why we are as we are (let alone account for how God might be present in or to human life). Yet I am not arguing for reading Kierkegaard as merely offering an exceptionally subtle and appropriately modern version of classical Protestant dogmatics. What, then, am I suggesting?

Kierkegaard as Christian Moralist

If Kierkegaard is neither to be regarded as a phenomenologist nor as a Christian dogmatist, what kind of thinker is he? I should like to suggest a tertium quid, namely that we might think of him as a moralist, albeit a moralist of a distinctively Christian kind. On this view, Kierkegaard's questions are not, how are human beings constituted; what are the features of human life that make the religious point of view the most plausible? or similar (questions to which phenomenology and Christian dogmatics each have their specific answers). Kierkegaard's question is a question about the good life, about how it is best for human beings to live and think, and is formulated as a question to a subject who is treated as being freely able to respond as he or she wills. The question itself goes something like this: this is how life looks, lived on non-Christian premises; this is how life looks lived on Christian premises; which kind of life would you, dear reader, prefer to live? The sting in the tail of this question is that, on a Kierkegaardian understanding, there are no external reasons that can decide our choice for us. There are reasons—but they are reasons only for those who stand on one or the other side of the choice. This means that whether the choice to live the Christian life is a purely arbitrary choice, rooted in nothing but the free will of the individual who wants to live that way, or whether it is prompted by the prevenient grace of God must entirely escape the eye of even the most empathetic phenomenological observer. Even when the believer emerges from trustful silence to bear witness to the desirability of desiring God, this will only be persuasive for those who wish to be persuaded. Not only Kierkegaard's substantial claims about the absurdity of religious faith, but also his manner of arguing for them, set a limit to the ambitions of phenomenological research in respect of religious existence. Believers and nonbelievers will, of course, draw very different conclusions from that, but, either way, Kierkegaard can still be read as offering significant perspectives on and provocations to thinking about the values, goals, and moral sensibility that best reflect the best possibilities of human living. A Kierkegaardian religious life will understand itself as founded on that which comes from outside the frontiers of human possibility:[30] but it is, after all, a human possibility to live such a life, and Kierkegaard can be read as helping us see why it might be desirable so to do if we are only willing to consider it. The refusal to offer grounds that might appeal to a neutral bystander separates Kierkegaard from the classically theistic mode of Christian apologetics, and the close description of human psychological states gets us only to the outer edge of the religious decision, thereby thwarting the ambition of an exhaustive phenomenology of the

God-relationship. Nevertheless, Kierkegaard's appeal to the freedom of the reader also separates him from those Christian dogmatists who see the human condition as intrinsically hopeless. Kierkegaard's belief that there is hope for those who want it does make it possible after all for us to read him as a kind of moralist, albeit of an exceptionally radical and challenging kind.

And one final point. Even though—or perhaps precisely because—God is so utterly concealed behind the incognito of human freedom in the Kierkegaardian account of faith and we can consequently have no knowledge as to whether God exists or not, the difference between believer and unbeliever is significantly relativized. Strange as it may seem, a nonbeliever might not in fact be prevented from believing in a Kierkegaardian manner in the forgiveness of sins and thus escaping despair, even if he or she didn't believe in the "existence" of God. The one thing needful would be the belief that this was an appropriate way of living out the most humanly valuable understanding of existence, whether what constituted its "value" was more closely specified in terms of its being beautiful, interesting, satisfying, morally excellent, or simply less boring.[31] It is hard to see how phenomenology might decide whether such a person was authentically fulfilling human possibilities or falling into a particularly contorted version of bad faith.

Notes

1. See my *The Philosophy of Kierkegaard* (Chesham, Eng.: Acumen, 2005), especially chap. 4.

2. Martin Heidegger, *Being and Time,* trans. John Macquarrie and Edward Robinson (Oxford: Blackwell, 1962), 62 (first German edition, 38).

3. See Heidegger, *History of the Concept of Time,* trans. Theodore Kisiel (Bloomington: Indiana University Press, 1985), especially chaps. 1–3. Other early lecture series (*History of the Concept of Time* contains lectures given in the summer semester of 1925) that deal with Heidegger's understanding of phenomenology include *Phenomenological Interpretations of Aristotle: Initiation into Phenomenological Research,* trans. Richard Rojcewicz (Bloomington: Indiana University Press, 2001), and *Einführung in die Phänomenologische Forschung, Gesamtausgabe,* vol. 17 (Frankfurt: Klostermann, 1994).

4. Edmund Husserl, *Logische Untersuchungen* (Tübingen: Niemeyer, 1993), 2–3.

5. Edmund Husserl, *Ideas: General Introduction to Pure Phenomenology,* trans. W. R. Boyce Gibson (London: George Allen and Unwin, 1931), 174.

6. Gavin Flood, *The Ascetic Self: Subjectivity, Memory and Tradition* (Cambridge: Cambridge University Press, 2005).

7. Heidegger, *The Phenomenology of Religious Life,* trans. Matthias Fritsch and Jennifer Anna Gosetti-Ferencei (Bloomington: Indiana University Press, 2004).

8. See Karl Rahner, *Foundations of Christian Faith: An Introduction to the Idea of Christianity,* trans. William V. Dych (London: Darton, Longman, and Todd, 1978).

9. A rather different modeling of possible convergence between Christian theology and phenomenology would be that exemplified in Michel Henry, *I Am the Truth: Toward a Philosophy of Christianity,* trans. Susan Emanuel (Stanford: Stanford University Press, 2003), a primary example of the so-called "theological turn" in French phenomenology toward the end of the twentieth century. Different again, although affiliated to the Husserlian tradition, is the religious phenomenology of Anna-Teresa Tymieniecka. See, for example, *Phenomenology of Life and the Human Creative Condition* (The Hague: Kluwer, 1998).

10. Jörg Disse, *Kierkegaards Phänomenologie der Freiheitserfahrung* (Freiburg: Alber, 1991).

11. Ibid., 15.

12. See Michael Theunissen, *Der Begriff Verzweiflung: Korrekturen an Kierkegaard* (Frankfurt: Suhrkamp, 1993).

13. I think it important to put it this way. The issue is not simply whether "God" is to be posited as some kind of Being (Supreme, Absolute, or Unconditioned, perhaps) beyond or outside the limits of human consciousness (though that may also be a question worth considering in its own right). Rather, what seems to be at stake for Kierkegaard is a very specific narrative configuration of how God relates to human beings and that narrative, he suggests, is not so much an interpretation of experience as an a priori that makes experience meaningful in a particular way.

14. Kierkegaard's notion of there being a religious a priori that precedes any actual religious experience is already testified to in the early journals and, not unimportantly, particularly in relation to his reading of J. E. Erdmann's *Glauben und Wissen.* See my article "Kierkegaard and Speculative Theology," *Bulletin of the Hegel Society of Great Britain* 56/57 (2007): 23–44.

15. *CI,* 9.

16. *EO I,* 174.

17. Ibid.

18. Ibid., 175–76.

19. *SUD,* 14.

20. Ibid., 8.

21. See Jon Stewart, "Kierkegaard's Phenomenology of Despair in *The Sickness unto Death,*" in *Kierkegaard Studies. Yearbook* 1997, ed. Niels Jørgen Cappelørn and Hermann Deuser (Berlin: W. de Gruyter, 1997).

22. Theunissen, *Der Begriff Verzweiflung,* 117, 133.

23. *SUD,* 77.

24. *JP* 6110.

25. For further discussion of "the woman who was a sinner," see my *Kierkegaard's Upbuilding Discourses: Philosophy, Literature, and Theology* (London: Routledge, 2002), 202–10.

26. See, for example, *EUD* 125–39; also, at greater length, see the discourse known as "Purity of Heart Is to Will One Thing" (after an earlier, freestanding translation), being pt. 1, "On the Occasion of a Confession," in Kierkegaard, *Upbuilding Discourses in Various Spirits,* trans. Howard V. Hong and Edna H. Hong (Princeton, N.J.: Princeton University Press, 1993). For further discussion, see Pattison, *Kierkegaard's Upbuilding Discourses,* 139; Pattison, "Philosophy and Dogma: The Testimony of an Upbuilding Discourse," in *Ethics, Love and Faith in Kierkegaard,* ed. Edward F. Mooney (Bloomington: Indiana University Press, 2008), 155–62; and Jeremy D. B. Walker, *To Will One Thing: Reflections on Kierkegaard's "Purity of Heart"* (Montreal: McGill-Queen's University Press, 1972).

27. See my *Kierkegaard's Upbuilding Discourses,* 92–100, and also my article "'Before God' as a Regulative Concept," in *Kierkegaard Studies. Yearbook* 1997, 70–84.

28. See *SUD,* pt. 2, chap. 2, "The Socratic Definition of Sin," 87–96.

29. Pierre Keller, *Husserl and Heidegger on Human Experience* (Cambridge: Cambridge University Press, 1999), 118.

30. And it is this understanding that grounds Kierkegaard's sympathy for Jacobi—but his positive commendation of Jacobi should not be misinterpreted as meaning that he regards the latter as having provided a satisfactory account of how this "outsideness" can become significant for an individual human life.

31. It might also, for example, be a life suited to those who experienced their existence as needing "infinite help" in the face of "infinite need," as Alastair Hannay discusses in connection with a remark of Wittgenstein's in *Culture and Value.* See chap. 13, "Solitary Souls and Infinite Help," in *Kierkegaard and Philosophy: Selected Essays* (London: Routledge, 2003), 179–89.

Contributors

JEFFREY BLOECHL is an associate professor of philosophy at Boston College. He has written, edited, and translated widely in contemporary European thought and philosophy of religion. He is founding series editor of *Levinas Studies: An Annual Review* and, with Kevin Hart, of *Thresholds in Philosophy and Theology*. He is also in the process of completing a book that proposes a post-Heideggerian phenomenology of religious life.

DANIEL DAHLSTROM is chair of the philosophy department and a professor of philosophy at Boston University. He is the author of *Das logische Vorurteil, Heidegger's Concept of Truth,* and *Philosophical Legacies.* He has published numerous articles, edited more than fifteen collections, and translated works of Mendelssohn, Schiller, Hegel, Feuerbach, and Heidegger into English.

MARK DOOLEY lectures in philosophy at the National University of Ireland Maynooth. He is also a columnist with the *Irish Daily Mail* and a regular broadcaster on Irish radio and television. He is the author of *The Politics of Exodus: Søren Kierkegaard's Ethics of Responsibility, The Philosophy of Derrida,* and *Roger Scruton: The Philosopher on Dover Beach.* He is the editor of *Questioning Ethics, Questioning God, A Passion for the Impossible: John D. Caputo in Focus,* and *The Roger Scruton Reader.*

DARÍO GONZÁLEZ, born in Argentina, teaches history of philosophy and aesthetics at the University of Copenhagen. He is an editor and translator of *Escritos de Søren Kierkegaard.* His many publications include "The Triptych of Sciences in the Introduction to *The Concept of Anxiety,*" "Suspended Reflections: The Dialectic of Self-Enclosure," "Sin, Absolute Difference," and "Essai sur l'ontologie kierkegaardienne: Idéalité et détermination."

BRIAN GREGOR is a teaching fellow in philosophy at Boston College. He has published several articles in the philosophy of religion, ethics, and aesthetics and is the coeditor of *Bonhoeffer and Continental Thought:*

Cruciform Philosophy and *Being Human, Becoming Human: Bonhoeffer and Social Thought.*

ARNE GRØN is a professor of ethics and philosophy of religion at the University of Copenhagen and cofounder of the Center for Subjectivity Research. His numerous publications mainly deal with the theory of subjectivity, philosophy of religion, and ethics. He has written extensively on Kierkegaard, for example, in two books, *The Concept of Anxiety in Søren Kierkegaard* and *Subjektivitet og negativitet. Kierkegaard.*

KEVIN HART is Edwin B. Kyle Professor of Christian Studies at the University of Virginia. He is the author of *The Trespass of the Sign: Deconstruction, Theology, and Philosophy* and *The Dark Gaze: Maurice Blanchot and the Sacred.* He is the editor of *Counter-Experiences: Reading Jean-Luc Marion* and coeditor of *The Exorbitant: Emmanuel Levinas Between Jews and Christians.*

GEORGE PATTISON is Lady Margaret Professor of Divinity at the University of Oxford. He is the author of *Kierkegaard, Religion, and the Nineteenth-Century Crisis of Culture; Kierkegaard and the Crisis of Faith: An Introduction to His Life and Thought; The Philosophy of Kierkegaard; "Poor Paris!": Kierkegaard's Critique of the Spectacular City;* and *Kierkegaard's Upbuilding Discourses: Philosophy, Literature, and Theology.*

HEIKO SCHULZ is University Professor of Systematic Theology and Philosophy of Religion at the Johann Wolfgang Goethe-University Frankfurt am Main. He is coeditor and cotranslator of the *Deutsche Sören Kierkegaard-Edition* (*DSKE*) and the author of *Eschatologische Identität: Eine Untersuchung über das Verhältnis von Vorsehung, Schicksal und Zufall bei Sören Kierkegaard.*

MEROLD WESTPHAL is Distinguished Professor of Philosophy at Fordham University. He is the author of *Kierkegaard's Critique of Reason and Society; Becoming a Self: A Reading of Kierkegaard's "Concluding Unscientific Postscript"; History and Truth in Hegel's Phenomenology; God, Guilt, and Death: An Existential Phenomenology of Religion; Overcoming Onto-theology: Toward a Postmodern Christian Faith,* and *Levinas and Kierkegaard in Dialogue.*